How to Find Love And Make It Last

A Practical Guide to Relationships

Book One

Includes: The 101 Question Compatibility Test

Virginia C. Gleser

Harmony Publishing

Published by Harmony Publishing, A Division of Sky Sail Productions
512 14th Street
Modesto, Ca. 95354
Join me: Virginia Gleser (author) on Facebook

First printing of *Love, Marriage and the Art of Raising Children* in Buenos Aires, Argentina. 2005
Second revised edition, (retitled) *How to Find Love and Make It Last, A Practical Guide to Relationships. Includes the 101 Question Compatibility Test.* By Virginia C. Gleser United States, 2016
ISBN# 978-0-9647247-4-7

Realizing Your Wizardness from *What the Bleep Do We Know*, by William Arntz, Betsy Chasse, and Mark Vicente was used by written permission from Health Communications, Inc., 3201 S. W. 15th St., Deerfield Beach, Florida 33442-8190

The typeface used for the text of this book is Times New Roman

I dedicate this book to my husband Robert, the father of our eight children, my capable captain, and lover for over four decades. Your dedication to change has made it possible for our relationship to grow and evolve. You are my magician mechanic, patient editor, brainstorming partner, manifestor of ideas, grandfather extraordinaire, and the best short-order chef around. Living out our latest dream, cruising with you in tropical climes aboard our sailboat *Harmony,* has filled me with happiness. Your adventuresome spirit and *joie de vivre* make me feel like I'm the luckiest person in the world.

Oh! To Be Lucky in Love

To those who have ears, let them hear.
To those who have eyes, let them see.
To those who have heart, let them love.
To those who have soul, let them dream.
To those who have a will to change, let them
Seek to move the world with their
Creative imagination and compassionate power.
For even the small steps of change that you make,
Become an expansive, illuminating step
For the universe,
Rippling out to the outer edges of the Unending void.
To you belongs magic.

With Love, Virginia

Table of Contents

Love surrounds us always. It's just a matter of tapping into it.

How To Find Love and Make it Last: Introduction to Book 1

When my teenage children were going to high school and starting to date, I began to write this guide to help them travel through the labyrinth of love with their eyes wide open. I hoped that the difficult lessons my husband Robert and I had learned during our then thirty years of marriage and the subsequent changes we had gone through, could help them make intelligent choices when they were looking for a partner. I wanted to shine a light on how to build a vibrant, ever evolving union. It soon became obvious that I was writing it for everyone not just my kids, and especially for those who have been through tough times in their past relationships and are still looking for "The One." I wanted to write the book I wish I had read when I was beginning to explore the erotic and mysterious world of dating.

Our young adults actually said that they found my manuscript useful when they were searching for their life partners. They circulated it among their friends who also gave me positive feedback. It wasn't until our children had flown the nest, and Robert and I were spending the summer of 2005 in Buenos Aires, Argentina that I finally had time to publish *Love, Marriage, and the Art of Raising Children.* Small print shops abound in that vibrant city and with the favorable exchange rate we were able to find a competent printer with a Heidelberg press and a layout team to make my book a reality. I soon received messages from friends and strangers, who wrote that it made a difference in their lives. It wasn't long before a high school teacher used my book in her life skills class, and I received precious letters from her and her students about how much it had meant to them. The enthusiastic response inspired me to release an updated and renamed edition *How to Find Love and Make It Last, A Practical Guide to Relationships, Includes: The 101 Question Compatibility Test.* I have divided it into two books since they address different stages of life. Book 1 will cover such topics as Finding "The One," Loving Yourself, Tools for Communication, and How to Change Your Incompatible Habits in order to make you a wonderful partner. Book 2 will cover Marriage and the Art of Raising Children.

***

Love is an action word. I would like to take you on a journey to the depths of love: to the psychic frontier where you can find truth through communication, where you can clean out old resentments, apologize for hurts, forgive past wrongs, dump mental garbage and unload childhood pain. With a clear and open heart, mind, and body, you'll be ready for a relationship that can operate in prime running condition.

> Love is an action word

How to Find Love and Make it Last is a Driver's Ed manual to help you negotiate the often, elusive route to a successful relationship. Our culture has a love affair with cars and the general requirements here in California for a driver's license is a written test and a vision check-up. Then you receive a permit, which qualifies you to take a training course before taking the final driving exam. It's easy to make a mistake during the road test and many nervous drivers fail the exam at least once. When you do receive your license, you gain the privilege to join the large, sometimes hectic and dangerous community out on the road.

When it comes to love, sex, dating, marriage, and parenting, unfortunately there are no required classes, tests, practice hours, or reality checks that might help assure a successful relationship. It is not surprising that statistics give a married couple around a 60% chance of success.[1] This land of fractured families is a disaster area, needing major relief! We are in the midst of a social crisis, and the children from this fallout suffer along with Mom and Dad. Whoa! Let's stem the flood.

These days four out of ten marriages fail, which is, believe it or not, better than previous decades, when it was closer to 50%. Unfortunately one out of every four households is headed by a single parent, and unwanted pregnancies are still way too high.[2] Mental and emotional issues caused by family upheaval usually are put on the back burner and no one wants to talk about them. It is only with a commitment to a personal quest for self-improvement that we can make a large societal paradigm shift. Equipped with relevant tools for communication, you can become aware of what it takes to have a successful relationship and avoid repeating those old destructive patterns. By understanding how a happy relationship works, physically, emotionally, and spiritually, as well as what it takes to have love stick around year after year, you can create a romance that is vibrant and full of joy.

When you find that deep, long lasting connection, there's a special feeling that only happens around true love. You wake up in the morning and you are greeted with your partner's warm hugs and whispers of how much s/he loves you. An easy communication exists and you can talk about anything and everything, especially about problems that would ordinarily cause hassles. When you share cooking, gardening, dancing, laughter, travel and adventure or whatever it is that you love to do, it brings you both happiness and expands your horizons. Of course, lovemaking is a beautiful time to connect and reach an intimacy that is healing to body, mind and spirit. Your career is inspiring and you bring home enthusiasm and new ideas. You value the time when you are by yourself and enjoy being together with your partner. Life is not stagnant or boring but continually evolving with exciting new discoveries and experiences, both inward and outward. The essence of your loving relationship is a deep respect for your partner, unobstructed communication, and a willingness to change. It feels like you've won the lottery; dreams become reality, magic happens, and love soars.

The essence of your loving relationship is a deep respect for your partner, unobstructed communication, and a willingness to change

It can actually be like this, but rarely in the real world does an idyllic, contention-free relationship start out this way. When trouble comes, often the old "fight or flight response" kicks in, and it might seem easier to run away or give up. One or both of you may have reached the point where you've dug in your heels and refused to make a change. Having a peaceful discussion about your thoughts and feelings can be next to impossible when the air is full of tension and nobody seems to be listening. Compromises are difficult to achieve, and both of you may feel stuck in a passionless void. To remain together "for the children," usually becomes an unhealthy choice if a foundation for a workable partnership has not been created. Inevitably frustration, anger, depression, and at the worst, domestic violence can enter into the scenario. With today's statistics, marriage looms as a risky proposition. The divorce rate is proof that what we have done up until now is barely working. If our society is to survive with a balanced state of mind and a contented spirit, then we need to find a way to build and nurture successful relationships.

Unfortunately, the toxic fallout of separation and divorce often lands squarely on the woman's shoulders and sadly, rains down on the children. Although women have made incredible advances in lifting the glass ceiling, there is still a 20% discrepancy in equal pay for equal work.[3] If there are children, she is often left with the responsibility of raising them. Shattered is the security, trust, and comfort that is found in a home where two people love and respect each other.

Currently, many young people are living together and shying away from the formal marriage agreement. Is the necessary commitment present if children enter the picture? The pressures of parenting can overwhelm a couple, from lack of sleep to keeping up with the bills, and there's little time or energy to get it on with your partner. It's at this point, where the agreement, formally declared in front of your family and friends can serve as a protective bubble around you even while it is being tested. If you have a supportive family that can help with the inevitable stresses that surface in a new partnership, count yourself lucky. I wish I had been given some clues about what a marriage entails and what to expect; and a few tools for how to communicate would have come in handy.

How to Find Love and Make It Last is a practical guide that gives you a perspective on problems that inevitably plague a new relationship, with an accompanying set of tools to deal with the inevitable challenges of life. The goal is to build a happy, healthy, and ever evolving union. The *101 Question Compatibility Test* brings up common situations that might arise as a serious relationship develops. With an insight into what to expect, you're on your way to dealing with problems when they occur. *The Answers* to the questions will delve further into the specifics, revealing what changes or compromises you can make to maintain a long-term commitment. Lucky in Love happens when preparation meets opportunity.[4]

***

Everyone is brought up on fairy tales about the Handsome Young Prince and the Lovely Princess. The radiant couple, after many trials and tribulations, continues on to have a glorious wedding, accompanied by dazzling sunbeams and birds' sweet songs. The celebrated couple walks hand in hand into the sunset, and then what? Is it happily ever after, or does the sun go down and darkness takes over, in a real and metaphorical sense? Reality sets in, life has its ups and downs, and no one seems to be immune from the struggles. Does a new couple have any idea what to expect when it comes to keeping the spark of love alive forever and ever?

Lucky in Love happens when preparation meets opportunity.

With the United States divorce rate hovering around 40%, the answer seems to be a resounding No! It is painful for everyone to see marriages fall apart. Not only is there the sadness and anger that people feel from having attempted to create a successful relationship that didn't work out, but there is also the deep conflicting emotions of the children who have had their world turned upside-down. Researcher, Nicholas Wolfinger found that 89% of the children of broken families are more likely to go through a divorce than people who were raised by intact families.[5] Their experiences have left them with distorted lessons about trust, commitment, mutual sacrifice, and fidelity.

When the heart closes down, love stops, and hard work is required to rekindle the spark. When there is bickering and hassling (of which Robert and I, unfortunately, have had plenty of experience) the energy is sucked out of the room and love flies out the window. When you do the work to unblock old destructive patterns, it leads to true love, an enduring marriage filled with passion, good times, and more than a few miracles. A functioning family is the inevitable product of a couple whose priorities are a commitment to love each other and keep the pathways to happiness free from obstructions.

Before the baby-boomer generation came of age, the number of divorces was extremely low, mainly because it was financially, culturally, socially, and religiously unacceptable.[6] These marriages were not necessarily happy unions.[7] Wives sometimes stayed with their partners under terrible conditions of abuse, drunkenness, and infidelity. Later, when the liberation movement came along, women realized that they didn't have to live under tyranny at home or at the workplace. For the first time, many women were capable of earning enough at their jobs to survive adequately on their own.

Clutching their recent independence, many young women moved in with their boyfriends prior to marriage on a scale never before seen in history.[8] The Baby Boomers brought up in the 1950's model of family life, wanted something not just different, but more authentic with equality between the partners. No longer were men the sole breadwinners while women stayed home with the children. Unfortunately, the charts for navigating the intricacies of working out a successful relationship had not yet been updated. There needed to be something new, but we didn't quite know what that looked like. The models we were getting from our parents didn't fit our ideas of what happiness was all about. By the 1960's there were so many fractured families that the press even gave it a name, "The Generation Gap."[9] The close ties and strong traditions that had existed only a few generations ago had in many cases disappeared.[10]

Following the cultural upheaval of the sixties and seventies, the dynamics of relationships were permanently changed.[11] Could the conditioning of thousands of years of a patriarchal system be overcome? In the relatively recent past, the Constitution of the United States was written by and for white, male landowners. The challenge continues to be to reach equality between men and women as rapidly and gracefully as possible.

During these turbulent times of the late 1960s, the Gay Liberation movement was in its early stages of coming out from the shadows. Homosexuality was against the law and gays had to hide their identity in the workplace and the military. The majority of Lesbians, Gays, Bisexuals, Transgenders, Queers, Intersexual and Asexuals (LGBTQIA) were in the closet, living with the fear of retribution if they should be found out.[12] To appear normal and avoid harassment both gay men and lesbian women were often in heterosexual unions (Marriages of convenience in Hollywood during the 1920's were called "Lavender marriages"). [13] Fortunately, there have been major strides in accepting LGBTQIA people, and we continue to move towards achieving equal rights.[14] Although I am speaking from a heterosexual point of view, this book can be relevant for everyone.

Times are changing; in the "olden days," after a period of courting, a suitor would have to go to his girlfriend's home and formally ask her father for his daughter's hand in marriage. It was definitely not okay to live together until the couple was married. Gay marriage was not even a whispered possibility. The classic fairy tale has the king demanding that the young prince perform a series of tasks to win the princess for his wife. Practically speaking, the conscientious father wanted to make sure that his daughter's admirer had the means to support her and the grandchildren. Did this beau have a good reputation in the community as an honest, hardworking, and loyal person? It was also the father's responsibility to prevent his daughter from marrying while "her head was in the clouds, being in love." In her current state, how could she have an objective long-range view of the situation? She was expected to have her parents blessing for this life-long decision. Her intuitive sense as it were, might or might not be honored depending on dear old Dad's feelings on the matter.

In current times, that rigid formality is mostly gone, but here is a story about how it was several hundred years ago. When my mother, Sophie Montgomery Crane was ninety-two years young, she wrote the memoirs of our family history in a book she entitled *Family Stories*. Her grandson, Luke Rainey, who was living nearby at the time, helped her with the computer work. The following is an excerpt from her writings about my ancestors, Col. William Gilbert and his "gutsy" wife Sarah McCandlass dating back to the early 1700's.

"William was two years old when his parents left Ireland and settled in Charlestown, Massachusetts. Years later, romance blossomed between William and Sarah, but Sarah's father refused to give his permission for her to marry on the grounds that William was too poor. Sarah reluctantly agreed on the condition that her father would not compel her to marry anyone else. However, much to her chagrin, her father decided she should marry a wealthy bachelor in the neighborhood. The wedding date was set, the guests gathered but, shockingly, the bride did not appear. Instead she walked out the kitchen door and through the garden gate, her trunk having been sent before to a neighbor's house where she became the wife of William Gilbert. The Gilberts left immediately for the 'Wilderness of North Carolina,' and she never saw her parents or siblings again. William was an energetic and enterprising young man and soon Gilbert-town, a small manufacturing center, was built with the couple prospering and living in luxury and elegance. He later became a member of the legislature and a Colonel in the Revolutionary War." [15]

History repeated itself when Robert and I eloped, like Sarah and William, without our parents' approval. I was twenty and my new husband was twenty-three, and we had no idea what we were getting into. We were in love and knew that we wanted to go on a lifelong adventure together. Both sets of parents were not happy that we were engaged. Robert was not of the same religion (Protestant) as my family, and I was not Jewish, which supposedly broke a five thousand year tradition. These were some of the stumbling blocks that prevented our parents from giving us their blessings. Fortunately, unlike William and Sarah, we continued to have civil relations with our families that improved over the years.

When a young person first leaves home, there is a transition from being a child to becoming an independent adult who makes his own money, finishes his education, finds a job, and a place to live, basically making major life decisions for him or herself. Relationship decisions usually play a large part of the "20 and 30 something" decades when you are discovering who you are, and what you like. Eventually you become acclimated to an independent lifestyle and have an understanding of where you are headed. Dating and trying to find that special someone to share experiences with begins to take up more of your time.

Have you been through a few trial runs that didn't work out the way you envisioned it in your dreams? Did you get dumped or were you the dumper? Was it a constant drama or did it just fade away to nothing special? With the right knowledge and practice your relationship can be filled with happiness and romance. You can create a meaningful union that will hold up throughout a lifetime, and achieve the loving partnership that you have always wanted. But there is a price to pay! Are you willing to compromise and change to become the wonderful lover that s/he is searching for?

When you move from being a single person to being in a relationship, it's no longer just about you. Your partner's ideas of how s/he wants things, favorite activities and dreams all come into play. To get along, both of you have a responsibility to make the changes that will create a compatible life. To keep your relationship current and to prevent issues from building up into something called "irreconcilable differences," there are the inevitable times when you have to "work it out." Most of the time you might think that whatever it is that is bothering you is not a big deal and you don't need to work it out. Then when you don't talk about it, this little thing can blossom into a big deal.

This working-it-out process was one of the basic agreements of our intentional community known as The Farm in Summertown, Tennessee. In the early 1970's during the back-to-the-land movement, 350 young people who had been meeting weekly for years in San Francisco bought 1000 acres in rural Lewis County, Tennessee. We considered our community a spiritual school not unlike an ashram, only American hippie style. One of the basic tenets of our practice was to work on creating peace and happiness in the world. We knew that the only thing that we have control of is ourselves and if we modify the behaviors that get in the way of cooperative living, and work on having harmonious relationships with those close to us, there was a chance that we could raise the happiness quotient up a notch worldwide. We had an agreement among all the members of the community to discuss any problems that came up. Giving and receiving feedback was our way of delving into the heart of the subconscious (things that were sub to our conscious self where many of our gremlins reside). The object was to find an agreeable solution and facilitate change. If a resolution couldn't be found, we would seek out help from our friends.

Most of the time you might think that whatever it is that is bothering you is not a big deal and you don't need to work it out. Then when you don't talk about it, this little thing can blossom into a big deal.

In today's world, "these friends" are often marriage counselors, but they can also be mentors who are in happy relationships. There were many nights when members of our multi-family household would sit around and work it out. Not being trained in counseling or psychology, we learned by trial and error what helped and what escalated the issues.

Creating an atmosphere of acceptance, trust, and compassion while working it out made it so our words didn't fall on deaf ears. Unfortunately, even when there is an agreement to work on change, resistance and animosity can rear its ugly head and requires patience, nonattachment, and unconditional love. It is one of the most difficult things to do, to listen and understand what is being said. When we make the choice to let down our defenses, knowing that the positive change will be good for both of us, a transformation takes place that creates a cooperative couple and a peaceful household.

There will be an in-depth explanation on this subject in the Chapters about The Subconscious and Communication.

Although Robert and I were deeply in love with each other, at times our relationship was a nightmare and required huge amounts of work before we could find stability. When children arrived, the adventure became more challenging, since we wanted the best for our beautiful boys and girls. The reward for making compromises created a connection that allowed for the love to expand each time we came to an equitable agreement. Working through the process within the crucible that was our school on The Farm trained us in a practice that has remained relevant throughout our forty-five years of marriage.

I am not a marriage counselor, psychologist or licensed health-care professional. My credentials are borne out of a long, happy, continually evolving, and fulfilling marriage and the raising of our eight happy and successful adult children. These ideas are a guide to help you understand what is required for a relationship to work. When children are in the plan, everyone wants to create a safe haven for them to thrive. When we evolve compassionately and communicate graciously, we keep the love vibrant and passionate which is a foundation for a well-functioning family and a stable society.

Please contact the author on Facebook under Virginia Gleser, author, if you have a question or comment, or find an error that needs correcting.

He/she, Him and Her

He and she, her and him, and sometimes s/he are used throughout the book interchangeably, often using only he or she for simplicity's sake. Make it relevant to your situation.

The Birth of A Flower Child

In 1970 at the age of nineteen, I moved to San Francisco to seek my fortune. I was the daughter that The Beatles were singing about in "She's Leaving Home," whose parents were left on the far side of the "Generation Gap" in tears and confusion at the disappearance of their eldest daughter. They couldn't comprehend in these rapidly changing times why she was unhappy and wanted to drop out of college when she'd been such a good student, the Valedictorian of her High School class. What was she doing attending marches and candlelight vigils for peace and civil rights?

I had grown up in South Korea, a child of Southern Presbyterian medical missionary parents who had also been brought up in Korea and China by missionary parents. My physician father was in the process of building a teaching hospital for nurses, interns, and residents, when the North Korean Army crossed the 38th Parallel into South Korea in June of 1950 sparking the Korean War. My parents were a part of the international community that was given a two-day notice to evacuate. They buried a few of their valuables including their wedding silverware, paid the hospital staff the money that they had on hand, and left their work in Jeonju, Korea. My mother was six months pregnant with her first child (me) and bounced along the rough, corrugated dirt roads to Pusan where a ship was waiting to take all the fleeing foreigners to Osaka, Japan. Since the conflict had started unexpectedly, the U.S. military did not have their medical teams in place and the wounded were being flown directly from the battlefields in South Korea to the Osaka Army Hospital in Japan.[16] When the armed forces officials found out that my father and his partner were surgeons, they asked if they would serve until replacements could arrive. My father agreed to help out if his child could be delivered there, so in the autumn of 1950, I entered this world, delivered by Captain Walter Bousa in the Army Hospital.

After the truce was signed in 1953, families were again allowed to return to their homes in South Korea. During my unsettled elementary school years I was home schooled using the Baltimore, Maryland-based Calvert School system, and spent two years each in Seoul, Korea where my father served in the U.S. Army in charge of a MASH hospital near the 38th parallel, and in Towson, Maryland where our family returned for furlough. From the seventh grade on I lived away from home at boarding schools in Taejon and Seoul, since our rural Korean town did not have an international junior or senior high school. During these formative years, I visited my parents during the major holidays and summer vacations. To avoid the cholera outbreaks that inevitably happened every summer we would spend time at beautiful Taechon Beach along the Yellow Sea. My father had a homemade sailboat and enjoyed giving me my first lessons in the art of sailing.

Every five years a missionary family is given a furlough back to the U.S., and in 1960 we visited my grandparents who had retired along the coast of Mississippi. I attended the fourth grade in a segregated school and I was amazed to see signs on gas station bathrooms that read, "Whites" and "Colored." In Korea my family was a minority and belonged to a different race, but we had been welcomed with kindness and respect. I have vivid memories of seeing the degrading treatment of our neighbors in the U.S.

When I was seventeen I traveled alone to the United States to attend college, and experienced intense culture shock.

The year was 1968, a time of enormous upheaval in our country. The Vietnam War was intensifying with our friends and classmates being drafted to fight a war that many of us did not believe in. Racial inequality and bigotry had persisted in the land of freedom and liberty despite the Civil War, the Civil Rights act, the Marches on Washington and Selma, Alabama, and Rosa Parks keeping her seat on that bus in Birmingham. I was a firm believer in civil rights for all and participated in candlelight marches from Martin Luther King, Jr.'s Ebenezer Baptist Church to the State Capitol Building in downtown Atlanta.

The women's liberation movement was also on the national stage, bringing long awaited equal rights to the work place. There was a resurgence of environmental awareness, campus unrest, and the assassinations of both Martin Luther King and Robert F. Kennedy.

Unfortunately the generation gap was never more obvious then when my father and I discussed the Vietnam War, our arguments escalating just like the war had during my teenage years. I was a child of war and I saw this conflict as a repeat of the sadness and disruption that had severed Korea in half and made it into a divided family. I couldn't rationalize the use of violence as a means of working out our problems. There had to be a better way of diplomacy and compromise. I thought it was deplorable that we could bring in our big guns and thousands of men half way around the world to sweep up someone else's mess. My father on the other hand was a firm believer in the domino theory of Communism! He thought it was the blight of the world, and if we allowed it to get a hold in Vietnam it would soon spread to Korea, Japan, and so on. His fears were not unfounded. World War II had recently ended and The Cold War was in full swing. There were rumors that were later confirmed about brutality and aggression by Stalin's Kremlin. In China and in Korea, my father and mother had seen atrocities and inhumane treatment with their own eyes. I understood our differences, but I was dedicated to the search for something better. I became active in the Peace Movement and proudly attended the half a million person Peace March on Washington in 1969. This was incomprehensible to my father who thought I was being brainwashed by the Communists. Years later the Berlin Wall fell and the former Secretary of Defense, Robert McNamara wrote his memoirs, "In Retrospect: The Tragedy and Lessons of Vietnam"[17]admitting that it had been a terrible mistake for the U.S. to go to war in Vietnam. Even then my father had a difficult time letting go.

With tensions mounting, I felt like I had to get away, so I dropped out of college and moved from Atlanta, Georgia to California with my small savings from a summer job. Joining a migration of thousands of my peers from all corners of the United States, who had come of age in the '60s,[18] I wanted to create a life that would be meaningful and might make a difference in the world. It wasn't that I didn't care about my family, but I needed to be out on my own, to see life through my own experiences and perspective and find my way to happiness. I was hungry for love, searching for my place in the world, and discovering where my choices would lead me.

I settled down in an inexpensive room at the YWCA on the outskirts of Chinatown in San Francisco and while I was there, my housemates and I huddled around a small, fuzzy, black and white TV in the lounge, and watched the Apollo 13 space mission fly past the moon. Most of us had recently left home and in between shouts of celebration, we were immensely relieved when the astronauts landed safely back on Earth after a malfunction forced them to abort the moon landing. I realized I was on my own voyage of discovering who I was, standing on the frontier of adulthood, and the last thing I wanted to do was return home.

I also adopted a vegetarian lifestyle. Growing up in post war-torn Korea, I would accompany my father on annual hunts for pheasant, deer, and duck for our winter meat supply. My brother and I went along as bird dogs, hauling the game over our shoulders to our old Willy's Jeep. I was particularly turned off to the whole carnivore experience when we had to trudge through snowdrifts and up steep hills carrying a dead bleeding deer. When I went off to college I made the radical (at that time) decision to become a vegetarian, with the idea of eating a healthy diet while living a peaceful lifestyle. I wanted to live simply with an awareness of my effect on the environment and promote peace by my choice to not even indirectly be responsible for animals being killed. It was easy to become a vegetarian with California's bounty of fresh fruits and vegetables purchased at the local produce stalls around the corner from my apartment.

Living near Chinatown during their New Year's celebration, I was kept awake into the early morning hours by firecrackers blasting off night and day and loud parades with colorful dragons dancing their way through the jubilant and rowdy crowd of revelers. Taking long meandering walks after work and on weekends through the city nestled between steep hills I would climb to Coit Tower and watch the sailboats scooting across white-capped San Francisco Bay. At night I would explore the coffee houses of North Beach and talk deep into the night with strangers about the pressing topics of the day, from Eastern religions to politics, and our future dreams for a utopian world.

Let's leave the late '60's for a moment and talk about you.

When there is light in the soul,
There is beauty in the person.
When there is beauty in the person
There is harmony in the home.
When there is harmony in the home,
There is honor in the nation.
When there is honor in the nation,
There is Peace in the world.[19]

Loving Yourself

Finding out how to accept yourself unconditionally is one of the keys to having love in your life. Your ability to love yourself opens up the door to sharing your life with someone else. There are many different interpretations for the word **love,** but there is only one ever-elusive what-everyone-is-searching-for true love. You were born into this world as a pure and wonderful person, perfect in your uniqueness. And then your parents, teachers, and life experiences molded you. If your caretakers were kind, honest, supportive, and truthful, chances are that you have an honest view of yourself. On the other hand, maybe your caretakers thought they were being kind, when they had no clue they were causing harm. Rarely is there a parent who is not trying to provide for their children in the best way they know how, but there is a tendency for the patterns of child-raising to repeat themselves from generation to generation. Unless you decide to alter deep-seated, destructive habits passed down from your parents, the legacy will most likely continue on down the line. If you are dedicated to finding true happiness, accepting and loving who and where you are right now is the first step. Changing unhealthy behavior is some of the work that is awaiting you. But for now, put your attention on all the positive and valuable qualities that make up who you are.

Finding out how to accept yourself unconditionally, that perfect, unique you, is one of the keys to having love in your life.

You can only love someone as much as you love yourself. When you continually discover how to better care for your emotional, physical, intellectual, and spiritual needs, you can develop those qualities that make a great partner. To keep the love flowing, there are choices to make each moment of the day. Do you choose a healthy diet for your mind, body, and spirit? What does it take for you to be happy with yourself? Can you appreciate periods of solitude? Do you spend time in nature? Can you visualize how powerful you are, and how intelligent, beautiful, imaginative, and talented?

Self-love is about making the right choices. Soul-searching with the intent to make conscious changes to improve yourself is a lifelong endeavor. Do you allow yourself a second big piece of cheesecake, or is it buying an expensive item that you can't really afford? Perhaps later when you find that you have added on a few pounds or run up your credit card bill, you realize that you should treat yourself better. Can you rewrite your script to make yourself into someone who you respect and admire? There is only one person who is in charge of your future, and you can create yourself in any way that you desire.

Here's a great quote from Carolyn Myss' book, *Why People Don't Heal and How They Can*: "Regardless of what needs surface as you learn to know and love yourself, the important points is to "give yourself the right of choice, self-expression, and self-respect."[20]

"Give yourself the right of choice, self-expression and self-respect"
Carolyn Myss

Realizing Your Wizardness

What the Bleep Do We Know written by William Arntz, Betsy Chasse, and Mark Vicente,[21] is a fascinating book that was also turned into a great movie. They talk about how all of us are capable of being wizards, people who create our own reality every moment of our lives. Unbeknownst to most of us, we have been unwizarded. Although we started out as the perfect Master of our own destiny, we have become compromised by family patterns, teachers, society, the media, our choices, our experiences and belief systems. Thanks to these brilliant authors, we have the Wizard Handbook showing us how we can get our Wizardness back. They have also provided us with the Unwizard Handbook that explains how we became compromised. With their kind permission, here are their wise words.

The Unwizard HandBook	***How to Get Your Wizardness Back***
1. Convince people that they are not magicians.	1. Remember your greatness: You are already a Magician.
2. Glorify in your victimhood.	2. Accept responsibility for your life.
3. Confound and crosswire Belief Systems.	3. Don't give power away to authorities and trust your own experience. Remember: Belief is the engine of creation.
4. Make New Knowledge scary and inaccessible.	4. Seek and ye shall find, Knock and it shall be opened to you.
5. Make Magicians creepy and being a Magician dangerous.	5. Find those who are wise and from whom you can learn and study.
6. Get Wizards to lie.	6. On the verge of a lie, ask yourself 'What's the worst that can happen if I tell the truth?' Is the lie worth sacrificing my magical heritage?
7. And Never Look Inside.	7. Don't listen to "Never Look Inside." Look Within.

When your have your Wizardness dialed in, you are on your way to Loving Yourself and being Lucky in Love.

Do you have a voice in your head full of fear or lack of trust? Paulo Coelho in *By the River Piedra I Sat Down and Wept* talks about "The Other" that resembles the devil and the angel sitting on each of your shoulders arguing and nagging about your every move. Is your default belief system set on the worst-case scenario? Are the adults around you telling you what you should and shouldn't be doing? [22] Are you stressed at school or work? Are you involved in a crazy relationship? Are you overdoing the addictive substances? Is it simply that you believe that everything should go your way or is it that you are destined to suffer? Are you glorifying in your victimhood and accusing someone else of causing all of your troubles?

Instead of getting bummed by the obstacles and defeats in life, can you take them on as your challenge? You are the writer, director, producer, and actor in your own movie. If you forget your lines or trip over the stage lights, it's okay. You can study harder and pay closer attention to where you are going. It's not a big deal because you can learn from your mistakes and make changes. Are the actors in your life enhancing your show or are they causing unnecessary drama? When you edit your film, do you do whatever it takes to create an outstanding piece of art? When you find flaws in the script, do you rewrite it? Have you chosen a direction that you want to go in and are you in charge of the show? That you are even attempting to climb this Everest of personal growth and evolution is something that should make you proud. Wizards learn from their experiences, find the silver lining when things seem to fail, and add that knowledge to their repertoire. You are taking the "road less traveled"[23] that will bring you satisfaction, and like Robert Frost said, "That has made all the difference."

Unconditional Love

When you make a poor choice in life, aren't you basically still a decent person? [24] Respecting and loving yourself despite all of your problems, mistakes, and faults is the essence of unconditional love. There's always plenty of guilt, remorse, shame, and regret to go around, but at any moment you can bring out the "guilt-off spray" and let go of these unnecessary burdens that weigh you down. You'll then realize that there are now endless possibilities to create a new you. Everyone makes errors in judgment; fortunately, we can learn from our mistakes. When you forgive yourself and move on, it can be the beginning of a meaningful search that leads to change and a better life. A way is opened to take a fulfilling path, live a life of integrity, and make the right choices.

You are more lovable when you make positive changes. Are you pursuing your interests and your dreams? Are you taking care of your beautiful self? What is it that you see in yourself that you would like to change? Are you eating unhealthy foods or smoking cigarettes? Do you fill your head with mind-numbing TV? Do you let angry words color your speech? Do you harbor prejudices and negative opinions about other people before you have walked a mile in their shoes? Do you notice and care that what you do affects those around you? Do you blame everyone else for how your life is going? If the answer is yes to any of these questions, you can set a new standard to work towards and that is loving yourself. You do have control over unhealthy behavior patterns. You can be brave and make amends for the rotten things you said or did. It's difficult and requires courage, but there are many benefits to making the right choices, and inevitably these changes lead to self-confidence. Loving your pure self, that you know deep down is the real **you**, can set you on the path to true happiness.

Respecting and loving yourself despite all of your problems, mistakes, and faults is the essence of unconditional love. There's always plenty of guilt, remorse, shame, and regret to go around, but at any moment you can bring out the "guilt-off spray" and let go of these unnecessary burdens that weigh you down. You'll then realize that there are now endless possibilities to create a new you.

The only way that love can last a lifetime is if it's unconditional.

"I saw that you were perfect, and so I loved you. Then I saw that you were not perfect and I loved you even more."
Angelita Lim

Love me when I least deserve it because that is when I really need it. Swedish Proverb

Karma and Personal Responsibility

Understanding the concepts of Karma and Personal Responsibility can help you take charge of your life by making choices that will enhance your happiness and success in whatever endeavor you wish to pursue. Karma is an Eastern term that has embedded itself into the vernacular and is loosely translated as: "For every action, there is an equal reaction." Common sayings about the universal law called Karma include, "what goes around, comes around," and "as you sow, so shall you reap." Karma can also be translated as "Luck" or "Fate." Another way of looking at it is whatever situation you find yourself in now is due to choices you have made in the past. If you don't like where you are, make better choices in the present. You might ask, "How could I have chosen such a terrible life?" Are you tempted to be angry at the universe, at God, or your parents? Or is somebody else the reason for your unpleasant situation? This seemingly awful life can be looked on as a teacher that you have chosen as an instructor to lead you to your passion, your purpose, and true happiness. How you live your life in the present each and every moment is the practice. Soon enough, you will discover if what you are doing is the right path. You always have the power to make adjustments as you go along.

Every moment there are choices to be made. You can learn from your mistakes or count on repeating them again and again. Life is that great teacher that won't let you slack off without consequences. Maybe when you have tripped up one too many times, you will have a realization that you need to watch where you are going, and live each day with awareness and personal responsibility.

How you live your life in the present each and every moment is the practice. **You have to start somewhere and that might as well be right here and right now.**

Every moment there are choices to be made. You can learn from your mistakes or count on repeating them again and again. Life is that great teacher that won't let you slack off without consequences...live each day with awareness and personal responsibility.

"Wholeness is not achieved by cutting off a portion of one's being, but by integration of the contraries."
Carl Jung

The Lucky Box

In the boating lifestyle that Robert and I have embraced, sailors are a superstitious lot. One of the things we cruisers have built into all of our boats is an imaginary "Lucky Box." When Robert helps someone get his HAM radio up and running, or helps fix an outboard engine, the good karma is added to our "Lucky Box."

Here's what happened to us when we were aboard Harmony sailing north from Ecuador to Panama, a 600-mile voyage, pushed along by a strong breeze behind us, and the favorable 2-3 knot Humboldt Current. Every once in a while, we would hear a strange pinging noise and when Robert went to check it out, he found that one of our steering cables was beginning to fray. We dug out our emergency tiller and, on the morning HAM radio net, let our fellow cruisers know that we had a potential problem brewing. At the time we were about 100 miles off shore along the Columbian Coast. Fortunately, everything held together and we made it into the southernmost island of the Las Perlas Archipelago south of Panama City and dropped our anchor in a quiet cove. There was only one other boat in the anchorage, and we hailed Otter II on our VHF radio and invited them for a get-together. When Don and Patricia came aboard, they said that they had heard of our steering cable problem on the morning net and as fate would have it, they had just replaced their steering cables for their 3000-mile trip to French Polynesia. Their old cables were not in bad shape, but as a measure of preventative maintenance they wanted new ones. They were glad to give us their used parts that also came with the necessary couplings. We couldn't believe that the only boat in the entire area had just the part we needed, and we happily made a withdrawal from our Lucky Box.

"He who wants to do good, knocks at the gate; he who loves finds the gates open."
R. Tagore Thakur

"Love is a fruit in season at all times, and within reach of every hand." Mother Teresa

Forgive and Let Go

Parents love their children in their own way, but inevitably they botch the job. Nobody has had the perfect childhood. Everyone has experienced memorable highlights along with events that were deeply hurtful. Some of these are small hurts and, unfortunately, there are occasionally major abuses. These events in your childhood helped form your personality when they caused fear, anger, insecurity, low self-esteem, and mistrust. When you take a look at past events and see how they molded your childhood, you can see how these struggles created the person you are today. On the other hand, you may find that some of your problems stem from how you reacted to those same situations. It is possible to clear out the negative aspects of your past and begin to heal that part of you that is an injured child. Becoming the parent of your inner child acknowledges and heals your child's hurts and leads to emotional health. By forgiving the offender(s) (your parents or anyone else), you shoulder the responsibility that is required to take care of yourself. You can then move forward with acceptance, forgiveness, and reconciliation. When you give yourself the attention and love that you deserve, you can expand your capacity to love.

By understanding who your parents were and how you have inherited both their positive and negative attributes, you can see where your strengths and weaknesses have come from. Sometimes your parents' negative qualities can become your strengths. For example, like many fathers of the day, my father was a workaholic. This is a socially acceptable addiction since it put food on the table and kept a roof over the family's head. He was a surgeon and did the great work of healing people, but his busy schedule sliced into family time. When I had children, I easily fell into the role of workaholic and super-mom. There was always so much needing to be done that I had to make a conscious decision to spend quality time with my kids while they were growing up.

Most of us have our share of family problems. Parents inevitably impose hurts and their own unresolved issues onto their children. By working through and dumping this negative baggage, you can free yourself, not to mention the next generation from the painful legacy that has been passed down to you. When you do the complex work of discarding outdated, dangerous, and useless belief systems, energy is freed up to follow your passion. You can be the one to stop the mistreatment. Instead of being a victim, you will become a hero; a seeker willing to go into the deep recesses to heal the damaged person within. You may need help since these things might have been hidden and suppressed all of your life, concealed behind thick walls of fear, mistrust, and anger. Are there moats with sharks swimming around protecting you, as well as preventing you from going into those dark, secretive places within? If your parents or caretakers were emotionally, physically, or mentally abusive, it may take professional counseling to help you find your way out of the maze of trauma that you experienced. It takes a brave and empowered person to seek the help that is needed to facilitate healing. You will not only be doing this work for yourself but for your partner, and possibly a future family. If our society as a whole was more accepting about how truly difficult relationship work is, there would not be such a stigma against asking for help.

There are healing exercises that you can do to help effect these changes. In their book, *Core Transformation*, Connirae and Tamara Andreas describe in detail the ways of delving deeply inside to heal hurts that have been hidden for years.[25] One of their exercises, for example, is to find a quiet place and become aware of yourself at each age of life from conception to the present. Become the parent to that little one and nurture and love that child within you. Take the time to imagine yourself in the womb, cuddle and play with your one-year-old self, your two-year-old self, your three-year-old self, and on up to the present. Each time that you do this meditation, you can concentrate on one year from your past. Mesh with that four-year-old for instance and imagine what it was like growing up in your family. Was there tension between your parents, were you mistreated by an older sibling, and were there not enough moments of love or quality time for you in between all that was going on? There may be times when you cry for the child that is you and acknowledge your child's pain. Instead of feeling like a victim for all the hard times you experienced when you were young, you can now choose to take charge. With that decision and commitment you become the nurturing parent to your child, treating him or her like you would have wanted to be treated, like he or she deserved.

As difficult as it may seem, you can also choose to forgive anyone who mistreated you (like your parents, teachers, or caregivers.) The freedom that you gain going through the forgiveness process will clear out and extract the negativity residing within and set yourself up for a future of clarity and wellbeing. You don't have to forget what happened, trivialize it, or make it seem less hurtful than it was: forgiveness frees you to move forward and embrace the rest of your life. Whoever has hurt you will be metamorphosed from being the monster that haunts you, to the person who has helped you understand the true meaning of forgiveness.

When you feel good about having healed your wounded child, or at least are reconciled with the process, you can take the next step. This may sound strange but the next exercise is nurturing your parents at their different ages of life. Let's take it for granted that most parents suffered through many of the things that you did, if not more so. They probably believed that they were trying to do a better job of parenting than what they received. But, if they have not done any therapeutic work, they are destined to inflict the same mistreatment on their own children. Unfortunately, one third of abused children grow up to abuse their children.[26]

If you have developed a relationship with an empathetic partner, you can ask him/her to do these exercises with you, nurturing and loving both of you for all of your years. When you share your past with each other, it can be an incredibly empowering and healing exercise. When someone outside of your family hears the truth of your life, they can share the burden.

The intention of these exercises is not to dredge up negative, hurtful demons, but to put you in charge of caring for yourself, and bringing you to the present with a clean slate. Love fills the vacuum and you feel charged up. Things should start to go your way. Magic does happen. Every day when you wake up happy and content with your life, the interactions that you have during your day will be rewarding and you will discover love.

What Do You Want to Change?

Why do the difficult work of making changes? You cannot rewrite past mistakes or your family history, but you can begin the process of coming to terms with them, and learn to forgive, let go, and become the person you want to be. With practice, your new approach will become a habit of your daily experience. It will be the groundwork that makes you a happier person who attracts love and good times. There are easy things that you can do to continue the process of creating a new you. Find a quiet place away from family and friends, electronic gadgets, and other distractions. Take time to be still and clear your mind. Have a pen and paper nearby, and write down all of your best qualities. Then write down your talents, your intentions, your dreams and your passions. Be imaginative! Open your mind and be flexible about where it takes you. Everything is possible while you prepare yourself for an exciting journey.

On the other side of the page, write down the things you would like to change in your life: any bad habits, negative family patterns, or your unpleasant behavior during previous relationships. These will be elements of yourself that you can aim to rework and improve. Recognizing these issues hardly eliminates them, but it is the initial step to taking charge.

A group of fun exercises to help you tap into how to make changes for yourself are found in Sharon Franquemont's *You Already Know What To Do.*

Our grandson gets a kick out of his Tae-Kwon-Do class where each month there is a new goal. Here is one I especially liked:

Change the things you can.
When you can't change it,
Change your attitude about it
So you can accept it.

We fall in love by chance; we stay in love by choice.

Tools for Creating the Love You Want

1. **Your positive attitude** affects the world around you. An optimistic approach to the hard times that life throws your way helps you find the blue sky peeking through the stormy clouds. It isn't only a cheerful face and kind words that makes up a positive attitude, but a heartfelt, turned-on feeling that emanates lightheartedness, honesty, integrity and sincerity.

2. **Patience** is when you remain unruffled in your "calm place" while the chaos, uncertainties, and fears of the world swirl around you. It is being tolerant with yourself; you are working towards improvement, not perfection. There are times when your patience is put to the test with your dealings with other people, but understand that they probably have their own issues that they are struggling with. A mellow perseverance will help you stay on your path while you make your way through life.

3. **Flexibility** allows you to flow with whatever life throws your way. People, often out of fear or insecurity, become rigid in their thinking and want to have control over everything. Are you open to change? Of course, you want to let go of hurtful, stubborn, unyielding ways. Flexibility allows new creative ideas and concepts to grow, launching you into a higher state of consciousness.

4. **Acceptance** gives you the ability to appreciate yourself as you are, and in doing so, allows you to make the inevitable changes gracefully. Accept the present and then go forward into the new moment. You are in the perfect place for now: Have you hit bottom? Uh, oh, made a mistake? Doing okay? Or living the Pura Vida? Whatever it is, embrace it.

5. **Forgiveness** helps you accept and love yourself and everyone around you. Yes, we all have our faults, but forgiveness allows you to move forward, absolving yourself and everyone else of all the wrongs from the past. Putting hurts behind you can eliminate grudges and those feelings of revenge. Forgiveness unlocks the chain around your heart that keeps you from loving and being loved in return.

6. **Non-attachment** is the knowledge and ability to deal with the fact that there are some things you cannot change. When you release that tight hold on something that is just not going to go your way, everyone wins. There are plenty of other possible directions to take, ways to be, things to do, and places to go. You can only change yourself; you can't change anyone else. You cannot grab someone else's steering wheel and show them where to go.

The Serenity Prayer

Grant me the Serenity
To accept the things I cannot change,
Courage to change the things I can,
And wisdom to know the difference.[27]

7. **Tolerance**: Our planet is filled with a fascinating diversity of cultures, races, religions, and political systems. Unfortunately mankind has this ridiculous, crazy-making tendency to want to look down on anyone who is different. Take your pick, black or white, men or women, poor or rich, immigrants, and so on. This way of thinking creates an "us versus them conflict." Biases and prejudices are usually handed down to you from your family and friends, and these teachings can be unlearned.

Seeing life from a different perspective challenges your ways of thinking and keeps you honest. Everyone who enters into your life has something to offer when you relate to him or her with friendliness and respect. Tolerance is one of the keystones for peace and understanding, and if we can get in the habit of practicing it in our homes, it can permeate the world.

8. **Gratitude** allows you to appreciate every experience or person that comes into your life. It's easy to be thankful for all the wonderful things that have happened, but when you are grateful for the difficulties and challenges that you have overcome, the reward is self-confidence and empowerment. When you can transcend the beliefs that life is unfair, and that your frustrating troubles are someone else's fault, you can live life to the fullest.

9. **Passion**: Whatever it is that brings fun and laughter into your life and inspires and excites you, that's where your passion resides. Enjoying quality time with my family and friends, sailing, writing, dancing, gardening, cooking, painting, giving and receiving massages, and listening to music are some of mine. What are yours?

Keeping these nine tools handy will help you deal with the "always somethings." The life you've chosen is hopefully full of beautiful scenery, fascinating fellow travelers, and exciting experiences, no matter how many potholes, and construction slow-downs you encounter. An appropriately cool bumper sticker says, "Obstacles or Adventure, It's all in the Attitude."

"Obstacles or Adventure,
It's all in the Attitude."

"Love is a force more formidable than any other. It is invisible – it cannot be seen or measured, yet it is powerful enough to transform you in a moment, and offer you more joy than any material possession could."
Barbara DeAngelis

Uh, Oh, Negative Habits

Here are nine positive actions that you can take to clear out negative habits:

Step One: Choose one of your negative traits that you have written down from the previous chapter, "What Do You Want to Change?"

Step Two: Accept that this is a part of you. When this happens, there's usually shock and denial, pain and guilt, anger, and possibly depression. There's a blues song that says, "I'm not what I want to be, but I'm better than I used to be, and I'm getting better all the time." The tendency is to put yourself down, but you can eliminate blame or shame and even cultivate that self-deprecating humor. Embrace this part of you and understand that up until now it has served a purpose. Perhaps you learned it by imitating those around you or you adopted it because you felt like you were invisible and needed to assert yourself. Was anger, stubbornness, or defensiveness a way to protect yourself or get your way when you were a child? Accepting yourself as you are is a difficult thing to do. Everyone has trouble with this realization. Lighten up, we are all a perfect whatever we are and, fortunately, if you don't like your behavior you have the power to change it.

Step Three: When you accept yourself as you are, you are empowered to change whatever it is that you want. There is a sense of freedom when you realize you can let go.

Step Four: Can you take note of where this unpleasant behavior came from? When you look around at your role models was there ugly language, laziness, or a bad attitude? Did you add it to your repertoire? It's probable that you don't remember when these habits first formed, but it's likely that it happened at an early age. When you become aware that this behavior is not to your liking and you decide to change, your free will is working for your benefit. Gregg Braden writes in *The Divine Matrix*: "At every moment there are infinite possibilities of choice of how you will be or act. Making the choice is free will."[28] When you take charge and use your free will, creating and molding how you want to be, you exhibit your power, your potential, and respect for yourself. It might seem complicated, but when the change happens, it's miraculous!

Step Five: Feel good about yourself when you exercise your power of free will. You are now someone who consciously chooses what kind of person you want to be and what habits to leave behind. Celebrate the person you have become.

Step Six: Know in your heart that the hard work will be worth it. Envision the negative pattern leaving your body, mind, and soul. Often during stressful situations, the old unhealthy trait may reappear. This is the ultimate challenge. When you find yourself indulging in the behavior that you have decided to throw out, take note and stop. You will feel empowered, knowing that you were able to identify something that you wanted to change and can actually stop doing it. It is possible to break a habit, but it will probably take many attempts to eradicate an unhealthy routine. Since it has been with you for so long, it is probably a part of every cell and neural synapse in your body. Be patient. Stay vigilant, and continue to evolve. You can develop the habit of change.

Step Seven: Forgive yourself when you fall back into old patterns especially in stressful situations, and have to make an adjustment again and again. For some of us, it may take a thousand run-ins with our demons to realize how deeply that habit is embedded in our psyche. Nobody is unscathed and we all need to be let off the hook. Forgiveness is a partner of unconditional love.

Step Eight: Seek out a mentor or a guide, someone who has gone through changes and understands what you are going through. S/he can be a teacher, counselor, therapist, spiritual guide, or someone who "has it together" and is a positive, wise, happy role model. This quest might be made easier when you ask for recommendations from family and friends.

Step Nine: When you acknowledge and begin work on a specific negative trait from your list, self-respect and trust grows. Celebrate this stage of your transformation. Appreciate the hard work you've done.

> "Love is a fabric which never fades, no matter how often it is washed in the water of adversity and grief."
> Robert Fulghum

Catch Me Exercise

When you decide to make a change to rid yourself of a negative pattern, try an easy one for starters, like, for instance, saying "Good morning" to everyone you meet, or not being rude to your family and friends. Write down exactly what change you would like to make. Then notice when you actually do it. Did you come up with a nice response rather than your "same old, same old" routine. What did you do that was different? When these wheels are put in motion, you are working towards an attainable goal. It's not uncommon to find yourself trying to get away with it, sort of like sneaking behind your own back? This is the "catch me" part of the exercise. Are you sabotaging yourself? Have you talked yourself into thinking that you can't do it because it is too difficult? It may be easier than you think; all you have to do is make the conscious choice. What emotions and thoughts flood through you when you try resisting an old habit? You probably need to face old hurts, acknowledge them, give them their due, forgive, and let go. You are seeing unconditional love in action. Self-confidence increases when you treat yourself well.

Perspective Counts

How about the idea of (hold on to your seats) the subatomic particle reality that states: **We are all One**? All of our flesh, bones, blood, atoms, thoughts, and ideas are all one entity. We breathe the same air and drink the same water. We share the same emotions and dreams. We want the best for ourselves, the earth, and all sentient beings. Whenever you look at someone else, you are looking at yourself. If you look at another person with compassion (feeling with them), you can learn about yourself. They will become your teacher. Plutarch quoted Cato the Elder in the first century AD, "The fool never learns from the wise man, but the wise man learns from the fool."[29]

"The fool never learns from the wise man, but the wise man learns from the fool."
Cato the Elder

When life flows easily in the direction you want to go, it feels like the stars are lined up. But when life throws a major obstacle in your path, you can only resist it up to a point. You may have seen the bumper sticker: "When people make plans, God laughs." In the sailing community we often say, "Our plans are written in the sand at low tide." Let reality be your guide and when you set out to live your dream, it usually becomes obvious which step to take next.

Let reality be your guide and when you set out to live your dream, it usually becomes obvious which step to take next.

Off to San Francisco to Meet My Love

The *carefree hippie experience was in full swing in 1970's San Francisco, but even with my live-simply-on-the-earth philosophy, the small savings that I'd earned at a summer secretarial job were dwindling and the rent for my $32 a month room was coming due. I needed to look for work, so in the early grey, damp fog, I set out to apply for a job at an employment agency in one of the downtown high rises that casts dark shadows on this burgeoning city's financial district. After finishing my interview and typing test, I closed the door with my fingers crossed hoping to land a much-needed position.*

While I was walking towards the elevator, a tall, attractive man was leaving an adjoining agency and we walked down the long hallway together, striking up a conversation about our hopes for employment. Robert asked me if I had a minute to visit an art gallery where he had been working part-time. It featured John Lennon's collection of black and white sketches and Bennie Bufano's gracefully rounded, stone animal sculptures. Robert had coincidentally found a path to my heart. From my earliest childhood, art had been an important part of my life, and some of my warmest memories were of painting flowers alongside of my grandmother, Florence Hedleston Crane. She was an accomplished botanist and landscape artist who painted scenes of Korea and the Gulf Coast of Mississippi. Strolling along the Embarcadero, discussing boats and sailing, we shared our passion for the ocean. Alternate energy was one of the topics of the day and we talked about the possibility of sailing ships carrying cargo once again. Walking me home, he asked me for my phone number, and he promised to stay in touch. That was one of two phone calls that I was hoping to receive. The employment agency was the first to call, Yes!!!, signing me up with a minimum wage job as an office typist and clerk at Baker and Hamilton, a wholesale hardware distributor on the south side of Market Street.

Every weekday morning I stepped outside my front door into the quiet San Francisco streets. Dressed in a maxi coat and tall leather boots, a cool mist swirled around me, caressing my waist-long hair. Hopping aboard a cable car to work was so unique and I clattered down Nob Hill, passing Union Square on my way to the seedier side of town. Every afternoon, I rode the cable car back up Powell Street, chatting with tourists from around the world. When the cable cars were full, I'd walk the steep hill home.

Robert held on to that slip of paper with my phone number and soon called and asked to see me again. When he came by to pick me up, he was dressed in corduroy bell-bottomed pants and a light blue, embroidered Turkish shirt that set off his clear blue eyes. Dating was exciting with so much to do in San Francisco! We'd go to Golden Gate Park or Ocean Beach, or just hang out with our vibrant city friends. We might browse art galleries, and occasionally baked fruit and nut breads that we sold to a health food store for spending cash, our first business together.

I'll take a break from the early romantic moments of my flower child days in San Francisco, but I'll come back to it soon. Economic reality meant I had to go to work.

Is Your Work Fulfilling?

What you choose to do for your occupation and career will ideally not only earn you a living, but it will bring you deep satisfaction in a job well done. In our modern world, money is the form of energy that we use to pay for our housing, school, food, clothing and incidentals. In the past we might have bartered, and there is a movement afoot that uses credits to trade useful resources and skills among people in a certain area, but that is the exception.

Here are five basic things that most people need for a happy life:

1. You like your work.
2. You like who you work with.
3. You like who you live with.
4. You like where you live.
5. You are in good health.

Work, sometimes referred to as one of those "four letter words" is how you will support yourself and your family. Since you'll be spending a lot of your time on the job, you want to choose an occupation that is challenging, and fulfilling. Discovering your passion and finding a career that captivates your interest can lead to a productive and satisfying life. It's the best when your occupation brings you pleasure, inspires you to wake up each day, and brings you a sense of joy and accomplishment. When you find the right vocation, there is enthusiasm, a sense of satisfaction, and empowerment, not to mention money in your bank account.

When work is interesting, and the pay is decent, we usually find a happy camper. Is there someone encouraging and supporting your vocational goals and dreams? Monetary wealth is not necessarily an essential ingredient for happiness, but it can be a result of a passionate life. Eleanor Roosevelt said, "Happiness is not a goal, it's the byproduct of right living."[30]

There is more to wage earning than merely paying the bills. Your vocation should include what interests you. If you are not enjoying what you do or the people you work with, and are struggling with a job that seems to be going nowhere, it will serve you well to look for better possibilities. Improving your skills to make yourself employable for a position in your chosen field may require an investment in school, including taking out student loans. If you are worried about going into debt, think of it as betting on yourself and who better to bet on! Usually the results will be job satisfaction and you will be more than compensated financially.

If you have the entrepreneurial gene, look into what it takes to start your own business, but don't quit your day job yet! In your off-hours, you can begin researching the possibilities in the field that interests you. There are mentors who can help you traverse the thorny path of obtaining a business license, keeping track of your accounts and inventory, networking, paying taxes, and selling your product. In our town of Modesto, Ca. there is a group of mostly retired business owners who use their extensive experience to help guide new entrepreneurs down the road to success.[31] The Internet has also become a great source of information.[32]

If you find yourself in an unhappy work situation or are having trouble finding a job, an interesting place to start is to make a list of your top five dream jobs. Then become proactive about pursuing what you love, while keeping your focus on your goals. Showing up every day to work or in search for a job, radiating enthusiasm even when you're doing the most mundane assignment usually gets you ahead. Everyone notices when you are on time, work with vigor, and be helpful to customers and your co-workers. With a positive attitude, good things start happening. If your job is disagreeable, but a necessary stepping stone to a better career and a more satisfying future, can you be comfortable with it for a relatively short time, while you go through the required hoops towards your goal?

If you haven't been able to find a job, how about volunteering for a local non-profit organization? If you are hardworking and fun to be with, it is likely that a paying job will open up for you. At the very least you will be able to network, and possibly find promising leads. When you help others, you end up helping yourself. More than likely, you will begin riding a successful wave into the future that you could only have imagined not too long ago.

You might enjoy reading Paulo Coelho's short book, *The Alchemist* about a young man who set out to pursue his dreams. Like all of us he needed to pay the bills and went from one mundane job to another. With each new experience, however, he gained skills, confidence, and connections that coincidentally opened doors that eventually led to the fulfillment of his dreams.[33]

Finding Our Community - Monday Night Class

On a clear, blue San Francisco Sunday, Robert and I decided to hitchhike to Golden Gate Park to see if there was a pick-up softball game or one of the spontaneous jam sessions that sometimes were on the cutting edge of the California music scene. We didn't have to wait long before a friendly couple picked us up in their old delivery van that they had converted into a colorfully painted camper home. We were enchanted by their mobile lifestyle, and while we were talking, they mentioned that we might be interested in a gathering called "Monday Night Class." The meetings were held at the Family Dog, located on the Great Pacific Highway, which was one of several concert venues in the city that featured the latest psychedelic rock groups. Most theaters are dark on Monday nights and the promoter, Chet Helms, was willing to offer his facility to the rapidly expanding class. It sounded like something we would enjoy and so the following week we arrived at the beachfront rock hall, where over five hundred mostly young people were quietly meditating while sitting cross-legged on pillows on the floor. Stephen Gaskin had started teaching this class several years ago at San Francisco State College. Sitting on a slightly elevated stage, he focused our attention by blowing a ram's horn and leading us in a long, resonating OM, the single note of so many voices sounding like the undulating rhythms of a symphony. It was magnificent and a tranquil stillness followed the last note. Stephen then gave an articulate, hip, and humorous talk about things Spiritual while making it relevant to the poignant issues of the day. The class continued with a dialogue that explored love, peace, sex, drugs, religion, lifestyles, and how these affect interpersonal relationships. Robert and I loved that first class; it was so inspiring and insightful that we continued to go week after week feeling that we had found a group of people of like mind who were talking about relevant ideas. At the time, the 60's into the 70's, there was a spiritual awakening in the West with an interest in Eastern religions and gurus like the Beatles' teacher, Maharishi Mahesh Yogi. Here in the U.S. we had our version of holy men and visionaries and many young people were seeking spiritual guidance in an attempt to understand their place in a rapidly changing world.

There were great discussions about esoteric subjects such as Tantric yoga, and how energy and telepathy work. A dialogue about being a vegetarian reinforced my ideas when it was framed in a way that made sense, a gentler way to live. There was talk of settling on a piece of land, living self-sufficiently, and raising our families closer to nature that fit in with our ideas of the future.

I was so happy being with Robert that even though we had only been dating for three months, I thought it was a great idea when he asked me to move into a small apartment off of California Street with him and his roommate, a high school friend from the Bronx. Robert never did receive any word about the job he had applied for and, destined to become an entrepreneur, he started the "Revolution Moving Company" with his old '57 Chevy pick-up.

San Francisco's housing was at a premium in 1970 just like it is today, and young people often lived collectively in crowded apartments and created living spaces out of VW vans and old school buses. These imaginative living quarters were artistically decorated as well as comfortable creations with lofts, kitchens, carpeted ceilings and warm stoves.

It wasn't long before we pooled our resources, and purchased a small van, creating our own home on wheels. After work Robert would pick me up in the truck we had named "Mother Oats," and we would find a romantic flat spot to park near the beach, or high on the hill at The Legion of Honor overlooking the Golden Gate Bridge. In the meantime he had become an apprentice mechanic with our cantankerous vehicle constantly requiring attention. He bought a small tool kit and found a mechanic guru who taught him the fundamentals of engine maintenance and repair, lessons that proved to be invaluable down the road.

"I have decided to stick to Love; hate is too great a burden to me."
Martin Luther King, Jr.

" And in the end, the Love you take is equal to the Love you make."
Paul McCartney

"All we are saying is, Give Peace a Chance." John Lennon

Dating

Wouldn't it be worthwhile if there were classes about dating? Popular newspaper columnist L.M. Boyd occasionally wrote as the "Love and War Man." He suggested that there be diplomas given out that define your level in the dating scene. You earn a "Bachelor of Singles degree" after living on your own and supporting yourself for four years. After meeting a serious partner an "Elementary Marriage degree" can follow. After two years of the beginner's course of "Elementary Marriage" plus an "Advanced Marriage degree" you can earn your "Masters of Matrimony." You need seven years total for your "Doctor of Domesticity." Associate degrees, something like Marriage Elementary can be awarded to those who cohabit.[34]

A friend of the family was telling me how he was engaged at nineteen and at the last minute ended up calling off the wedding. He said that he was forever grateful since he was having so much fun being single, and was just not ready to settle down. Maybe there would be less cheating and extra-marital affairs later on down the line, if young people could enjoy dating a variety of people before settling down and getting married. Your true love may not turn out to be the glamorous person who was your first choice, but the person who truly cares for you and treats you with respect. Perhaps that person is from another culture and expands your horizons. Music teachers say, "Practice, practice, practice." Make mistakes, make changes, know each other, and know yourself. What's your hurry? Dating is fun and games, a time to become acquainted while taking lighthearted adventures.

Courting is an old concept that is almost completely overlooked in our fast-paced society. Up until the early part of the last century, there were rules of courting that kept relationships progressing at a deliberate pace. The couple could not put undue pressures on themselves since parents made sure that things went slow. In those days, some of the first dates might include asking the parent's permission to take the girl on a walk, talking on the front porch, or in the parlor. Later the suitor might be invited to dinner with the family, or would take her to a dance or social event like the county fair. A chaperone might escort the couple on their outings. There were specific times set for coming home. The parents wanted to make sure the gentleman was treating their daughter well, and pursuing his schoolwork or an apprenticeship towards a career. Back then there was no welfare or food stamp safety net to support women and children if the marriage did not survive, so the burden fell on the parents to ensure their daughter was well provided for. When her beau had a job that proved that he could support a future wife and family, he was then permitted to broach the subject of an engagement with her father, and ask for his daughter's hand in marriage. Parents were looking for a man who was mature enough to take on his new responsibilities.

So much has changed and our modern society has allowed many of these constraints to go out with the horse and buggy. Parents generally allow their adult children more freedom to make their own choices. Instead of courting, **dating** is the word (Is that still the word?) we use for a trial run to see if there is a chance for a lasting relationship. Dating is all about doing things that you both enjoy, without the pressure of a commitment. Certainly, there are amazingly cool things about your new boyfriend or girlfriend, and inevitably some behaviors that are not very savory, which your partner doesn't even seem to be aware of. You are seeing what I am going to call "the subconscious," something that is beneath his or her consciousness. There are also situations that will inevitably come up that will test your bravery, and challenge your ability to work things out to your satisfaction. When you have narrowed it down and found someone who feels like the one, are you able to talk freely and openly about everything including your feelings? How do you "work out" your disagreements and arguments? And what is this thing that we call the subconscious and why is it relevant to a relationship?

Situations come up between two people that inevitably require a tune up or repair. Why is she so moody? Why is he so controlling? What is she nagging about? Why is he so aloof and cold? What did I say that caused that argument? There will be ups and downs in any relationship and how you work out the hassles determines how successful the relationship will be. Taking care of issues when they pop up is the lubrication for a smoother ride.

More about this on Pg. 102-109 in the chapter "The Subconscious," but let's begin by talking about safety first and how the body works.

> When you realize you want to spend the rest of your life with somebody, you want the rest of your life to start as soon as possible. "When Harry Met Sally"

How the Body Works

A short Anatomy 101 course will show how the human body is a well-designed combination of science, beauty and art; this physical architectural wonder is magnificently engineered inside and out, a matrix of intricate systems that mostly runs without our conscious involvement. Understanding how your physical body grows, develops, and operates can inspire you to take special care of yourself for a lifetime.

For millennia, biologically speaking, the female's concern has been to mate with a suitable male who can provide a safe environment for her offspring. The male of the species, on the other hand, has a drive to mate in order to ensure the continuance of his line. Sex is one of the driving forces of a relationship and since we generally live longer now than in the past, it's not unusual for couples to wait until their late twenties or thirties before starting a family.

Scientists who have studied our biochemistry have found that hormonal changes appear in our bodies during different life stages: dating, settling down, having children, and the empty nest years.[35] Teenagers, for instance, have a notoriously difficult time rising early in the morning, but have plenty of energy for staying out late. Middle-aged folks have the stamina to rise early and put in a full day's work to provide for their families. Parents tend to get up with their babies in the middle of the night and are happy to go to bed at a reasonable hour. Elders tend to wake up with the sun and go to bed not long after sundown. Waking up during the middle of the night to read or do whatever is not necessarily insomnia, but part of an ancient biorhythm. It's only since the electric light and our modern schedules that are run by alarm clocks that we label waking up in the night to be a problem. Our bodies evolve while we age and chemical and hormonal changes keep us in sync with our biological clocks.

Female physiology is amazingly sophisticated and elaborately evolved. Sometime between the ages of nine and sixteen, the hormones and the chemicals in a girl's body[36] miraculously change and she begins her menstrual cycle. The eggs that she has stored in her ovaries since birth are released, one egg a month, coincidentally synchronized with the cycles of the moon. The woman's body then builds up a comfortable nesting place in the uterus for fertilization to take place. There is a small window of approximately two to three days when a woman is ovulating. When the egg remains unfertilized (from not having intercourse that results in a pregnancy), estrogen hormone levels slack off and progesterone levels increase, and within a couple of weeks, menstruation begins. This blood is the sloughed off uterine lining that was built up to nurture a baby. After menstruation, the cycle repeats itself and the body starts preparing for the next release of an egg. Once this cycle has begun, a girl has biologically become a woman, and in many cultures it was not uncommon for girls to have a rite of passage, marry, and start a family. These days having children is often delayed to finish an education or start a promising career that can help support a family.

Regular monthly cycles are fairly predictable, and a woman can become pregnant approximately halfway between the cycles or fourteen days before menstruation. However, irregular cycles are quite common and are caused by various stresses like exams, travel, illness, and undue anxiety. In plain terms, if you are going to have sex, use protection rather than play the guessing game. However, there is no sure method of birth control. Certainly the withdrawal method or the rhythm method is risky.[37] Pulling out or withdrawal before ejaculation is a dangerous game of chance since sperm does drip out in small amounts whenever a male is aroused. Natural methods of birth control, such as the temperature method or 'Natural Family Planning,' [38]can be effective with the proper knowledge and diligence, but they are far from 100% safe. Although the odds are much better with the pill and condoms, only abstinence is 100% foolproof.

Hormones affect a woman physically and emotionally, and during ovulation she is usually vibrant, sexy and turned on. Like all mammals in heat, she is biologically attracting a partner in order to procreate. Men of course respond to the obvious subliminal messages that are being broadcast. Clearly it is a time to be cautious. If sex does take place and contraceptives are not used, there's a good chance that the woman will become pregnant.

A week to five days or so before a period can often be a touchy time for a woman. Progesterone hormones are swirling around, emotions can seem blown out of proportion, and arguments can be dramatic. PMS (Pre-Menstrual Syndrome) has made its appearance. Most women have it to a certain degree, and some more than others. These hormones can give a woman clearer insight into who she is, what she wants, and what is bothering her. This can occasionally cause her to bring up issues that she has allowed to slide for the rest of the month. Usually, the things she feels are valid, but can seem pent-up and explosive. If her partner is caring and pays attention to her needs, he remembers that this is a time to be particularly sweet and tender and listen to what she has to say. Men may have to read between the lines, and if he is a compassionate listener there can be a serious discussion about what she is feeling. This may actually be the time when new agreements are made that can bring your relationship to a higher level.

Men also have hormones[39] and cycles - daily, monthly and seasonally - and although not as pronounced and regular as a woman's cycle, they are just as real. He can be emotionally up and down and occasionally has enormous spurts of energy that are balanced by times when he just wants to chill. There are studies still underway about how testosterone and even estrogen affects men's bodies and emotional health.[40]

See Reading References for informative books about sexuality and your body, Pg. 284.

> The human body is a well-designed combination of science, beauty and art; this physical architectural wonder is magnificently engineered inside and out, a matrix of intricate systems that mostly runs without our conscious involvement. Understanding how your physical body grows, develops, and operates can inspire you to take special care of yourself for a lifetime.

Safety First

During a driver's education course, the class watches gory films of car wrecks to see the devastating things that can happen when you drink or text while driving. Believe it or not, in 2013 there were 6 million wrecks on U. S. roads involving 40,000 fatalities and 3 million injuries.[41] Wow!

On our highway of love there are also speed limits and stop signs designed to help you avoid the emotional and physical wreckage. The gory films in the course on sex include HIV/AIDS and other sexually transmitted diseases (STDs), rape, unwanted pregnancies, abortions, neglected children, divorce, and poverty. When a new love relationship begins to blossom, it's time to think about safety. Hopefully you will take care of yourself and be respectful of your body. (The sages don't call it **playing with fire** for nothing.) Talking with your partner about contraception, birth control, STD testing, and commitment in your relationship before you become intimate demonstrates your maturity and empowers you to act responsibly.

What if the worst happens? Do the gory films and harsh warnings in the Driver's Ed classes prevent accidents? Unfortunately, they do not. Life often throws a curve ball like an unplanned pregnancy, an STD, or a partner that freaks out and leaves you to deal with the consequences. However, you can become empowered despite your mistakes. A hard-knock lesson from the universe can jolt you into the realization that you have a responsibility to take care of business. Can you forgive yourself, forgive the other person, and learn your lessons? Visualizing yourself in such a situation should grab your attention enough to slow you down. A sincere relationship requires thoughtfulness and caution.

You can become so enamored and tied up in your love affair that you fail to see what is happening around you. Is your entanglement preventing you from remembering your contraceptives? Is your date wanting more than what you are willing to give? Can you say "No" and are you able to stand up for yourself? Part of protecting yourself is keeping drinking and drugs to a minimum, especially with a new acquaintance or someone you are not comfortable with. Consider self-defense training; it not only teaches you how to protect yourself, but builds up your physical strength while increasing your sense of empowerment and confidence.

How are your discerning skills when it comes to how sex is portrayed in the media? Recently a popular TV program showed a great example of how our media sometimes bombards us with destructive images.[42] The middle-aged male character, recently separated from his wife but not yet divorced, asked a female coworker to have a beer with him, and they then went out for dinner. On the date they said, "Let's play it by ear." There were no words about safety. No lines like, "Wait, this is going too fast," or at least, "I have to find my condom, honey." They just jumped into bed! Before turning on the TV, I had just heard that one of my daughter's friends had accidently become pregnant. They must have "played it by ear" too, but the ear is too far away from the action. The message is: **It is easier to have sex than to talk about it.** What could have been a thought provoking and interesting story became trash. Unfortunately, the media is slow to change, still portraying cigarettes, alcohol and violence as romantic and sexy. How many ads are full of subliminal messages that suggest that if you buy this car or drink that beer, you will be rich, surrounded by beautiful, happy, young women and men and have a life like a movie star? How many times is violence used to solve problems?[43]

Garbage In Equals Garbage Out.

When you practice the art of discrimination and filter the useless or harmful stuff that is cluttering your mind, you'll find yourself making smarter and safer choices. Mike Dooley says, "Thoughts Become Things, Pick the Good Ones." [44] Stephen Gaskin in his book, *This Season's People* says, "Attention is Energy. Whatever you put your attention into, you will receive more of," [45] The computer geeks say, "Garbage in equals garbage out." **Be Safe** and Drive your mind and body responsibly.

"Thoughts Become Things, Pick the Good Ones." Mike Dooley

"Attention is Energy. Whatever you put your attention into, you will receive more of." Stephen Gaskin

Birth Control, Pregnancy and Abortion

During your teenage years, intense hormones are screaming through your body, begging you to reach out for closeness and the thrill of a sexual relationship. In the passion of the moment, it is hard to think straight about what you are doing. There is an old expression that says, "There is not enough blood in the body for an erect penis and the brain at the same time." Do you know what it takes to protect yourself from an unwanted pregnancy or a sexually transmitted disease? Women who are in charge of their lives take care of their bodies.

Before you rush into exhilarating sex, take a look at what happens when you become "accidentally" pregnant and be aware of the heavy choices that are involved. You can keep the baby, give it up for adoption, or have an abortion. But why weigh your life down with these difficult choices when you can plan responsibly from the start? Why not use protection? Did condoms feel like you were wearing a raincoat? Did you forget to take your pill? Did you think you could keep your man around if you had his child? Did it make you feel more like a man, stronger and more powerful, to have impregnated a woman? You have probably seen the billboard: **Making a child does not make a man. Taking care of a child does.** It is hard to realize your full potential when you are tied down with an unwanted child. Being a parent drastically changes your future. Life paths you may have planned to walk down will take a detour.

If you are already pregnant, did you want to get pregnant or was this an unplanned pregnancy? Are you married? Do you have a stable, financially solvent relationship? This can be one of the most wonderful times in your life. However, if it's an unwanted pregnancy, life is providing you with a tough lesson. Is your boyfriend ready to take on the responsibility of a child? Has he completed his education and does he have a decent job? If he is not ready to support a family, in the classic scenario, he doesn't take care of his family and the child is born into this tension. If on the other hand, both of you rise to the challenge of becoming responsible parents, there will be hard work ahead but the rewards are great.

Unplanned teenage pregnancies are a major concern in the United States. Do these young women not have enough love in their lives, thinking that having a baby who is totally dependent on them will fill that need? Or is it that having a baby will make their boyfriend stick around? Whatever the reason, if these young people could develop self-respect and confidence, empowered to do whatever they dream, they wouldn't have a vacuum to fill and they could take charge of their lives. Finishing an education, for instance, and finding a good job is what provides a young person with a secure future. When you are in charge of your life, there is no need to desperately search for a boy/girlfriend. Instead, work on becoming a well-rounded, self-assured individual, not hungry for love, a half-person searching for the other half. A relationship will develop naturally, a byproduct of good choices and living a happy life.

What choices do you have if you are pregnant with an unwanted child? Did you think, "This will not happen to us?" Or did you have a wild night and are now considering taking the morning-after pill? This pill can prevent the pregnancy, but there can be unpleasant physical or psychological side effects. Is this why your parents said to "go slow?"

Everyone knows that abortion is not a simple solution. It is one of the alternatives that can leave emotional scars and possibly physical ones as well.[46] It would be a positive shift if there could be a progressive dialogue between the Pro-Choice and Pro-Life organizations. There is a bridge across this controversy. It is possible to find the common ground that is not separate or exclusive. Encouraging women to become empowered and respect themselves and their bodies would go a long way to changing the need for abortion.

A woman has absolute responsibility for her actions and control over what happens to her body. Her body is not a part of the public domain, and basically her pregnancy is nobody's concern but her own and her medical practitioners. A judge, lawyer, member of Congress, or a congregation should not have a say over a woman's body. If the situation were reversed, would men want anyone telling them what to do with their private business? Abortion would almost become obsolete, only necessary to save an endangered mother's life, if people considered their options before they have unprotected sex. Abstinence is the best contraceptive, but for those who are sexually active, using birth control pills or condoms usually prevents a pregnancy. When you take personal responsibility for yourself and your partner, you consider the consequences, make intelligent decisions, and save yourselves a huge amount of heartache.

When there's a firm commitment between the two of you to be together for the long run, a pregnancy is a joyful occasion. Certainly, the time of conception is a magical experience.

Sexually Transmitted Diseases

If you decide to become sexually active, birth control pills taken as prescribed can keep you from becoming pregnant, but they do not protect you from STDs. Condoms are a safe way to prevent disease, but they aren't 100% safe. There are ever-evolving strains of Sexually Transmitted Diseases, (STDs) including herpes, chlamydia, gonorrhea, syphilis, and AIDS. According to www.hhs.gov there are 20 million cases of STDs among 15-24 year olds each year and 4 in 10 sexually active teen girls has an STD that can cause infertility. Males age 15-19 are 2/3 of the new HIV cases each year. Also 34% of the Gonorrhea cases and 39% of the Chlamydia cases are in ages 20-24. Young people and gay and bisexual men are at the greatest risk.

Love means protecting each other against diseases. Shouldn't you talk about this before you have sex? Open communication shows your mutual respect and maturity. Currently all of these diseases are at epidemic proportions,[47] and both of you will, of course, want a negative test before you have sex. Remember that STDs are serious and can cause chronic health problems and infertility.[48] Take care of your sweetheart. It's easy! You can be tested at any local public health clinic, and Title X family planning clinics give low cost testing and contraceptive services for all.[49]

The Sixties Revolution

The Sixties revolution was all about change, particularly when it came to our views about sex and sexual freedom. The majority of the Baby Boomer youth, my 'g, g, g, generation,'[50] seriously questioned the values taught by our parents. The seemingly calm, middle class upbringing of the 1950s within the confines of convention screamed of hypocrisy, materialism, and contradictions. As teenagers and young adults, we often questioned authority and experimented, challenging the institution of marriage along with everything else. Eventually a certain percentage of us returned to the old cultural traditions, while others brought new ideas into the concept of marriage, or refused to have anything to do with it.

Having promiscuous sex was a life and death issue before penicillin became widely available. It probably was one of the reasons for the prudishness of the era that lasted until the dreaded syphilis and gonorrhea became curable with a series of penicillin injections.[51] Also, after birth control pills became widely available in the 1960s, for the first time in history a woman could have sex without the fear of becoming pregnant or contracting an incurable disease. The sexual revolution flowered in this window of opportunity. But, when AIDS came along in the 1980s, once again, the idea that sex was "free" and safe was over.[52]

During World War II, when the 'Rosie the Riveters' went en mass to the workplace to help with the war effort, and women were no longer primarily dependent on men for their livelihood, the dynamics of relationship and marriage were forever altered.[53] Since then, while the struggle has continued, changes have happened. Women have asserted their equality, and men have had to welcome them into the workplace. While the tendency for women to want to be as powerful as men sometimes causes them to negate their femininity and adopt negative aspects of their male counterparts, there are men, while trying to accommodate the change, have become passive and allow the women in their lives to run over them. Creating balanced relationships when it comes to the sexes is ongoing and hopefully getting better all the time.

The fallout from the dramatic changes of the 60s and 70s is the high divorce rate and its effect on the children born into this turbulence. We are now continuing to chart an improved course that achieves happiness and cooperative equality between men and women.

In the middle of these chaotic times, Robert and I struggled to negotiate our way through the maze of our interconnected psyches to discover true love.

We are now continuing to chart an improved course that achieves happiness and cooperative equality between men and women.

On the Beach at Sunset

The Summer of Love in 1967 was a distant memory, but San Francisco was still magnificent and ever vibrant when I arrived in 1970. The back-to-the-land movement was in full swing with self-sustaining communes and farms cropping up from coast to coast. The Northwest beckoned and we packed up our rebuilt van and drove across the Golden Gate Bridge, heading for our next adventure. There was a plan of sorts; we wanted to see if we could live out of the truck and pick fruit in Oregon and Washington starting with the cherry season. It seemed like a romantic vision at the time, following the seasonal harvest of apricots and peaches, and finishing up several months later with the apple harvest. We meandered through the redwood forests to Washington and, when we landed at our first gig, we learned first-hand how difficult that work can be. Even though we were young and fit, we were no-match for the hard-working, migrant workers who pick enough to make a living wage. Since our big plan hadn't worked out, Robert talked me into flying to New York City, his hometown, to rejoin the family musical instrument business, something he had rejected several years before. I had misgivings from the start about this new idea since we would be far away from the beautiful Pacific Northwest that we had fallen in love with in our recent travels. New York's hard edge combined with temporarily living with Robert's parents soon became our undoing. Our relationship was not strong enough to handle these stresses, and I flew home to my family who had in the meantime resettled in Nashville, Tennessee.

It had been a wild and crazy ride moving to San Francisco with so many eye-opening experiences. Even though our relationship was on shaky ground, I had tasted something extraordinary and I was still in love. I had a good visit with my family while Robert wrote me love letters filled with poetry like Paul McCartney's, "The Long and Winding Road." He had once again come to the realization that it wasn't working out for him in New York, and besides that, he missed me. At the time, drive-away-cars were a popular way to travel one way, and he drove south to visit me in Nashville. What was I thinking? And of course, my family was not keen on the idea. Robert was not at all what they had in mind for my beau. I told him that I wanted to settle down and return to college. We had a sweet visit, made separate plans to travel back to California, and promised to stay in touch. I sent applications to the University of California and was thrilled when I received my acceptance to the new campus of UC Irvine. I was excited to be moving back out to the West Coast; I found an apartment in Newport Beach with two other students and a secretarial job to supplement my dwindling bank account until school started. Robert returned to San Francisco, and we continued to write to each other. I missed his love and companionship.

One week before school was scheduled to begin, Robert drove south to see me with another one of his "great ideas," which turned out to be life changing. Strolling on the beautiful white sands of Balboa Beach, we couldn't stop talking about all the things that had happened while we'd been apart. Robert had been enthralled with Monday Night Class, and by the fall of 1970, teacher Stephen Gaskin had gained a national reputation for speaking about relevant issues in the language of the day. He had been asked to travel on a lecture tour to colleges and churches across the United States, with the possibility of bringing a semblance of peace and understanding to an unsettled country. The campus unrest had been ferocious and, in Ohio, four students were killed at Kent State University during a non-violent march for peace in Vietnam. Demonstrations against the war continued nationwide, and the civil rights activists kept working on breaking down the walls of discrimination. Stephen let us know that he was canceling the class for the next four months and that anyone who could supply their own transportation and expenses was welcome to come along on what was to be simply called "The Caravan." This was something that Robert felt was important to him since he'd finally found a teacher and a community who could help him find his path to a saner life. Touring the country in converted school buses, vans, and even a Cadillac made into a camper also seemed like an exciting adventure.

That evening while sitting on the beach watching a romantic sunset, Robert asked me if I would marry him and travel with "The Caravan" across America. I couldn't believe that after I had enrolled in school, had an apartment and a job that this exciting but crazy opportunity presented itself. My emotions were torn. I was a product of my times and caught in a personal and cultural trembler of large seismic magnitude. It was obvious that we were in love but what about the details? It was the most difficult decision of my life, and I was thrown into a spiral of confusion and discomfort. The choices were a life of adventure with my sweetheart or following the conventional path through college. There was no doubt which choice would please my parents. I was stepping across several cultural boundaries when I even considered marrying Robert.

It was out of this turmoil that we began our lives together. Like every woman in this situation, I had to make my own choice and I chose to follow my heart and go for love. The following morning, I went to the University's admissions office and un-enrolled; I quit my job, packed up my few belongings, *and we drove together in my $500, 1963 Volvo (bought by my Dad) back to San Francisco.*

Finishing college would have been the practical and sensible choice, but I knew that I wanted to go on a life-long adventure with Robert and that he was the "One" for me. When we recently visited our son, Saul in Newport Beach and walked the shoreline reminiscing about our engagement, Robert commented that maybe I should have stayed and married the doctor I was destined to be with; that I would have owned half of Newport Beach by now. But I laughed and gave him a hug because through all the highs and lows, I've never regretted the choice that I made those many years ago.

"The Greatest thing you'll ever learn
Is just to love and be loved in return."
"Nature Boy"
Written by Eden Ahbez

The "One"

How do you find the "One?" You might have had a few dates or relationships that for one reason or another didn't quite click. You know from these experiences what you don't want and are narrowing down the essential qualities that you think will be right for you. You've realized that you don't want someone who is quick to anger, selfish, arrogant, lazy, negative, or any number of traits that haven't allowed your past relationships to soar. You know that you want someone who is kind, tender, happy, intelligent, humorous, fun loving, among many other good qualities. In the end, you usually have to make some compromises because no one is perfect. But if you find someone with the basic qualities that you have in mind, and you are firing together on all cylinders, then you may have found the "One."

Finding this special person can be elusive. Are you having problems discovering a perfect match? Is the problem him or her, or is it you? Is it both of you? **Certainly, the myth that your Prince/Princess Charming will come someday and sweep you off your feet is a fairy tale. The perfect 'One' doesn't exist.** After all, are you that perfect prince or princess, the ideal mate? The potential is there, but as yet unrealized. The magical transformation appears when you want the best for each other. Love makes great things happen. With mutual respect and persistence to forge new agreements, you can turn a frog into a prince, and Cinderella into a princess. If the requisite characteristics for a wonderful lover are there, you can create your beautiful partner. S/he will grow into your expectations, and there lies the rejuvenating power of love that can create passion and beauty out of mere mortals. If a man is open to evolving and growing into his highest potential, a loving woman can manifest him into a King, a Warrior, a Magician, and a Lover. And likewise, if a woman is willing to follow a similar path, a caring man can create his lover into a Queen, a Goddess, a Sorceress, and a Venus.[54]

Of all the billions of people in the world, you'd think this search for the "One" would be easy. Where do you look for and find this person? You might find this someone who shares your same passions wherever you go for your enjoyment. It might be on a nature hike, at a dance, walking your dog, at work, at the gym, or on an Internet dating site. The serendipitous meeting of lovers is epic, and you never know where you are going to run into the person of your dreams. The question might be, "Have you made room in your life for this new love?" Do you hold a vision of her in your mind; can you see this person walking down the street to meet you? Do you have room in your heart for her, where she could easily step in and share a life with you?

There is an exercise you can do to make space for a partner. Sleep on one half of the bed, leaving plenty of room for your future lover. Clear out your closet and leave half of it empty for her clothing. Clean up the garage and leave a parking space for her car. Conjure up a kitchen with both of you cooking delicious meals together. Is your living room a welcoming place to sit, chat, or cuddle up together? Making physical and emotional room for your sweetheart to bring not only her stuff, but also her unique creativity will make it feel like home.

Attraction is a fascinating and wondrous phenomenon. Harville Hendrix in his book *Getting the Love You Want* writes that **who you attract is "the composite of all of your**

caretakers," [55] that is your parents, older sibling/s, grandparents, or guardians. You have charmed your partner in the same complicated web of love! Out of the crowd, out of all the numerous choices, what makes two people come together? Hendrix's basic premise is that the person that you are attracted to will have both the positive and negative aspects of the caretakers who raised you. So it is no wonder that this person, who looks like a prince or a princess one-day, may look like a toad the next! The exemplary qualities of you and your partner are the constant reminders of why you love each other, and the disagreeable qualities are where your challenges lie and what you will work on. Part of being in love is being able to change. Hopefully, s/he will make the decision to grow, change, and evolve with you. With the magic working, both of you will transform into the beautiful "One;" the person you've been looking for, the love of your life.

When I first met Robert, there was an electrical energy that masked our differences of culture, religion, race, family background, and upbringing. I had lived overseas in Korea and he had traveled for several years through Europe, the Middle East, and Central Asia. I felt a kinship with his worldview, which was one of the qualities that I had been looking for in a partner. We weathered breakups, separations, bouts of anger and days of silence, but still we kept coming back to each other. There was a vibrant chemistry and a purpose that bound us together on a deep level. For the first time in my life, I knew what it was to fall in love.

Family's Perspective

Your family and friends with their unique perspective want to help you avoid the potholes in life's highway. What are your close friends saying about your new boy/girlfriend? How about your parents, grandparents, uncles and aunts? Or is it too early to introduce your sweetheart to your "wacky" family? It is always interesting to ask the adults in your life how it was for them when they were your age. Who was their first love and how did they meet? What changes did they go through in their relationships to arrive at where they are now? Looking back, what would they have done differently? There's a possibility that you will repeat the same mistakes that they did. The question is can you side step these familial land mines?

A word of caution. If there was abuse or violence in your family, it is understandable that they are not the ones you want to confide in. Some families are not ideal examples to emulate, but are great examples of what **not** to follow; that is their gift to you. You may find that there is no common ground to discuss personal matters. In that case, begin the search to find the mentors or guides who you can trust and who have your best interest at heart. Your family members might have a certain amount of neuroses that has been passed on to you, but this can be overcome by perseverance and hard work. Fortunately, most of us have decent enough families who love and want the best for us.

Keep it Slow

The electrifying sensual infatuation is the physical attraction and the first step that can lead to the real thing. From there, love is a growing process. It takes time to know if you both share the same interests and have the same values to build a foundation for an enduring friendship, the basis of a long lasting partnership. Dating lets you see how you each behave in various situations. How is the give and take? Are there any obvious *red flags*? Are his/her friends cool? Have you met the parents?

In the dating process, consider the pace of your relationship. A consistent refrain from parents is, "Take it slow. Take it slow." Even though your bodies and hormones are pointing in that age-old direction, getting it on is only a part of what makes up a relationship. Does he feel like the one you have been waiting for all your life? You don't want to find out later that he was only interested in sex. What about the trust and the warmth of friendship? What about enjoying common pastimes and dreams and developing an emotional bond? Rushing into a passionate physical relationship without going through the friendship stage overlooks potential problems that can cause trouble down the road. Also, if there's a break up, you have to live with rejection and that feeling that you have been taken advantage of. And then there's the worst-case scenario - how can we have this discussion without it - an unwanted pregnancy. Before that happens, let's find out if both of you have the willingness to do the hard work required to make a relationship last. It does take time for a loving friendship to blossom. Let's not be impatient and give out your **best stuff** before you really get to know each other. If you are having sex, use protection!!

Ask any parent; they know from experience and undoubtedly have had their share of failed love affairs. Most likely they came to realize that moving too fast can compromise the relationship and you can end up feeling cheap, trapped, hurt, jealous, sad, and angry. Isn't this exactly the opposite direction from the one you have chosen for yourself? Fortunately, there's plenty of time to turn around, and follow the map that can guide you down the path towards true love.

Love is a growing process. It takes time to know if you both share the same interests and have the same values to build a foundation for an enduring friendship, the basis of a long lasting partnership.

Thinking of you keeps me awake.
Dreaming of you keeps me asleep.
Being with you keeps me alive.

Red Flags!

Obvious signals warn you of "red flags," indicators of possible trouble ahead. They caution you to take it Slow, maybe even Stop, and naturally to Watch Out for Children. The following six questions can alert you to some pitfalls that can cause you grief.

1. Do you feel pressured? Does s/he want you to become more serious than you are ready for, or urging you to have sex, go drinking or take drugs? Perhaps you feel like you are riding in a car with a slightly drunk driver and seat belts are optional? Enough of that! Can you make a call to a parent, friend, or taxi to come pick you up if you find yourself in an uncomfortable situation? Is he hitting on you before he has even gotten to know you? On the other hand, perhaps you are the one pressuring your date. Do you feel that s/he is manipulative, clinging, or controlling? If he doesn't listen when you say "No," things will be off to a bad start.

2. When you talk with your amour, is there a comfortable give and take or is it a one-way conversation? When one partner dominates the interactions and only talks about him/herself and how great or terrible things are going, or only about his or her activities, or views, then you have a one-way street. Standing in the shadow of someone who is self-absorbed and doesn't show an interest in you and your world will soon grow old. You are merely decorative trim. Or was it you who went through the evening talking only about yourself? Are you the one who is self-engrossed and bloviating? Did you take an interest in your partner's life, and

his/her perspective and visions for the future? Keeping love around for the long term requires 100% from each of you. When you learn about your sweetheart, you inevitably learn more about yourself.

3. Does a pessimistic, bored, antagonistic, or apathetic attitude predominate your partner's personality? Is he or she prejudiced, looking down on other people? Does s/he badmouth his/her parents and friends? It's easy to find fault, but is that where you want to put your attention? Eventually that negativity may be turned against you. Nobody should be treated that way. An uncooperative attitude will drive friends and family away, leaving you isolated; on the other hand, possessing a positive attitude towards people and life will sustain you over the long term. It's the "Law of Attraction"[56] that when you look for the good in everyone, you will increase the odds of attracting a compatible partner and a varied group of optimistic and happy friends.

4. Do you like doing activities together? While going along with your partner's idea of entertainment is a nice gesture, there should be some things that you do together that you are both passionate about. A close partnership is often based on sharing common interests.

5. Can you talk about anything and everything? Can you discuss your feelings? If it is uncomfortable to have a conversation about something, dare you go there and find out what is lurking in the shadows? Before it becomes "the heat of the moment" have you talked about contraceptives or family planning? What about tests for STDs and STIs (Sexually transmitted diseases and infections)? There's so

much to talk about: future hopes and dreams, sex, politics, religion, finances, philosophy, and anything else that comes to your creative minds.

6. Are you willing to make changes for your love affair to work? Compromise is one of the keys to happiness. If you are inflexible, the relationship will wear your partner down in a hurry. Are you holding on to bad habits? Can you give up cigarettes or excessive drinking, or how about something really challenging like reining in that crazy-making anger? Can you come to an agreement about something with an equitable give and take? A balanced and workable relationship will allow both of you to go where your dreams take you.

"Being deeply loved by someone gives you strength,
While loving someone deeply gives you courage. Lao-Tzu

The Caravan, An Epic Honeymoon

The communal effort to launch The Caravan had begun several months before Robert whisked me away from Southern California. There were about seventy other people from Monday Night Class who were in our same circumstances, needing a mode of transportation. We had meetings and decided to pool our money to buy used school buses to take us on the cross-country speaking tour for peace. Members of our "bus family" scouted the orchards of the Central Valley and the back corners of car lots, and purchased eight buses to divide among our group. It was easy to buddy up with 8-10 people: several couples and a few single men and women. For only $250, we bought a 1947 ACF Brill, Greyhound type bus that had been the former tour bus for Marty Robbins and his band. We found it crippled in a hayfield near Napa, Ca. with a blown clutch. With only his apprentice level knowledge of mechanics, Robert replaced the clutch and we along with nine other friends were on the road, catching up with the rest of the Caravan in Yellowstone National Park.

Stephen was speaking at colleges and churches around the country and when we landed in Ann Arbor, Michigan, our 1000 cubic-inch Hall-Scott gas engine with six monster cylinders was backfiring and needed a valve job. The November weather was turning cold with snow flurries accumulating in the parking lot of an ice skating rink where we had pulled in to make repairs. The owners had been to Stephen's talk and had graciously allowed us to park and use their facilities.

What seemed like a slew of obstacles, turned into a chance to meet wonderful friends, including Kathleen who threw in her savings of $360 and joined our bus-family. While *our mechanics were taking the engine apart, the rest of us found part time work to make gas money (only 26 cents a gallon) and purchase food for the rest of the trip. I was paid to be a test subject for a research project about memory in the psychology department of the University. We restocked our dwindling supplies of food at the local health food store, and they gave us deals on 5-gallon buckets of honey, peanut butter, and brown rice. Several weeks went by waiting for parts but finally with freezing fingers, the mechanics torqued down the head bolts to 220 pounds, and the colorfully painted "Freeway Flyer" was back on the road.*

We had only missed a few stops and soon caught up with the rest of the Caravan in Washington, D.C. Despite obstacles and adventures, detours and breakdowns, our four months on the road was an amazing experience. It was so much fun we didn't want it to end.

Many veterans from the bus-family had been branching out and buying their own buses and vans, and after returning to California, we stumbled across a 1942 Dodge school bus in Monterey, for $150.00 (an inexpensive price even then). It had been converted into a camper with a bed, kitchen, and bathroom. We found a secluded parking spot near the ocean and with lavender and blue surplus paint, we decorated the outside of our new home.

After The Caravan returned to San Francisco, this expanding group of adventurous travelers realized that we had morphed into a village on the road. There had been an ongoing conversation about starting a community on a nice piece of land somewhere. With young children and a few of the women pregnant, it was time to start thinking about where we wanted to settle down and raise our families. At one of the meetings, it was decided to look for land and form an intentional spiritual community where we could live in a peaceful, natural setting.

Before we set out again across the country to look for our new home, Robert and I made a pilgrimage to the gold-gilded, domed City Hall in downtown San Francisco, where the Justice of the Peace performed a legal marriage. While waiting to attend the last Monday Night Class, a good friend, Louis Sampson, with his new $5, Modesto, California issued Universal Life Minister certificate, presided over our marriage ceremony in his school bus parked alongside Ocean Beach.

Knowing that neither of our families would approve of our union, we avoided any confrontation and eloped. Following our dreams and our unusual path was not what our parents wanted and this could have been a sign that we had a rough road ahead with a big chance of not having a successful relationship. On the other hand, and lucky for us, the difficult times built our bravery, confidence, trust and respect for each other, our togetherness, and our love.

We prepared our newly painted bus to travel across the United States, this time to Tennessee where the people had been welcoming and the land was affordable. We once again worked along the way to pay for our expenses across the country.

After making this second long trek across our beautiful nation, our idealistic community pooled our resources, and purchased 1000 acres of land located on the Cumberland Plateau south of Nashville, Tennessee, that we named simply The Farm. Robert and I began our married life living far out in the woods in our old bus parked between two large hickory trees leaning close together in nature's embrace.

By now our group had swelled to around 350 people (most of us in our 20's), who parked their vehicles and pitched their tents beside old logging roads that crisscrossed our Promised Land.

> When I say, I love you more, I don't mean I love you more than you love me. I mean I love you more than the bad days ahead of us, I love you more than any fight we will ever have. I love you more than the distance between us, I love you more than any obstacle that could try and come between us. I love you the most.

A Supportive Family and Community

Traditionally, the community at large has been involved with premarital instruction and the mentoring of married couples. The health of the household and the society depends on the childbearing couple's ability to be supportive and cooperative, and to bring up the next generation in nurturing and positive surroundings. Couples who act responsibly gain the trust of their families who are looking out for their best interests and want a dedicated commitment before the couple has children. A clan would not last long if it did not set guidelines learned through generations of trial and error. When young adults have their freedom and independence as well as a support system to fall back on in times of stress or hardship, heartache is kept to a minimum.

During a couple's courtship, meeting each other's family and friends is one of those steps in becoming acquainted. Hopefully, everyone is thrilled with your new love, and is giving you positive feedback. Or has someone mentioned that they see trouble ahead in your choice? Your family and community will be there when you need their strength and support.

Certainly, in our modern society, a sense of community can be difficult to nurture especially when a job has taken you far from your extended family. Except for the Native Peoples, we are all historically recent immigrants or their descendants. For a while, several generations lived nearby in order to survive in their new country. While parents often struggled learning an unfamiliar language and culture, their children adapted quickly to their new secular world. Today, if you can rely on a functional extended family, consider yourself fortunate. If you are living far from your clan, creating your own social support network is the next best thing. From humble beginnings, your nuclear family can merge into a new community of friends and neighbors of like mind, based on common ethics. Making friends with your neighbors can soon develop into play dates for your children and someone to keep an eye on your house when you're away.

There are ways to stay connected that can create a supportive bubble around family, where problems are resolved and each member feels included and responsible to the whole. Holding a meeting from time to time takes care of issues that are floating around causing bad feelings. Our family meetings usually began with a quiet time when each of us tried to relax, meditate and become centered. Entering this kind of a meeting in a receptive and mellow mood made it more likely that issues would work out to everyone's satisfaction. Do you need a "talking stick" that you can pass around to whomever is speaking, indicating that they won't be interrupted? If two people have a conflict, have them speak directly to the group about what is happening and not necessarily to the person with whom they have the problem. This can keep things from flaring up with finger pointing and anger. When the entire group has respect for the process, there is a good chance that problems can be resolved with love, insightful wisdom, and compassion. If a format for running a meeting is needed to solve a nagging problem, there are excellent group conflict resolution guidelines found on the Internet.[57] Why wait until the relationship is on the rocks before asking for help? If the family has trouble sorting things out, counseling can be a rewarding way to pursue your happiness and growth.

Let's return to my story of living on the old commune. We collectively decided to create an intentional community to see if we could actually effect a change in our close relationships, in hopes that we could make the world a better place.

> There are ways to stay connected that can create a supportive bubble around the family where problems are resolved and each member feels included and responsible to the whole. Holding a meeting from time to time takes care of issues that are floating around causing bad feelings.

Living the Utopian Dream

The Farm was not the 'you can do whatever you want' style of commune, but was built intentionally on practical and spiritual agreements that we had talked about at Monday Night Class. Our ideal was that we could create peace and harmony in the world if our individual lives and the community were structured with certain values and priorities. We were vegetarians, actually vegans but that word hadn't been invented yet. It's a healthy diet when the legumes and grains are balanced with sufficient fresh fruits and vegetables. We didn't drink alcohol, smoke tobacco, or wear leather and were trying to be so chemically pure that we didn't even use birth control pills. Living peacefully with our families, our households, and particularly with our local neighbors was our main focus. Instead of the 'free love' lifestyle that was commonly associated with the hippie commune experience, we believed that if a couple was living together, they were engaged, and if they were pregnant, they were considered married with a responsibility to create a happy home for their child.

The door to become a member of the community was not easy to enter, but was wide open for anyone who wanted to leave. One of the basic tenets of The Farm (the catch) was an agreement to 'work it out' with our partner and other members of our community in order to create peaceful households. Our marriage included the agreement to work on changing ourselves for the continued positive growth and evolution of our relationship. One of our basic beliefs was that all we really have control over is ourselves and if we can change, we might be able to make a difference in the world.

The need for this level of commitment became clearer when I became pregnant. This precious life soon to be entering the world added a huge responsibility to our relationship. When we decided to get married, Robert and I had discussed how love was at the heart of our marriage agreement, and all of our travels had tested our commitment to each other. But, being married did not solve the many issues that we brought to our union. I was groomed to be a professional woman in the workplace and live "the good life," married to a competent specialist of some sort, not barefoot and pregnant in the backwoods of Tennessee with a group of people who threw all of their money into a common pot, signing a Vow of Poverty! We often joke that if we hadn't enrolled in this school of hard knocks, Robert and I would have landed in divorce court, dividing up our San Francisco real estate empire.

It had been a year since our marriage at the Justice of the Peace in San Francisco. Our first son had been born and we were settling onto the newly purchased land that we called The Farm in Tennessee. Stephen Gaskin became the official "minister" of a congregation of about 350 people and was legally allowed to preform weddings. He officiated at our second wedding and so we have two anniversaries in February, sharing the week with Valentine's Day. On a cold, rainy winter's day, my parents and siblings attended the ceremony in the only indoor gathering place, the barn. The horses were in their stalls, neighing and pissing and we sat on hay bales with a large, iron woodstove standing in the middle of the floor keeping us warm. The Sunday service opened with meditation followed by a symphonic OM. This time we received blessings from our family and our honeymoon consisted of enjoying the hospitality of my parents in their home near Nashville, Tennessee and watching the Winter Olympics on television. What a propitious beginning!

We were happy with our choice to begin our family living in a community of likeminded people. Settling in large households with other families, we shared the chores and child raising responsibilities. Having our babies delivered at home with our community midwives in attendance allowed a special bond to form. In the soft light of a kerosene lantern, supported by my husband and competent and nurturing friends, I gave birth to my children. Not only did the kids grow up within their nuclear family, they felt at home with other adults and "cousins" in the household. By then we had purchased 1750 acres of land where the children could roam and explore with streams, fossils and arrowheads, horses and ponies to ride and take care of, a bike shop, a local radio station, and a school.

Robert and I were doing alright and we worked well together. We were adventurous and committed to our marriage and felt compelled to pursue this 'noble experiment' called The Farm. However, we had serious differences to work through, and my husband, I realized, had a hard time making changes and it looked like there was going to be some heart-wrenching times ahead. We were young, independent, and stubborn, and there was an obstacle-ridden path to follow before we were able to find our marital bliss.

> *All we really have control over is ourselves and if we can change, we might be able to make a difference in the world.*

The Subconscious

This section will delve into the intricacies of our psyches, and how we can overcome obstacles on the path to happiness and peace.

Disclaimer: The advice that is contained in this book is presented for informational purposes only. The material is in no way intended to replace professional medical care or attention by a qualified psychiatrist or a psychotherapist. If you find that you are disturbed or overwhelmed by anything about this subject, it might be prudent to seek professional counseling. This book cannot and should not be used as a basis for diagnosis or choice of treatment.

Most of our life-long habits, both positive and negative behaviors, have been learned from our parents or guardians and the majority of these habits were instilled in us from a tender age and solidified through the years.[58] Our annoying ways of being are not specifically designed to be provocative, but are rather subconscious, or unconscious, behavioral patterns. Since we are for the most part not aware of these mannerisms, there is little chance for us to make any changes. Unless someone puts a mirror up to our actions so we can see ourselves, these behaviors remain beneath our awareness, dwelling in our subconscious or even deeper in our unconscious.

What is the difference between the conscious, subconscious, and the unconscious mind? R.J. Corsini and D. Wedding in "Current Psychotherapies"[59] distinguishes the three:

1. Conscious mind is "awareness in the present moment." We are conscious of what is happening around us.
2. Subconscious mind has access to information when you direct your attention to it. In the meantime it stays **sub** (under) your conscious mind. Once we have mastered the skills like driving a car or a bike, speaking a language, or typing on a keyboard, they come naturally to us when we need them. If we do not use our abilities for a while we may become a little rusty, but as soon as we use them again, they are there for us. Memories and ways of behavior can be accessed more easily than the unconscious.
3. Unconscious mind sounds like you are medically out cold, but in psychological terms it is the part of the mind where we don't have easy access to the memories or information stored there. It includes childhood memories that we can't recall, and "beliefs, patterns and a subjective map of reality that drives our behaviors."

We are oblivious to disruptive or unhealthy traits that are *sub* or beneath our conscious minds. To keep it simple, I will use the word subconscious to include the subconscious and the unconscious. The practice that I'll be discussing is how to bring the subconscious to the surface by listening to feedback. Most of these life-long habits have become our automatic, spontaneous responses to the world around us. From an early age, we often unknowingly indulge in anger, fear, shame, manipulation or running away to protect ourselves from harmful or fearful situations. In any couple's relationship, where intimacy is the embodiment of love, these behaviors create tension and distance. Once you become aware of your subconscious behavior, you are free to discard unhealthy habits that can sabotage you while you pursue a successful life.

When you begin to let go of the habitual reactions of moodiness, ranting, withdrawal, self-medicated addictions, or any other negative characteristic, you emerge out from the cocoon that has protected you from the complicated and sometimes stressful and hurtful world in which we live. The eventual result of releasing these negative energy habits is a lifting away of the blockage that prevented love from flowing freely. You will then become empowered and courageous, ready to deal with any of your demons that challenge your happiness.

When you have a basic agreement to talk about things that are bothering you, an open channel of communication is created. This is a relatively simple agreement, but it has far reaching consequences. Breaking down the walls and barriers to unveil our subconscious to the light of consciousness releases amazing amounts of pent-up energy. The things that are troubling your partner about you are often subconscious and are hidden and prefer not to be revealed. However, when harmful or annoying behaviors are brought to your attention in a kind and loving manner, it becomes possible for you to become aware of them.

When you have a basic agreement to talk about things that are bothering you, an open channel of communication is created.

When you explore the subconscious mind there's a realization that certain patterns have become outdated and harmful. When you study their origins you can determine how you want to change these embedded belief systems and patterns of behavior that may have been your reaction to a scary or hurtful experience, or come down to you through generations of your family or societal and cultural conditioning. Doing this work can melt the ice around your heart and free the love that's been squelched. But before you can have a clear understanding of what your partner is trying to tell you, s/he may have to tell you about it numerous times. This is normal and gives both of you the chance to practice patience. It may take a while for you to see yourself through someone else's eyes, and then you can make the effort to change subconscious destructive habits.

To dredge up the muck in your emotional garbage dumpster is a touchy process. Often the tendency is to deny it, find excuses, counter-attack, or use other creative defensive mechanisms to keep from churning up the status quo. When you step too close to your partner's bad habits, there is a chance of raising such clouds of smoky confusion that you may forget what you were talking about. S/he might make you feel like you are the problem for daring to bring it up! And then there is that inevitable time when your sweetheart brings up something that is bothering *him/her.* We all struggle at this point. The challenge is to just listen and not immediately get up your hackles and say, "No, no, no!"

Can you understand what your partner is talking about? What is the content? Now is the time to be objective while you refrain from fighting back. When you take a deep breath and let go, you may realize in your deepest soul that s/he is on to something. The challenge is to welcome the feedback and make new habits.

The Ego wants to keep things as they are, and not rattle any cages.[60] Any time you have suffered and did not grieve or work through the hurt, you repressed your misery in the inner, locked recesses of your emotional self. We all have walls built to protect us from real and imaginary threats, and only with fear and trepidation would we want to tear them down and reveal our vulnerability. Who is this mate of mine? Can I trust him or her enough to let down my guard? Open up my heart and soul? Clear out the pain of old hurts and leave myself unprotected and exposed? If your answer is "yes," it still takes courage, dedication, trust, and an open heart to say, "It is okay to go deep into those places because I have a partner who loves me enough to help me through it."

It's all about trust.

It's all about trust. What about the anger we feel when our trust has been violated? Did someone say they would do something for you, and then they didn't? Certainly, mothers occasionally run late picking up their children, and a kid may feel great pangs of abandonment thinking that his mother doesn't love him. Parents are not usually negligent or forgetful; they just run into unforeseen events like traffic snarls, or even naively think that a few minutes won't matter. These experiences helped create your early feelings of fear, mistrust, and neglect. Apparently we all have these instances that mold our lives and flavor our actions.

And then there are the times when everything breaks down and you blow it. Did your hair stand on end, did your eyes take on a fierce, piercing glare, and your voice snap out ugly words? Instead of helping you come to a mutual understanding, anger tends to escalate the situation. If you are serious about working on anger issues, perseverance and letting go can change your life.

When things start to go wrong, it's easy to blame someone else for all of your problems. Wallowing around in a state of victimhood leaves you in turmoil that can adversely affect your physical, mental, and emotional wellbeing. You end up creating negative energetic mischief that engulfs everyone in your vicinity with bad vibrations. How are you going to pull yourself out of this hole? How about letting go of the belief system that someone else can be in charge of whether you are happy or not. You are the creator of each moment, and no one can take that away from you. When you take a minute or ten to breathe in and breathe out, you can let go of this worn out belief system and acknowledge that you are in charge of your life.

You might take it a step further. How about apologizing to anyone and everyone who had to absorb your angry rage? Certainly a humbling experience, but it releases you from the drama and puts you back on the right track. If she is a nice person and receives your apology, she might feel like she played a part in this situation and can apologize too. You may now have created a common ground to talk about what came down and start building trust again. If things begin to change for the better, you might be thrilled to find out that s/he is what you thought all along, a decent person with integrity.

We are all reluctant to hear about our subconscious and being ready doesn't mean that we will be comfortable when we hear it. When you have the agreement to be each other's mirror into your inner workings, you will be able to discuss anything you want. Asking nicely if you can talk about something helps introduce a touchy subject. When you prepare yourself with a few deep breaths, you will be receptive and able to do this work. You can't be attached to a person listening or changing. It is hard to stay gentle and patient with your partner while they work through something, but know that you will appreciate the same tender treatment when it's your turn to toss out some of your old, stale habits. There probably will be times when you don't want to hear feedback about things that you need to work on. Even though you may have made an agreement to modify your behavior for each other and work it through, there might be times when it feels overwhelming. It's fine to stop and give it a break. If you want to have a wonderful partner, be a wonderful partner. When you consistently make the effort to weed out unpleasant habits, your sweetheart will be impressed and even more enamored by you.

The search for true love doesn't come without challenges, and it takes courage to face your faults and weaknesses. When you can get over your fear of changing, and let go of these patterns, it frees you to find your true and authentic identity. When two people compassionately work together on this challenging process, the end result is usually a happy union.

Ten Steps to Illuminate the Subconscious

The following is a ten-step recipe for bringing the subconscious into consciousness. This practice can help a relationship evolve into a loving and intimate partnership, while going through a challenging metamorphosis. These steps build a foundation on which your love can deepen, mature, and maintain its vibrancy and romance.

1. Make an Agreement with your partner that you can tell each other about bothersome subconscious habits.

2. Remain compassionate, kind, and patient, with a large dose of humor and unconditional love.

3. Listen respectfully to what your partner has to say. Try to understand what s/he is saying about your behavior. Your partner has been courageous enough to bring up something that s/he knows will be difficult for you to hear. Resist the ego's urge to make excuses, lash back in anger, walk out, or put it back on your partner. S/he is not your enemy, but is merely the messenger. S/he is carrying good news, liberating news. When little and big issues are taken care of, and each of you has listened and agreed to work on changing for yourself and each other, the relationship sparkles.

4. Continue your commitment to work on changing the habit. Notice the breakthrough that happens when you become aware of what your partner is trying to tell you while you are in the middle of doing it.

5. Laugh at yourself when you are caught in the act. Stopping in mid-stream to enjoy the process means you are on your way towards a happier self.

6. Recognize and revisit the events, beliefs, and teachings of your past that caused you to adopt this un-useful behavior, and acknowledge that you don't need it any longer. When you arrive at the realization that you don't need this toxic "friend," you will understand how your unhealthy habits and old belief systems may have made it difficult for you to be in a satisfying, intimate relationship.

7. Release old patterns and experiences: a radical shift that takes place deep within your body, your mind, and your emotional self, even down to your DNA. Every cell moves over to accept the change. Waves of light and energy flow within and around you, relieving you of the burdensome weight that you have unknowingly been carrying around for so long.

8. Forgive yourself, and make the change deep within out of love and respect for yourself and

your partner. Move forward on the path that will attract happiness and freedom.

9. Stay vigilant. There is always the possibility that over time, in a weak or stressed out moment, you might revert back to your old comfortable ways, your default setting. Your loving and patient partner can then gently remind you to pay attention to your yoga.

10. Resentment can show up when you don't talk about your partner's negative behavior that bothers you. Frustration can grow when you bravely bring something up and your partner doesn't want to hear it and then gives you a hard time. Is there sufficient trust in the relationship to believe that what you are asking him or her to change or modify will actually improve your lives together? When stubbornness is overcome, and there is courage to change, s/he can find peace of mind.

A negative behavior pattern can often feel like a comfortable old friend who unfortunately is no longer an appropriate or healthy influence. There is a tendency (everybody does it) to fight change and dig in your heels. There are all sorts of rationalizations to hold onto your old ways, going so far as to lash out in anger, come up with outlandish excuses, and run away denying that you ever wanted to change in the first place.

But your higher self knows better and can triumph. When this happens, you Let It Go, Let It Go, Let It Go. This amazing release brings tears of joy to replace the tears of desperation, anger, and self-pity. Emotionally cleansed, you feel lighter and happier. You feel both confidence and humility, mixed with joy and thankfulness.

This ten-step process is one of the hardest things that you may have ever done, but when you are willing to create the new you, it brings the biggest payoff, infinite love and happiness.

Let It Go, Let It Go, Let It Go

Communication

With compassionate communication, you can have happiness and success in your relationship. The alternative is to struggle along trying to bridge the ever-widening gap of solitude that prevents knowing what each other needs and wants. Researchers Drs. Robert Levenson, John Gottman and Howard Markman, working at the University of California, Berkeley and more recently at the University of Washington, explored the ways that couples argue and fight.[61] By observing how the partners communicated, they were able to predict with amazing accuracy the relationships that would have a good chance of surviving and which ones would fall apart. The scientists found that the most destructive behavior for a marriage was contempt and criticism, followed by stonewalling and defensiveness. Hoping to minimize this behavior, they introduced a set of simple ground rules for peaceful and productive communication based on Robert's (not my guy) Rules of Order.[62] They discovered that this orderly format could restore reason and civility to any necessary discussion when the situation has deteriorated to a contentious mess. These guidelines may seem rigid, stiff, or too formal, but if you customize them to your own taste and then use them on a regular basis, they can become a lifeline by which you and your partner can pull yourselves out of the abyss.

An Updated Robert's Rules of Order

1. Only one person speaks at a time.
2. The person speaking states the problem while the other listens.
3. The listener shows that s/he understands by stating the problem in his or her own words.
4. The person who originally brought up the problem confirms that the listener has grasped the issue correctly.
5. The original speaker states how he or she would like the problem solved.
6. The listener makes concessions and agreements.
7. If there is another side to the issue, the same rules apply, but first the original speaker receives satisfaction.
8. If anyone has felt offended or mistreated, a heartfelt apology, or a show of tenderness can clear the air.

In addition to these guidelines, the following chapters provide more suggestions to help you and your partner create the mood for compassionate communication.

Tools for Your Communication Toolbox

TIMING. Timing is Everything. Resentments start to creep in and multiply when something is bothering you and you don't talk about it. Ideally, it's best to address the issue when it happens. But if you have missed the opportunity to say something at the time, you still deserve satisfaction. If you worry that it will cause trouble, or is trivial, or it would be better to just forget about it, this is probably an indication that you still need to talk it out.

When your partner first walks through the door after a long stressful day at work give him/her time to relax before bringing up the problem. The situation has a better chance of working out successfully with fewer explosions, when you wait until after a shower and a nice dinner. Realizing that there is a source of irritation itching to burst out and ruin the mood, take ten deep breaths and then gently ask if you can talk to him or her about something. Leave plenty of time to sort things out. After all, your job is relatively easy compared to the hard work s/he has of receiving and changing.

Making a habit of sorting out disagreements when they first pop up prevents issues from accumulating down the road. Unresolved hassles do not vanish but smolder and eat up the love in the relationship.

ASKING PERMISSION. When our kids were young, there were times when Robert and I needed to talk to them about their unacceptable behavior. We expected them to listen with respect and develop new habits for themselves. We understood that our children were our mirrors, and when the dust settled and we had time to reflect on what was happening, their negative behaviors were more often than not a direct reflection or reaction to the way we were. Like all children, perhaps they were simply testing us to understand the limits of their boundaries.

Then in a relatively short time, the children grew into adulthood and one fine day one of our daughters requested that we please ask her permission before we gave out advice. At first we were surprised since aren't we the parents who get to say whatever we want? But she was right and when we embraced the concept, it turned out to be a healthy step that changed the parent/child relationship into an adult/adult friendship. It was a reasonable request, which led to a more trusting and respectful dialogue. Our other adult children appreciated the change too, and the discussions between us became more receptive and respectful. Asking permission worked in our own relationship as well, eliminating a whole level of confusion, negativity, and chaos when we deal with touchy issues. It also prompted us to take it a step farther. We wanted to define what this request for permission meant. We called it "The Contract."

THE CONTRACT. Before you begin these, often, loaded conversations, **ask your partner if this is a good time to discuss a problem**. If she agrees, then continue. By giving her permission, she feels that you are not in "attack mode" and the conversation can smoothly continue. Of course, she may answer, "Uh oh, what is it now?" But when you make this process a habit, trust builds. While the answer still might be "Uh, oh," when she knows that it is for the best, she may also say, "Okay, what do you have for me?" Both of you have displayed courage: you to bring up this uncomfortable issue, and your partner for agreeing to hear what you have to say. If your partner isn't ready and would like to choose a more opportune moment, it is likely that she will then have a more receptive ear. A consistent refusal to sit down and talk about things could be a deal breaker and a "red flag." Without communication, the relationship is heading for a breakup or perhaps worse, the debilitating, stagnant life of mediocrity. A common complaint from married couples is that the spark has been doused like B. B. King sings in his song, "The Thrill is Gone." "Where is the exciting lovemaking we used to have? We just come home, eat, watch TV and go to bed when we used to talk for hours about everything." When either of you is not willing to talk out problems, the love, respect, and trust drains out of the relationship.

When you do not discuss and resolve the issues, you allow the garbage of unresolved conflicts to collect. The pile can grow so high that sooner or later a couple may split up, insisting that there is too much stinky refuse to deal with. The legal terminology for this mess is "irreconcilable differences." Changing partners usually doesn't help if you haven't embraced your feedback and evolved. You are still who you are and the garbage will just start to collect again. Dumping the trash on a regular basis and working through the changes is routine maintenance, essential to long-term happiness.

Below are guidelines for making "The Contract," and steps you can take when you ask your partner permission to talk about something that is bothering you.

Take some deep breaths. Scan yourself making sure you are in a kind, forgiving, and unconditionally loving frame of mind.

1. And then ask, "Can I talk to you about something?"

2. What I am about to tell you will be helpful to us both, and it is necessary for our wellbeing. I will say it nicely and with respect.

3. It takes bravery to bring this issue up and more courage to hear and receive the message gracefully.

4. Please listen respectfully and consider what I have to say. I would like a full agreement, but a "maybe" is satisfactory. A "no" is unacceptable. A "no" response indicates to me that you do not trust my viewpoint enough to consider that what I am saying has merit. A "maybe, I will consider it," is not what I prefer but is an adequate response.

5. You can call off this discussion at any time, with the understanding that it can be continued later.

6. Please note: If someone gives permission reluctantly, feeling like they are being pressured, or says "Okay," without sincerity, you probably shouldn't continue. Inevitably the situation deteriorates into an angry, frustrating quarrel and rarely can any progress be made. **Your message is not going to get through. Ask if there is another time to talk when he or she will be more receptive. You cannot be attached to someone else's enlightenment.**

MAYBE IS OKAY. When your partner brings up an issue, he clearly knows what his concerns are. Hopefully you will listen to the whole story without interruption. He might not have all of the correct facts, and he probably is adding his own fears and subconscious attitudes to the situation, but that's not the point. **Try not to have your first response be an argumentative "No."** Or do you say "I didn't do that," "You don't know what you are talking about," "You have it all wrong, I totally disagree," or do you put it back onto your partner and say that it is "all his fault?" These are all defenses that prevent change from happening. Perhaps instead of these retorts, you can anticipate the inclination to say "No," pause for a moment and contemplate what he is saying. At least give him a "Maybe, I will consider it, or I will think about it." Your partner would prefer a "Yes, you are right," but a "Maybe" is so much better than a "No, you are wrong, I didn't do that." Hopefully your response can evolve into saying, "I understand what you are talking about; it rings true." Ideally you will realize that your partner has a valid point and you can give him or her satisfaction by appreciating what s/he is talking about.

Once we had made this agreement we were amazed at how responsive each of us was to what the other had to say. There was also the added bonus that when Robert wanted to tell me something and asked permission with that tone of annoyance and irritation, I could ask him to take a chill pill, and ask me again later. When he cut loose of his uptight attitude, the message was easier for me to hear. Asking permission relieved the stacked, tense feeling, and talking about it could then begin on a relaxed footing.

HUMOR. Laughter chases the blues away and a light-hearted touch eases the challenge of making changes. Even when things seem terribly serious, a humorous remark or a smile of recognition can make the workout easier to stomach. When you have plowed through the muck, anger and pain, and understand what your partner is trying to say, it becomes an occasion for laughter and celebration. Laughing at yourself is a sign of maturity as well as making you fun to be with. Your humor makes light of the mystifying, ugly, and sometimes scary monsters that hide in the depths of your psyche. When you do not take yourself so seriously, it's easier to let go of grouchy and stubborn attitudes, and they evaporate into thin air.

You can make a potential hassle into a fun experiment that often turns into a laughing matter. When you've asked for a change, you generally have a clearly formulated scenario in your mind of how you would like it to turn out. How about instead of an angry tirade, starting off with a tender touch like, "Darling, I love the way you .... (fill in the blank) There's just a small thing I'd like to talk to you about. Would this be a good time?" When you play act and recreate the scene using the words you would like to hear alongside the words that were said, it gives a new perspective on how things could unfold. There is usually a wide chasm between what you each have in mind. When you say your new lines, it might feel like you're stumbling along in a different language. It often comes out sounding funny and you can't help but laugh. Humor is an art worth cultivating, especially when you can laugh at yourself. It is those humbling moments when you realize you've been an ass that can allow an uncomfortable situation to dissolve into laughter.

THE TALKING STICK. When you interrupt each other, communications disintegrate into an unpleasant shouting match. The person speaking should have the respect of the listener. It is a custom in some Native American meetings and ceremonies to have a stick, pipe, feather, or some valued object that is passed around the circle to each person who has something to say. It is understood that while that person is holding the "talking stick," she can speak without interruption and be listened to with undivided attention. The speaker then passes the "talking stick" to the next person wanting to speak, and then he too receives the same courtesy. As the discussion proceeds, each person has the time and space to complete his or her thoughts. Is there an object that holds special value to both of you which you could use for this purpose?

TAKE TURNS. Taking turns is one of those things that we hopefully learned in kindergarten, and when it comes to communication, you respectfully take turns listening to each other's points of view.

Let us suppose your partner has built up her nerve to bring up a topic that is bothering her, something that she would like you to change. Is she worried that you will become stubborn and come back with a barrage of excuses? When one person comes up with enough backbone to open up a possibly explosive discussion, there is a tendency for the other partner to see this as an opportunity to unload his or her pent-up issues. This is your partner's turn and you need to be sensitive to her by genuinely listening. Of course there are other sides to the issue or maybe other issues, however, you may have to wait for another day to discuss your gripes. Eventually, there will be time for you to have your say, but only after your partner feels that there has been a satisfactory resolution to what was on her mind. If you can gracefully receive the information about yourself, maybe when it is your partner's turn to listen to you, she will reciprocate in kind.

TAKE A FEW BREATHS OR TEN. To make sure that you are not "uptight" when you bring up a subject, it helps to check yourself by taking a few deep breaths. This can put you in a meditative mindset that is more expansive, compassionate, unattached, and gentle. Then in the kindest way possible tell her what's on your mind and she will sense your good intentions. It also helps to take, let's say, ten breaths when your partner asks you if she can talk to you about something. It creates a relaxed and receptive mood that makes it easier to let things go.

LISTENING. Being a good listener is essential for respectful communications. It's so easy to talk on top of each other, thinking you have something more important to say. Do you jump into those pregnant pauses, not allowing your partner to stop and formulate his or her thoughts, and interrupt or finish the sentence for him? How about even if your partner isn't totally perfect in his or her delivery, can you slow down enough to understand and grasp the content of what he is saying and make closure with that? Taking offense at the emotional content and his lack of confidence will make it harder to find common ground. Becoming defensive during discussions also squelches your understanding of your partner's perspective, and you hear only what you want to hear. When you take it personally and become upset, feeling like you have been attacked, minimized, and victimized, your reaction is likely to be one of resistance and denial. Inevitably you then miss the crucial point that your partner is trying to make. If you can mellow out and drop your defenses, remembering that the love of your life is trying to break through your stale habits, you can listen when he says his "peace."

GIVING AND RECEIVING. In a normal conversation, communication flows easily back and forth. Even when a discussion meanders and goes on detours and tangents, both of you can feel included, knowing that in the end you will both be heard.

However, when someone is always giving and the other partner is always receiving, it's a one-way street, and one person will feel resentment and animosity while the relationship is diminished interaction by interaction. There is the story about the passing of the gold coins, for instance, that our mentor, Stephen Gaskin, liked to tell. Two friends pass a gold coin back and forth. If one of them is stingy or selfish, he will shave a few slivers off of the coin and pass it back, accumulating a small pile of ill-gotten gains. Eventually, his friend will feel short-changed since he didn't receive an equal share, and the friendship inevitably erodes away. When the two-way street of give and take is open, communication is on track and you can easily talk about anything.

SATISFACTION. When your partner tries to talk to you about a touchy subject, there is often a tendency to counterattack. This is an offense used as a defense, with two people pointing fingers at each other and never connecting. Let's say, for example, that your partner brings up the time when you went on that shopping spree. He says that you are not living within the budget while racking up ridiculous interest on your credit cards. Without acknowledging what he said, you reply that he never takes you out anymore and, besides, he is stingy. One problem is now layered on top of another.

Your partner probably agonized all day over how to bring up this explosive subject of finances. Respect him for having the nerve to talk about your overspending. Do you know that you are out of control about this? Can you resolve the initial issue to his satisfaction before introducing another problem? Just because your partner opened the gates of a discussion, does not mean you can flood the conversation with your agenda. You may need to look into what prompts you to spend too much. It's responsible economics to stay within the budget and pay down debt, leaving you with a set amount of expendable cash for each month. When you resolve the credit card issue to both you and your partner's satisfaction, perhaps he will not be so worried about finances and will feel like taking you out for a night on the town.

RECEIVING FEEDBACK GRACEFULLY. It takes courage to hear what she wants to tell you, and it feels so good when you receive it gracefully and agree to process the baggage. Imagine touring New York City on a beautiful clear day, and you are taking the elevator towards the 102nd floor of the Empire State Building where you will have an expansive view. On the way up when the elevator stops at the third floor, you wouldn't think of getting off. Why would you leave the relationship stranded at a boring level rather than follow it to its highest potential?

APOLOGIES. If you can rise above the cultural prejudice that considers an apology to be demeaning or a sign of weakness, it will become obvious that asking for forgiveness clears the air. Trust, respect, love, and even repairing friendships are now possible. There's an understanding that you've done something that you regret and you want the situation to improve. It's an opportunity to make things better for yourself, your family, and friends. Apologizing is the initial step of giving up the energy that your unkindness has snatched away. Making a sincere apology may be one of the hardest things you'll ever do, but it begins to turn an unhappy situation around for the better.

If your partner has made a valid point in the heat of an argument, saying "You are right about that," and "I am sorry," can alleviate the tension. It's normal to feel vulnerable when you admit that you were wrong or that there is something you need to change, but when you apologize it opens up your heart.

Women and men have a different approach to apologies according to two studies done at the University of Waterloo in Ontario, Canada. Elizabeth Bernstein writes that it might seem that women apologize more than men, but according to the study, both men and women apologized about the same amount. It came as a surprise that people apologized more to their friends (46%) than to their romantic partners (11%), and more to strangers (22%) than to their family members (7%). Men tend to worry that an apology lowers their standing with their peers and is not beneficial in a competitive business setting. Women often use an apology to smooth out a rough spot in a friendship or to empathize with someone like, "I'm sorry you've had a tough time,"[63] rather than admit that they have done something wrong. But when an apology is an admission of guilt and a promise to do better, it becomes a valiant and even heroic step of taking responsibility for your actions with the intentions to make amends. To continue on and complete the metamorphosis is the real test, but a heartfelt apology can be the start of a liberating transformation.

There is a certain percentage of people who just can't seem to admit that they are wrong and since they are never wrong, they don't need to apologize.[64] When one of you says, "This is who I am, you can't ask me to change anything," is this The Popeye Syndrome, "I yam what I yam?" If this sounds familiar, at the very least the partnership will lose its vitality. Is it worth being so stubborn that you jeopardize this relationship? Many couples who have separated can go back and remember exactly when one or both partners dug in their heels. Did one of them challenge the status quo and insist on change, while the other person refused to budge? When you realize how much time, work, and emotional energy, you have invested in your relationship, the decision to adapt is obvious. Remember why you picked this person out of the crowd, out of all the many people that you dated? What made him or her so special? Didn't you think s/he was the best companion possible? Weren't you so in love?

CHANGE. In order to keep a relationship flourishing, it needs to continually evolve. When you have been asked to change something by your partner, the essence of who you are is not on the chopping block and neither is your style, your sense of humor, or your personality.

A certain amount of discipline is required to eliminate long-standing habits that sabotage happiness. For instance, when two people are communicating and one of you is being selfish, not wanting to hear it, getting angry, or being rude, the other person is insulted and resentment builds. The love is whittled away.

Often the hassles become so intense that the "grass seems greener on the other side." People separate and decide to try their luck with a new partner. If you are not in the habit of working things out and evolving, eventually your new partner will confront the same issues since you are still you. Your personal baggage remains with you no matter who you are with. Serial monogamy does nothing to chase the gremlins out of your subconscious. They do not disappear until you consciously usher them out of your life. If you can make an agreement to work things out, you can **"love the one you're with."**[65]

The part of you that is difficult to be with is behavior you can change. These annoying, divisive, unhealthy, and harmful habits can include anger, unkindness, arrogance, envy, stubbornness, and defensive quirks, to name but a few. If you refuse to modify your actions, you can end up in a lonely, grouchy rut, whereas changing your habit carries you to a higher level.

SURRENDER. It takes monumental courage to allow a transformation to happen. Do you know what it feels like to totally surrender? Loosening up enough to "let go" may make you feel defenseless, exposed, weak, or frightened. From time to time, it's healthy to find that quiet place deep within. Practicing with your partner is the true test. When you've made agreements to alter your response during a particular situation, it helps to focus on your intention to change with a mantra like: "Relax, relax, or let go, let go, or zip it, zip it" ("Zip it" is keeping your mouth closed when your tendency is to say something snippy or unkind that only makes the situation worse). Giving up pride and stubbornness may appear to threaten your very essence, and yet, it is actually good for you, empowering your lighthearted self to emerge.

Like plaque blocking an artery that brings on a heart attack, stubbornness, pride, anger, and fear block the joy, sweetness, and happiness from our lives. And then when your heart is finally opened, immediately you are vulnerable. Take a step towards love and, inevitably, there is the possibility of pain. Here you are in love, and your partner is bringing up issues that have been comfortably repressed and tucked away. S/he is exposing them to the light of day, and it is no doubt distressing. A successful relationship requires 100% commitment from both partners; it's all or nothing. Only by giving up everything and letting the walls come tumbling down can you unblock the flow of love and allow yourself to be loved in return.

TIMEOUTS. This process of working things out comes with a warning. Your partner may have given you permission to talk about an issue, but when it was presented ever so nicely by you, for some reason or other, he refused to hear it. It was too painful or embarrassing, bringing up such a deep hurt, or challenging his pride, or the very nature of who he thinks he is. Was his first impulse to "kill the messenger?" The issue hasn't gone away, and you still have to deal with the problem and make it better.

How about a fifteen-minute timeout or the proverbial walk around the block? The situation can become so heated that you need to disengage and take a break, with the understanding that the discussion is simply being placed on hold. You are not going to forget about it and neither should he. Let the issue sleep while the "cease-fire" is in progress. When cooler heads prevail, come back and pick up where you left off. There is a tendency to avoid **getting back into it,** but if you let things slide, they will come back to haunt you. Going to bed with an unresolved hassle is a no-no! This is different from "bagging it" because you are able to continue working it out after a break.

BAG IT. Sometimes you just have to agree to disagree. After everything is said and done, and there is still a disagreement consider "bagging it." That is:

1. State the problem clearly.
2. Tie it up neatly and bring it up again with a trusted third party.
3. You then have the luxury to forget about it. There is no reason to tear up a relationship over one issue. Outside help is available when you need it.

Sometimes while mulling over what transpired, a new perspective sheds light on the subject, and the **big** person comes to an understanding that his/her partner has a point. If this realization should come to you, don't hesitate to admit that s/he was right. Perhaps this was the missing piece in the first place and things can then work out easily. You may not need that third opinion, and you can realize how your acknowledgment and/or apology can re-energize the discussion and make way for an equitable conclusion. It takes **two to tango** and after taking time to reflect on the issue at hand, both of you may gain insight that clears the way for new agreements.

THE FAIR WITNESS. When you cannot reach satisfaction on an issue, the two of you can take it up with a trusted third party, which is a lot better than bringing it to a divorce court. A fair witness can be a diplomatic friend, a happily married person or couple, or a relationship counselor who you both feel comfortable with. The friendly referee, who is obviously not emotionally involved in the argument and may have seen it many times before, usually has a clear insight into the problem. This person brings a fresh perspective and often a lighter approach to help you work things through to a successful conclusion. An impartial viewpoint is simply a mirror held up for you to see things more clearly.

Are there issues that you have decided to leave unchallenged, the dangerous "shared subconscious" that leads to enabling each other's destructive behaviors? A mentor can help you through the difficult stages that are common in everyone's life. Another person's viewpoint can give you objectivity and a refreshing, new way to deal with your problems.

NEGATIVE ENERGY HABITS. Imagine that you are a bucket full of water. Arguing, complaining, angry words, stubbornness, and being grouchy are holes in your bucket where your energy drains out, sapping the strength and vitality from your relationship. Patching up these holes by working on changing these negative energy habits will change the whole dynamic, bringing love back into your life.

It's easy to become caught up in a toxic drama when you react to your partner in the same old predictable way. Around and around the negative vibrations go like a "loop." Every time this pattern comes up, the same scenario unfolds. The tendency is to want **the other person** to change. **The secret to ending a 'loop' is changing what *you* are doing**

and refraining from your habitual response when the loop comes 'round again. When you change, the loop collapses, frustrations subside, and healing takes place. This allows a door to open making it easier to deal with the real issues that the loop represents. The recipe is simple enough: speak the truth, fear no one, be kind, even humorous, and hold your temper.

BE KIND. Most of us indulge ourselves with rationalizations of why we can be angry, crabby, accusatory, shaming, or unkind. We come up with the excuse that we can be this way because of what our partner did, or due to a situation outside of our control. You might feel frustrated and feel that you have a right to take it out on someone else and the closest target is often your sweet companion, the love of your life. There is a certain comfort zone in this ugliness. These reactions then become normal behavior, which leaves you both drained by the end of the day. You can make an agreement with your partner that **there is no reason to be nasty, despite any offense.** An angry attack, a tirade, sarcasm, or any unkindness only creates resistance and resentment instead of the positive results you are seeking. The cure can be taken from a page in the kindergarten manual; be nice, be kind, share, and with a gentle touch, anger and stubbornness can be banished. Amidst all the dust and smoke, jumping down off of your high horse clears the air and lets you move forward.

The cure can be taken from a page in the kindergarten manual; be nice, be kind, share, and with a gentle touch, anger and stubbornness can be banished. Amidst all the dust and smoke, jumping down off of your high horse clears the air and lets you move forward.

Feedback

Constructive feedback, a compassionate appraisal, can let you know how you appear and how your actions affect those around you. When you are on an angry tirade, you'd be shocked to see a video of your actions. You can't imagine yourself looking that disgusting. And you'd never let anyone talk to your sweetheart that way. When you acknowledge what you are doing and begin immediate steps to amend your behavior, you'll avoid being that clueless person who wonders why their partner just up and left.

Most people's first reaction to feedback might be to feel hurt or insulted, as if it's a stab to their self-esteem, and what they think is their very essence. Yet with reflection and time to evaluate what your friend is saying, you as an individual can realize that a valuable, hidden part of you has been uncovered. When light is shed on one of your negative qualities and you feel uncomfortable, maybe even angry, off-balanced, and embarrassed, it is possible through all the smoke to understand at least an inkling of what s/he is talking about. You may even realize that, "I've heard that somewhere before." Being open to feedback is never easy, but if you don't take it personally, and agree that these valuable changes can make your life better, you might say, "Bring it on! What do I have to lose, a dysfunctional, crazy-making ego?" [66] Life generally gets sweeter when you dump the garbage.

When you cultivate the skill of listening to your feedback, a transformation can happen. Sharpening your discerning skills will allow you to see what other people are saying and whether their feedback is right for you. You can recognize your true friends because they are the ones who will appreciate you despite your flaws. No one says it's easy to hear what is being said, but s/he is trying to tell you the truth about yourself, and does have your best interests at heart, doesn't s/he? Your first impulse, like most of us, is to fight back, argue, put up smoke screens, walk away, bring up all sorts of excuses, or defend yourself. It doesn't hurt to take a break at this point because after all, you can't hear anything in that agitated state.

When you are ready to be receptive, understand that your friend is trying to help by giving you his/her perspective. It may not necessarily be something you think you need or want to change, but it is certainly worth your time to listen and consider the feedback. Can you, without being paranoid, evaluate where he is coming from and what his motives might be? If that all checks out, can you add his suggestion to your to-do list, something that you work on for your own good? Resist the temptation to say, "No, I don't do that! Leave me alone." When you consider what is being said, can you say, "Maybe there's some truth to that? I'll consider it." A "Yes, yes, I know what you're talking about, and Thanks." would be the best response, but a "Maybe" will do.

This practice of being open to feedback can be cultivated throughout your lifetime. Is your tendency to insist that you are always right? Let's suppose a friend tells you that your deodorant isn't doing its job. Do you feel humiliated? Consider your buddy's point of view. S/he is the other half of the discussion, after all. What is the big deal if you take more showers or change your clothes more often? Or how about when a friend is brave enough to mention that your temper is out of hand; do you feel your anger rising? What can you say to diffuse the situation without blowing your top? Learning to handle anger is a difficult thing to do, but you'll find your life changes for the better when you make the effort to stay cool when your hair stands on end. Anger can be a positive emotional response to injustice, intolerance, and mistreatment. How you channel that anger into positive results can make things better for everyone. You want to be able to talk about your feelings and about the things that bring up anger inside of you, without ranting, throwing things, or hurting yourself and others.

Accepting feedback requires that you make a commitment to change. Having decided to walk down a path to a happy life, and agreed that you have changes to make, there are still times when it seems like this practice is requiring too much. Maybe you want to go back into your old shell and be the way you've always been: rage at the world and refuse to listen to your partner. Okay, but how does keeping all that negativity in your life make you feel? When you look at all the changes you have already made and the new opportunities that have come your way, before long you'll be ready to take another leg of your journey towards a higher consciousness. We all lose our way from time to time and that is what makes us human. But even the detours turn out to be our teachers, so not to worry.

When you have made the choice to accept your feedback, it becomes a personal growth opportunity. Your partner will appreciate it, and you might ever so kindly and gracefully, try some day to give her feedback too. Will she follow your example? When you evolve with one another, your love strengthens.

Can I Bring You a Drink of Water?

You never know when you might receive some feedback. You might be going along doing what you always do, when out of the blue, you have someone mentioning something that you weren't aware of. This happens to everyone, and Robert and I are no exception. We were aboard our sailboat, Harmony, one beautiful day in a calm, pristine, anchorage in the Sea of Cortez on the Baja Coast of Mexico. An osprey chirped in her nest atop the jagged pinnacle rocks and Robert, passing by on his way to the galley, asked if he could bring me a glass of water. I immediately jumped up like I usually did and said, "Oh, Don't bother, I can get it." He said, "It's okay sweetheart, let me bring you a drink of water." By not receiving his offer gracefully, I created a blocked channel of good energy coming from him to me, and we both lost in the transaction. When I looked deep within, I realized that I had been raised in the traditional manner of my generation where it was expected that women would give more than they would receive. When our many children entered the world, there was rarely a moment from my nurturing role that I could call my own. However, I was a person wanting approval, acknowledged when I was giving and good. Giving and achieving were my tickets to the love that I needed, but this early life lesson turned out to be a defective belief system. The simple, ordinary act of accepting a glass of water became a big deal, the beginning of a deeper understanding of give and take. I might have always been generously taking care of everyone, but by not receiving, not wanting to be any trouble, or a burden to anyone, it prevented my friends and family the pleasure of giving. When Robert talked to me about how he wanted to be able to bring me something without me jumping up and getting it for myself, it made sense. It was such a simple request that it was easy to accept what he was saying. For years after this first happened, I still had the tendency to help myself whenever anyone asked me if I wanted something. It was a visceral response that seemed entwined around my very DNA. Part of my struggle was living in the modern age of feminism: the assumption that any intelligent and capable woman should be able to do things for herself. In the 21st century us women are still trying to balance doing things on our own and receiving gracefully. I finally decided to try and let go and I felt relieved and happier. Slowly over time I have been able to arrive at the place where I can say, "Thank you, sure I'd love a drink of water," and stay in my seat and enjoy the honor of being served. [67]

It's usually a surprise or a shock when someone tells you "where it's at." Our relationship is a fine example of the ups and downs of taking feedback. Robert was dedicated to rewiring his behavioral patterns from the many dysfunctional habits that he had picked up during his lifetime, but when it came down to actually making changes, it was a nearly impossible struggle. Several times he left me, and The Farm, sometimes for a month or more. He once picked oranges in Florida, hard labor under a hot sun and, as karma would have it, with a throbbing toothache that didn't make it easier. Eleven years into our marriage he left again and during that separation he banged up against the world and had the realization of how important making some crucial changes would be to keeping him sane and his family intact. He knew that he could rely on me to help him, and he returned with a resolution to do whatever it took to make things work. He had finally decided to make that big metamorphosis that allowed us to move on.

Not long after that, having lived the "noble experiment" for twelve years, we decided that maybe we were strong enough as a team to make it out in the real world. We wanted our children to be acclimated into the general society and attend public school in order to be prepared for the university system. Fortunately we are still in touch with The Farm community and we visit our friends and attend reunions and gatherings. We, of course, continue to have multiple conversations on social media.

> *The simple, ordinary act of accepting a glass of water became a big deal, the beginning of a deeper understanding of give and take.*

> "True love has no expiration date."
> Artist Carl Larsson

Are You Ready To Take the Compatibility Test?

Each day that you are involved in your relationship, you are making an investment. Perhaps when the savings have grown large enough, you agree that you want this union to be permanent. Traditionally, when a couple continued along this road, it led to an engagement. Today, some couples go the traditional route and others decide to live together to test drive the relationship. Is this someone you want to share your life with and someone you truly love? Is it pure joy being in each other's presence? Are you living on your own? Have you graduated from school? Are you financially independent? Have you discussed having children, and the details of how to support your new family? Are you ready to take the next step?

Throughout the dating stage of a new relationship, primarily pleasant experiences fill up your time. Are you comfortable and relaxed with each other? Can you say anything that's on your mind, and does s/he listen to you? If your camaraderie continues to grow and love blossoms, a new stage in your life has begun. When you have been with your sweetheart for a long enough time to have enjoyed activities together, had an argument or two, and experienced a few highs and lows, are you still best friends? Maybe you have taken a break from each other and are back together knowing that you are both in love and want this relationship to work out for the long run. Do you feel safe and secure? Is it a give and take relationship? Are your family and friends happy for you? If your answers are yes to all of these questions, Congratulations, you are ready to take the 101 Question Compatibility Test!

The History of "The Test"

I first became interested in creating The Test when we were working for Plenty, the non-profit division of The Farm. We were living in Miami at the time and helping to support the Guatemala project that was rebuilding a town that had been devastated by a large earthquake in 1976. We had a roofing company at the time that supported our project and made enough extra to finance the forty people working in Guatemala. We lived in a large house that we called the Age and Youth Center since we had elderly and physically challenged people that we cared for along with our numerous children. One of our seniors read the Miami Herald every day, and she showed me a newspaper article[68] that talked about the need for guidelines when a couple is contemplating marriage. The premise of the article was that there would be successful marriages if there were premarital testing and counseling before people took the plunge. I liked the idea of a list of questions to give to our children when they began to develop serious relationships. I wanted to create a test that was relevant to our times, would touch all aspects of life, and could even be used in a school setting to open up discussions about relationships. Even though our children were in elementary school at the time, I promised myself that someday I would work on this project. The Test needed to be appropriate for any couple beginning to date, and when my children became teenagers, I began to compile not only The Test, but also to supply the answers. My kids were gracious enough to take the test and let me know where it needed to be refined, and it wasn't too many years later that they used it for real.

If Robert and I had taken a similar test, and talked about what to expect, perhaps we could have avoided some rough patches in our marriage. When we were engaged, we began to relax our walls, and the first obvious issue that came up was his anger. Also problematic was that I was not courageous or confident enough to stand up for myself. We didn't have an inkling of the probable difficulties that we faced and what work was required. We were more typical than we realized and we could have easily been one of the statistics in the alarmingly high divorce rate.

Fortunately, there has been a concerted effort to fix this problem, and the pace of divorce, though still ridiculously high, has slowed. In our town of Modesto, California, a columnist, Michael McManus, is known as the Johnny Appleseed of the pro-marriage movement. He was influential in creating a community marriage policy requiring any couple that wished to marry in a house of worship (86% of couples) to go through ten two-hour counseling sessions and take a personality test to detect possible problems. He met with the local spiritual leaders and reached an agreement with most of them to participate in his plan. About 10% of the couples who took part in the program found that they were not ready or were not compatible and ended their relationships. Ten years after initiating the program, Modesto's population had grown by 40%, while the divorce rate dropped 7%. Over 200 communities across the country have adopted this program, and a 2004 study showed the divorce rate was lowered by 17.5%. The plan also emphasized the need for mentoring married couples when problems arise. So now peers in the program who have come back from the brink of separation pay it forward and counsel other couples. [69]

A successful marriage is based on love, hard work and dedication. The payoff is peaceful happy families living in cooperative communities. The children grow up surrounded by love and support, and a positive legacy continues on for generations.

A successful marriage is based on love, hard work and dedication. The payoff is peaceful happy families living in cooperative communities. The children grow up surrounded by love and support, and a positive legacy continues on for generations.

Taking the Test

Find a comfortable and quiet place away from your partner where you can take the test without being rushed or distracted. Try to resist the temptation to give answers that will please your love. Be true to yourself.

Later, in a relaxed setting, compare and discuss the test. The subjects where you see eye to eye confirm your compatibility. The answers that are different are the issues that need exploration. Can these differences be reconciled? Can there be a compromise? Can you change your ways enough for this new partnership to continue? Now is the best time to sort these issues out and reach a clear understanding.

Below you will find the 101 Question Compatibility Test. In the back of the book are two tests for you and your partner to complete. Answer the questions with Agree, Disagree, Unsure, Yes, No, or Maybe. Be prepared to talk about why you chose these answers. While you go through the test, place a star by any questions that make you uncomfortable or that you would like to discuss further.

The 101 Question Compatibility Test

Mark each sentence with: Agree, Disagree, Unsure, Yes, No or Maybe

1. Do you enjoy your work?
2. Will you make a good parent?
3. Are your future in-laws comfortable with your culture or religion?
4. Does your partner's sense of humor sometimes bother you?
5. Do you enjoy spending time with your partner's friends?
6. Do you have any doubts that you have made the right choice?
7. Are you concerned about the significant age difference between you?
8. Have you grown up with a healthy attitude about sex?
9. Do you agree on your roles of caretaker and/or breadwinner when rearing your children?
10. Do either of you have large debts?
11. Do you know where you are going to live?
12. Have issues concerning premarital sex, former lovers, and/or ex'es caused you problems?
13. Does your partner become angry, making you afraid that s/he will hurt you?

14a. Are you worried about you or your partner's use of tobacco, alcohol, or other addictive substances?

14b. Do one or both of you enjoy drinking or using recreational drugs in moderation?

15. Do you have an agreement about how to handle your finances?

16. Are there conflicts concerning your religious beliefs?

17. Is your partner frequently moody or depressed?

18. When there are problems to be discussed, does you partner refuse to talk about them?

19. Are you uncomfortable with you partner's public show of affection?

20. Do you enjoy discussions about religion, philosophy and spiritual matters?

21. Are you taking an active part in the wedding plans?

22. Is one or both of you a workaholic?

23. Do you agree about whether or not to have children?

24. Do you work out your problems by having sex?

25. Does your partner make condescending remarks to or about you?

26. Are there family members who will cause friction between you?

27. Will your partner make a good parent?

28. Does your partner encourage you in your interests? (Your career, hobbies, sports, art, music, yoga, etc.)

29. Have you talked about how you want to maintain your home and do your household

chores? (Doing the dishes, laundry, the lawn, vacuuming, cleaning the bathrooms, etc.)

30. Does your partner have certain habits that annoy you? (List them.)
31. Are you uncomfortable when you are with your future in-laws?
32. Do you feel pressure to choose a certain spiritual or religious path?
33. Is you partner jealous and possessive of you?
34. Is your partner or you not on speaking terms with a member(s) of your family?
35. Does your partner refuse to compromise on a particular issue? (List it.)
36. Do you believe in the power of love to heal the body, mind, and spirit?
37. Do you have 'my' and 'your' friends, but only a few who you share in common?
38. Do you believe that sex is an important part of marriage, and are you open to exploring the art of lovemaking with your partner?
39. Does your partner want to get married sooner than you do?
40. Do you agree about how you are going to discipline your children?
41. Are you confident that your income will cover your expenses; can you live within your budget?
42. Does financial help from your family have strings attached?
43. Do you both have promising careers?
44. Do you and your partner handle your personal problems in a reasonable way?

45. Does your partner’s behavior at social events sometimes embarrass you?
46. Do one or both of you always have to be right?
47. Do you or your partner have a tendency to be lazy or unmotivated?
48. Do you agree on how to furnish and decorate your home?
49. Do you know what is sexually satisfying for your partner?
50. Do you agree on how much of your budget will be spent on housing?
51. Are there homosexual, bisexual, or trans-sexual tendencies and preferences in your relationship?
52. Is it difficult to talk about your true feelings with your partner?
53. Are you feeling pressured into marriage by the family?
54. Do you worry that problems you experienced in childhood will affect the way you raise your children?
55. Are you nervous and uncomfortable about revealing your body to your future partner?
56. Can you count on your partner to be a good listener?
57. Are you worried that you do not have adequate insurance coverage?
58. Do you and your partner trust each other with members of the opposite sex?
59. Are you unhappy with one or more of your partner's interests (career, hobbies, sports, etc.)?

60. Are you sometimes embarrassed by your partner's appearance?
61. Do you disagree about the type of wedding you want?
62. Do you try to avoid arguments or disagreements with your partner?
63. Does your partner handle his/her finances responsibly?
64. What are your expectations for your children?
65. Do you have doubts about your love for your partner?
66. Are you uncomfortable with your partner's family and friends since you have come from a different social, cultural, or economic background?
67. Can you count on your partner to give you support when you are feeling down?
68. Is your partner too dependent on his or her parents?
69. Are you ready to accept the responsibilities of being a parent, (3 A.M. feedings, a sick and crying child, "terrible twos," rebellious teens)?
70. Is there a difference between love and sex?
71. Are you comfortable with your partner's politics?
72. Are TV and video games a satisfying and inexpensive pastime for you?
73. When you are angry, do you say or do hurtful things to your partner?
74. Will your different educational backgrounds cause problems?

75. Have you talked about using birth control to plan your family?
76. Are you satisfied and happy with how your life is going?
77. Are you afraid that you might be sexually impotent or frigid?
78. Are your ideas about raising children compatible?
79. Can you foresee problems resulting from an interracial marriage?
80. Is there a conflict about your views on adoption?
81. Is your partner involved in community activities at the expense of you and the family?
82. Does your partner support your future goals and ambitions?
83. Are your partner's eating habits a source of contention?
84. Can you talk with each other about any subject?
85. Do your partner's prejudices bother you?
86. Will getting married solve some of your problems?
87. When you have time off, does your partner choose all of the activities?
88. Do you agree that both of you will be working outside of the home?
89. Do you embrace the basic principles of the traditional marriage vows?
90. Are you and your partner on the same sleep cycles?

91. Will the physical and/or mental health of one or both of you cause any problems?
92. Does your partner place too much emphasis on neatness?
93. Do you have trouble agreeing on major expenditures (House, car, vacation)?
94. In the middle of a heated argument, can you agree to a cooling-off period before you try to resolve the issue?
95. Are you living too close to the parents?
96. Were you mentally, physically, emotionally or sexually abused as a child?
97. Has pregnancy affected your marriage plans?
98. Have you had sex before this relationship?
99. Are you in agreement about how you like to spend your vacation and holiday times?
100. Have you talked about how your life will be after the wedding?
101. Do you feel relaxed and comfortable with your partner?

The 101 Answers

After both of you have taken the test, you can now discover the contrasting nature of some of your points of view. On most subjects, you are going to agree and that's worth celebrating. When there is a difference of opinion on any questions, these will be the subjects that you will delve deeper into and find ways to compromise and reach a happy medium. I have written the following answers from my perspective, but there are also excellent books on the subjects, and many sources of information available on the Internet to help you go deeper into the issues. Also, don't hesitate to talk to your counselor or guide.

1. Do you enjoy your work?

When you wake up each day to a satisfying, challenging and decent paying occupation, it can feel more like going to play than to work. That enthusiasm will permeate your life on the job, and you will bring it home with you. Consider yourself lucky if you actually have the perfect employment situation, since jobs can often be stressful.

On the other hand, do you have trouble dealing with a boss or co-worker? Does jet-setting travel or a long commute keep you away from home for long periods of time? Do you feel uncomfortable with your partner's chosen field? Are the workplace politics full of negativity? Is the pay too low to support a family? Is your chosen vocation not a "right" vocation, meaning is it environmentally destructive, is it

ethically or morally repugnant, or does it require you to compromise your beliefs, standards, health, or integrity? If your job is an unsatisfying but necessary stepping stone to a better career will you be comfortable with it for a relatively short time, while going through the required hoops toward your goal? Are there any improvements that you can make in your present work environment? Is your partner willing to help support you while you go to school? Can you put off having a family until you are on your way to a higher paying career? Who is the wage earner now? Are you both working? How about when children arrive? When you truthfully answer these questions, you can begin to make the positive adjustments towards your dream job. Visionary and creative out-of-the-box discussions can bring up the many possibilities and opportunities available. When you are brainstorming about your work choices, keep an open mind, be flexible, and allow your ideas to soar.
See the chapter: "Is Your Work Fulfilling?" Pg. 57.

2. Will you make a good parent?

Selflessness, dedication, patience, consistency, flexibility, youthful exuberance, playfulness, and a sense of humor are some of the characteristics that make for good parenting. When the two of you have basic agreements about values and discipline, you'll be on the same page when your children arrive. When parents manage their family as a cohesive, compassionate team, the children usually thrive. Different styles of parenting are fine as long as there is an agreement about the boundaries and consequences.

Do you and your partner have fun interacting with little ones? Do you have a sense of humor and an adventurous spirit, or is there a reticence or fear when you are around kids? How do you handle the situations that pop up, including fighting, not sharing, whining, shyness, being picky about food, tantrums, and clinging to their parents? What are your feelings concerning time-outs, spankings, or other disciplinary methods?

What religious orientation do you want for your children? Are you in agreement with your partner on this issue? It's amazing how much resentment there can be when parents force children to attend religious services especially when one or both of the parents does not participate. What you do sets the example for your child's behavior.

Will you give your child the husband's surname or a combination of your names? Will there be a circumcision for a boy? Will there be a baptism for the baby? How would you handle a child with special needs? Will you vaccinate your children against polio, diphtheria, tetanus, measles, mumps, rubella, and whooping cough? Knowing that you agree on answers to these basic questions will make things easier when the time comes.

What about day care? Are you planning to be a stay at home parent or do you need both of your paychecks to pay the bills? How are your finances if only one of you is working? Will the cost of day care be so high that it might be worth staying home and raising your child? Crunch the numbers and be imaginative. The four or five years between the birth of your child and the beginning of primary school are a relatively short but important time in the development of a child's mind and body. By living simply and cutting back on extra expenses, you might be able to stay home and share in your child's daily growth and progress. If your finances don't allow you to give up your career or work, and there's no close relative nearby, the search then begins for a daycare that is compatible with your beliefs and values. Will you send your child to public school, or is a charter or private school an option? There are also parent-run cooperatives and state funded home schooling programs available.

Parents want to do their best to raise their children to be happy and healthy and be able to take care of themselves when they grow up and strike out on their own. The subconscious tendency is to raise your children the same way that your parents raised you. How did your parents treat you, both positively and negatively? Changing negative patterns requires delving into both your happy and unhappy memories of childhood. In the book, *Core Transformation* by Connirae and Tamara Andreas,[70] there are exercises that teach you how to parent the child of your youth. When you give the hurt or misunderstood child that lives within you the love, tenderness, and nurturing that was sometimes absent when you were a child, you can transfer that same compassionate care to your own children. It feels good when you treat him/her like you always wished you had been treated. It helps to make agreements with your partner that you will work on changing harmful patterns of parenting that you might have experienced. When you change negative behavior within yourself, you remove a legacy that would otherwise be passed on to the next generation. Knowing how you want to raise your children will make it easier when issues arise. Creating positive and loving patterns in your family will give your children and your descendants the most valuable gift you can possibly imagine.

3. Are your future in-laws comfortable with your culture or religion?

It is a most wonderful gift when the in-laws give their blessings to your union. The family bonds remain tight and supportive, and the sage wisdom of past generations will be carried on to the next.

Cultural and religious differences can enhance and broaden your relationship. Unfortunately, in some instances, these differences can be a source of contention. If you have a problem with the in-laws, your partner may bring some of the tension and even the parents' personality traits or biases to the relationship. However, being argumentative or defensive with your partner or future in-laws usually only makes matters worse. If your love doesn't want to continue these negative behaviors and has been working on changing them, this bodes well. Tolerance is a virtue especially when you are dealing with religion, politics, and in-laws. Since religious or spiritual beliefs are personal decisions, it's wise to respect each person's choices.

In our case, my husband and I came of age in the cultural turmoil of the sixties when never before had so many couples married across religious, racial, economic, and cultural boundaries.[71] Our marriage went against the wishes of both of our parents. For me to marry a Jew and for my husband to marry a Christian was cause for anguish on both sides of our family. Nevertheless, we followed our hearts and hoped that our parents would come to accept our union, which they ultimately did. However, many marriages cannot withstand the stress. When you enter a relationship with cultural and religious differences, there will undoubtedly be issues to work out. Though your in-laws might have good intentions, they may also have hurtful biases you will want to ignore. Hopefully your in-laws will voice their concerns clearly and compassionately, and then accept you and your partner's decision gracefully. It's well known that meddling in-laws can be a sore point in the lives of a newly married couple. Families have all sorts of reasons for not accepting your union including race, religion, culture, economic standing, age differences, or maturity levels. Anyone marrying across these boundaries is likely to have extra tensions to deal with.

Then there are families who do not approve because they have preconceived notions of who is "good enough" for their son or daughter. Parents worry (that's just what we do), and they do not want to see their child suffer undue stress. When you address their concerns and objections and respectfully try to understand their viewpoint, hopefully, things can be more agreeable. Why is the family not accepting of this person, your amour? Are they trying to warn you about a dangerous character flaw that they see and you don't? When issues come up, do you have a tendency to slide over them as if they are unimportant?

If you do decide to marry without your family's blessings, building a supportive community of friends and mentors will serve you well. After all is said and done, do what is right for you.

4. Does your partner's sense of humor sometimes bother you?

Laughter is the language of a happy heart, and humor is an art worth cultivating, especially when you can laugh at yourself in those humbling moments when you realize you blew it. A successful relationship flourishes when you can make each other laugh. Is the humor off-color, tiresome, corny, or sophomoric? What is so funny? Does your partner often paraphrase a hurtful comment with, "I was just joking?" If this is common, look closely, it is not a joke. What is really bothering him? Without squelching your partner's true sense of humor, let him know how you feel about any jokes that disturb you. Will your partner change his behavior or become resentful? As far as compromising goes, this seems like a small thing to ask. Discovering his true feelings hiding behind the hurtful or degrading jokes can free him up to be truly funny.

5. Do you enjoy spending time with your partner's friends?

Enjoying each other's friends should be easy. The trouble comes when your partner's acquaintances have a detrimental influence on him or her. Do you dislike them because they have "weird" attitudes or behaviors, or is it a personality conflict? Is it drugs, alcohol, or is he spending too much time away from you? If this is causing a strain on the relationship, it's time to talk about it.

Friends are a reflection of who you are. Are there times when you want to hang out with your pals without your sweetheart? A happy couple doesn't need to feel jealous or threatened by their partner's freedom and independence. Being away from each other can enhance your love. When you spend time away from each other, you want to feel secure in his or her love, trust, and loyalty. Of course, if this bothers you, is there something that is triggering your jealousy or do you need to work on being more trusting and assuming his/her good will?

Does your partner exclude you from his/her gatherings? Does your relationship feel threatened by his/her friends? Is there a tendency to cling and not let him/her out of your sight?

Is one of you more gregarious and extroverted while the other is shy and introverted? Do you love each other for these qualities? There are times when the social butterfly will want to go out with friends, while the quieter partner stays home to do a project, read, or watch TV. There can be dates when you go out together and other times where you can both have a sweet time at home doing what you love. If something is creating a strain on the relationship, find a way to make it good for both of you. Being flexible and compromising always helps.

6. Do you have any doubts that you have made the right choice?

Marriage is a risk and it is not for everyone. There are no guarantees that it will work today, after children arrive, or when there's a mid-life crisis. Love opens up your heart and makes you vulnerable. When you fall in love, your defenses come down and it can be a scary thing. You might get hurt, and therein lies the risks. Therein also lies true love. Honestly taking and discussing this test can give you and your partner an accurate picture of where problems may surface, how you compromise, and whether you are ready to take the plunge.

What is the reason for your 'cold feet?' Is there something terribly wrong or is it those typical butterflies in your stomach? Are your family or friends warning you about something? Are you afraid of ending up divorced like your parents even before you've begun? Do you want more time to date before you make a serious commitment? Do you have a valid objection? Is there someone else who you think you might be in love with? Whoa!

Bring up all of your doubts now, not after the wedding. If you are uncertain, it's almost a guarantee that there will be trouble later. You just might want to postpone any wedding plans until these misgivings have been cleared up to your satisfaction.

7. Are you concerned about the significant age difference between you?

In ancient China, matchmakers and fortunetellers considered it a good match when the man was four years older than the woman. Recently a survey about longevity found that the best match was when a man was four years and four months older than his mate.[72] It is often thought that young women mature faster than men. However, there is no cut and dry rule about whether you should be the same age or years apart when you marry, but there are things to consider. When you are within five to ten years of each other, you grew up during the same era and enjoyed the same music, dances, fashions, and cultural innovations. You lived through the same time in history, with all of its scientific breakthroughs, political and technological changes.

If you are interested in having children, the woman's biological clock is an inevitable time constraint. A certain number of women these days are having healthy babies into their forties, but having a child after the age of 35 is considered a high risk pregnancy.[73]

Is this a Father issue? Mother issue? Was one of your parents absent, and you are searching for an older mate? Or were you "Daddy's Little Girl" or "Mama's Favorite Little Man," and you're looking for a father or mother replacement? Are you thinking that a youthful partner who is cuter with fewer lines on her face will bring you happiness? Or are you searching for an easy ride with a "sugar daddy," who is financially secure?

Perhaps you are just starting out in your career and excited to put all of your learning into action, while your partner is planning to retire soon and wants to go on a worldwide traveling adventure. Or you may be ready to have children, but your partner is divorced with grown children and may not want to start a new family. Are you ready to be a stepmother to his children? Can you find some common ground on these critical questions?

All couples go into a marriage wanting it to last. If there are 15-20 years between you, when you are 60, your partner will be 75 or 80. Consider the possibility that your older partner might have health issues, leaving you with the burden of caregiving while you are still in the prime of life. But then again, there's no telling what might happen in the life we choose. This doesn't have to be a deterrent if as the poet, Virgil, says, "Love conquers all!" Consider having discussions about what Erik Erikson called the 8 Stages of Life. [74] Where do you and your partner fit into the stages, which include college, work, having a family, mid life, empty nest, and retirement? This perspective will allow you to anticipate what to expect and appreciate the choices that you make.

8. Have you grown up with a healthy attitude about sex?

It's only been in the last few generations that there has been a societal loosening up of inhibited attitudes about sexuality and lovemaking. Was sex one of those subjects you could comfortably talk about in your family? How did you learn about sex? Have you had a bad experience with sexual harassment or abuse that is still haunting you? If you are feeling that you are not acquainted with the finer points of love making, there are numerous books, videos, and manuals to guide you towards a wonderful experience.

If you are shy or insecure, your partner can take the time to gently and patiently help you relax. Does he make you feel beautiful and sexy? If he is sensitive to your needs, he can turn you on. Don't be afraid to tell your partner what feels good and how you'd like to be touched.

Have you ever looked at yourself and explored yourself in a sexual way, feeling comfortable with your body? Masturbation is generally considered to be normal, but in the past, there have been harsh measures against it. However, it has been shown through numerous studies that this self-love is a natural and healthy human response.[75] Regardless of your opinion or belief, having a healthy respect and love for your own body allows you to give and receive sexual love that enhances your physical pleasure and emotional health.

Lovemaking is an experience where both partners' sexual needs are met. Women generally take longer to reach orgasm, but in a stable relationship women have orgasms as often as men when the subtle techniques of lovemaking are explored.[76] When the woman is in touch with how her body responds and knows what she wants, she can guide the lovemaking to the high place of shared satisfaction and sheer ecstasy.

9. Do you agree on your roles of caretaker and/or breadwinner when raising your children?

The first years of your child's life, before he enters school is a precious time. Your baby, toddler, and preschooler is growing at a furious rate, physically, mentally, and emotionally. The question to ask is will you be able to stay at home to care for your baby or will she go to day care? Are there other options like grandparents or close family friends nearby who would be willing to watch her? There are couples who have decided to work on different shifts so that a parent is always home. A baby-sitter or grandparent can fill in the few gaps that pop up in the schedule. How long will mother take off from work, or will she go back to work at all while your child is young? Will Mr. Mom manage the household while mom continues on her career path? How will you handle the financial change if one of you stays home? Arranging times to be with your friends and neighbors who have children can lead to supportive discussions, play dates, and childcare cooperatives.

I stayed home and cared for our children when they were young, nursing them until they were at least six months old, and more often for a year. Each baby was a part of me for nine months in utero, and we were still closely connected after each birth. These ties that were formed in my children's early years continue to be lifelong connections.

In comparison, a father's role in society today is changing rapidly, and now Dads are more involved with the care of their young children. Traditionally the father was the patriarch and manager of financial matters, leaving home each day to earn a living. He made all the major decisions and led the family. When a child was being born, he was relegated to the waiting room, nervously pacing until he was called in to see his new baby. Fortunately, there is now a more equitable sharing of responsibilities between partners. Dad is often present at their child's birth, supporting the mother during the delivery. This intimate bond that forms during this life-changing experience often results in the father taking a more active part in the care of his little one. Also, when both parents work, roles become interchangeable.

With fathers becoming more involved in child-rearing, we are seeing imaginative innovations that are practical and fun. We were visiting our daughter and her family when our son-in-law found a way to make changing diapers enjoyable for both, him and his baby. It became a car race with "Brmmm, Brmmm" and "Honk, Honk," both the baby and Dad laughing until the clean diaper was on.

Unfortunately, when a father hasn't had any role models as an interactive dad, he may feel insecure with these new responsibilities. Also, there are mothers who have had difficult childhoods where mothering skills have been lost. It is said that most mothers, however, have an intuitive sense built in from millennia of practice and that even when they feel unsure they usually know what to do. [77] If Mom is comfortable with being a mother, patient, firm, humorous, and intuitive, Dad can take some clues from her and look to her as a skilled mentor. When parents can agree about how to raise their children, the kids can thrive in a secure environment with consistency and appropriate boundaries.

10. Do either of you have large debts?

You might think that extra-marital affairs would be the number one reason for a marriage to fall apart, but it actually comes in second to financial issues.[78] Is there a large credit card debt? The financial pundits recommend that you pay if off as quickly as possible. Ideally these cards, which generally have a high interest rate, should be used as a 30-day free loan and paid off entirely within the grace period. If you are purchasing a larger item, try to pay more than the minimum payment each month. It's a trap that can ensnare you if you are not diligent in paying this kind of debt off as quickly as possible. How about using it only to reserve hotel and airline tickets or to purchase needed items at online stores when there are great deals?

Is your large debt a student loan with affordable monthly payments at a reasonable interest rate? If you are keeping up with the payments, good for you! If you happen to have a surplus, you can pay your loan down sooner. If the interest rate is high, can a refinance lower your bill? Even better, look into student loan forgiveness programs that pay off the loan if you work in an under-served area.

If your large debt is a mortgage on a house, is it time to refinance to a lower interest rate? Do both of you like the home's location, size, and cost? A few years ago there was the sub-prime mortgage fiasco and many people just starting out were caught in the mess. Fortunately, there are programs to give people relief. The rule of thumb is: Don't consider buying a home unless you plan on being in that location for at least five years.

On the other hand, renting a home allows you time to accumulate enough savings for a down payment and to be sure that this is the area where you want to settle. If you have children, are good schools close by? Is there easy access to work and shopping, and a warm community feeling with neighboring families? Do you have family living nearby?

Perhaps the debt is an indication of a larger problem, for example, compulsive spending, binge shopping, or gambling. Before you are married, talk about how you would budget your finances and what you would do with any discretionary income. If there is a problem, seeking financial counseling can help get you on track with your money issues. Balancing a checkbook and budgeting your income is rarely taught in school, but is critical to a financially savvy relationship.

If one of you came from a wealthy family or has already accumulated a fortune, are you willing to have a shared account or do you need to consider a pre-nuptial agreement? Check with a lawyer or an accountant to see how this is done. [79]

Finally, there are books, seminars, and workshops about finances that are available everywhere. Suze Ormond's,[80] *The Nine Steps to Financial Freedom,* and Dave Ramsey's[81] *The Total Money Makeover* are both easy to read with a no-nonsense, balanced attitude about financial matters. These books have helped us manage our resources, and we thank them for their excellent advice.

11. Do you know where you are going to live?

In 2007, the United States Census Bureau estimated that a person moves an average of 11.7 times during a lifetime, and most of the moves are made before a person reaches the age of 45.[82] Many things determine where you live. Are you still attending school? Are you going to move for better employment? Does your job require travel or relocating? Do you like living in the mountains, near the ocean, near relatives and friends or are you interested in searching out new horizons? While you are dating, are you talking about traveling sometime in the near future? It's not uncommon for young people to take off exploring the world, often on a shoestring budget, before they settle down and have a family. Although, young children move easily, once the kids enter junior and senior high school, they are more reluctant to leave their close friends and school activities.

Are you planning to rent an apartment, purchase a home, live in a big city, small town, or in a rural area? There are banks that offer programs that help first-time homebuyers purchase a home. Is the house big enough? Is it going to accommodate the family size that you have planned? Is it too big with high utility bills? If you want to live simply and have discretionary income to spend on travel for example, then smaller square footage might be a better option. Is the price affordable?

Lastly, is the location convenient and close to where you work? A long drive puts a strain on a relationship. However, a temporary distant commute might enable you to save up enough to buy a home closer to your place of business. In today's computer age, many bosses allow you to telecommute from home. A converted bedroom could be used for an in-home workstation. When you lay out all the options, a practical solution usually presents itself.

12. Are there issues concerning former lovers and premarital sex?

Practicing abstinence until the wedding night is a long-held tradition in many cultures although often not followed these days in our modern Western society. Apparently humans are promiscuous animals, with 97% of people in the United States having engaged in premarital sex up from 89% in 1950.[83] Do you feel like you would like to have a little more sexual experience before you tie the knot? Is one or both of you wanting to abstain from having sex before you are married?

Jealously and insecurity can rear its ugly head if you bring up past sexual encounters. If two people truly love each other, being sensitive and tender are the ways to alleviate these feelings, especially when you say sweet things like, "I'm so happy to be with you," and, "You're the only one for me." Your past relationships taught you valuable lessons about being with a partner, but they came up short for one reason or another. Hopefully, you have learned from these experiences and know what you do and don't want in your long-term partner. Have you grown and matured and are totally satisfied to "love the one you're with?"[84]

If you had children in your former partnership, nurturing good relations with the mother or father will make it easier for everyone to adapt to the new situation. Do you have an equitable joint-custody arrangement or is your ex disruptive? Is there jealousy between your new partner and your ex? Can everyone please be civil and get along for the sake of the children?

Are you unable to cut loose of your ex? Is s/he on your mind and are you constantly comparing your partner to him or her? Undoubtedly, this will cause friction in your present relationship until you can let go and move on. With gnawing doubts removed, all your love can flow to your partner and your marriage will survive and prosper.

If a former boyfriend or girlfriend still holds a piece of your heart, perhaps you should place your current relationship on hold while you go back to make sure that s/he is not "the One." What could be worse than being married to one person while wishing to be with someone else? Marriage is a long-term commitment and one of the most important choices of a lifetime. It should feel absolutely right. When in doubt, don't.

13. Does your partner become angry, making you afraid that s/he will hurt you?

Time to raise the red flag! If a partner has a bad temper, flying into a rage over minor things, being mean, destructive, or threatening physical harm, everyone in the family suffers.[85] Are you "walking on eggshells," trying not to make him angry and hoping that things will stay calm. Living under these conditions inflicts emotional and sometimes physical wounds that are hard to heal and can leave lasting scars. Avoid this situation and don't just walk away, but run...FAST!

Regrettably, many physical, mental, and emotional abusers show signs of being abused and are insecure and immature with no idea how to deal with life's problems and stresses. They take their frustrations out on whoever is closest and have no idea how this frightening emotion is affecting his/her loved ones. If other people are trying to warn you of this danger, listen to them!

If your partner's temper is not under his/her control, your marriage will be under siege, and you and your children will be in danger. Anger is used to maintain control and exert power. When your partner manipulates you with rage, s/he is attempting to take away your free will. Ask yourself, why are you enabling this harmful behavior?

The Dance of Anger by Harriet Goldhor Lerner Ph.D.[86] includes an excellent rundown on the causes of anger and how to deal with it. If a bad temper is part of your own personality, make a dedicated effort to understand the root causes of your discontent and learn how to manage it before you complicate your life with a partner.

What can you do to alleviate a hot temper? It doesn't go away without serious work. Only with a commitment to change will this problem be mitigated. Is your partner angry and even violent, and then afterward very sorry, sweet and remorseful? In this situation, it is common to hear "I will never do anything like that again," and "I'm sorry" over and over. You may believe that the sweet person who you love has returned and all will be well. Is it true? Not likely.[87] Don't be fooled by the intermittent peaceful times. What are you going to do when it happens again?

Anger is an innately human emotion that alerts us to something that requires our immediate attention and action. It can be a call for justice and fairness and gives us the necessary energy to act against a danger. It may be a proper response or, more than likely, a default-response used to hide emotions like sadness, confusion, insecurity, and feelings of inferiority. If you are not accustomed to talking about your feelings or venting them in a healthy way, when life's stresses weigh you down, your first response is to erupt in uncontrolled anger. When you feel the flush of rage, stop for two minutes and breathe deeply. In those short minutes, you can choose to act in a mature and responsible way instead of blowing your top. You may think you have a good reason to be mad, but there is never a good reason to hurt someone else or take it out on your family.

There are things you can do to bring a situation to a satisfactory conclusion without resorting to hostility. When you find creative ways to channel your energy, your habitual response can be changed. What is the core reason for your hot temper? Can you drop the issue until you are calmer and able to talk out the problem, approaching it with self-control and love, rather than letting it get the best of you? In the long run if you commit to changing this pattern, and doing the difficult work required, it will bring relief to you and everyone around you.

Counseling can help find the root of the hostility and show him/her how to work on managing his/her emotions. You can also discover what attracted you to him/her in the first place. You don't deserve to be mistreated. Is there a pattern of emotional abuse in your family and are you tolerating the same treatment because it is your comfort zone? Gary Chapman and Ross Campbell in their book, *The Five Love Languages of Children* and Gary Chapman in his book, *The Other Side of Love* are resources on understanding rage, and how to distinguish between valid and distorted anger. [88]

14a. Are you worried about you or your partner's use of tobacco, alcohol, or other addictive substances?

If either of you have an addiction to alcohol, tobacco, or drugs, the dependence can take precedent over a happy home. The power that these substances can have over your body is difficult to control. In the worst-case scenario, an addiction can take over and rule a person's life until the substance is more important than his or her partner, the children, the marriage, or the home. An addict often loses his/her job, siphons off the money, and there may be DUI's (Driving Under the Influence) and jail time.

When there is a concerted effort to clean up one's act and find out what the underlying issues are then progress can be made. In many cases, a subconscious behavior can create a situation where a person feels like nothing is helping, and with that hopelessness, s/he is driven to self-medicate. Once his/her body has been taken over by the physical addiction as well as the psychological dependency and emotional relief felt from the substance, it is difficult to take the steps towards recovery. However, many people have made the pledge to take control of their lives and pursue happiness. Alcoholics Anonymous and Al Anon (for families), for example, have been lifesavers for many individuals.

Substance abuse affects everyone in the family. For instance, smoking during pregnancy causes problems for the newborn. Young children of smokers have more instances of asthma, bronchitis and other ailments than those of non-smokers.[89] Also, the money spent on the substance could be used for healthy food, clothing, books, travel opportunities, and cultural enrichment.

Are there addicted members in your families? Are they in denial about their problems or are they fighting the good fight to quit their dependency? Are you and your partner following family patterns by indulging in addictive substances? Unfortunately, a habit doesn't improve over time especially when the alcohol or drugs cause undesirable personality changes. If you or your partner are willing to seek help, there is hope, but be cautious and do not rush into this relationship. Managing an addiction only happens with effort, commitment, and sheer force of will. No one can do it for you. Before you commit to living together, give your partner or yourself time to recover from a harmfully dependent lifestyle. You can be helpful and supportive, but put a serious relationship on hold until a major directional change in life has taken place.

.

14b. Do one or both of you enjoy drinking or using recreational drugs in moderation?

When individuals partake in moderation, there is usually not a problem. But what is your definition of moderation? A romantic night out together can be fun and relaxing, and there are usually no lasting side effects. New research has come out that says that a glass of wine is apparently good for your heart.[90] Do you and your partner have a mature attitude and behavior when it comes to drinking? Do your families or friends drink a little too much on the weekends and holidays? A habit or addiction often develops when there are physical, mental, or emotional problems and the person seeks relief through alcohol and drugs. Self-medication can lead to dependency, and eventually the drug of choice takes over through a physical and/or psychological addiction. [91] This usually only intensifies the original problem that hasn't gone away.

On the other hand, organic psychedelics have been used for hundreds, or probably even thousands of years. Indigenous cultures often use small amounts of tobacco or hallucinogens like cacti (peyote), marijuana, and mushrooms as part of their ceremonies. The Native American Church uses peyote as a sacrament during their services. They use a reasonable amount at the right time, and with an attitude of respect and reverence. An experienced guide or road chief is there to create a validating rite of passage, a healing experience, or an insightful celebration.

Herbs and ales are popular in our modern culture as a way to enjoy life and "get high." The question is can you handle it, or are you once again going down that slippery slope? If you find yourself over imbibing, can you stop, or do you need to join an AA type group, or go into a detox program that can help you break your addiction? Without doing this difficult work, a happy, stress-free relationship doesn't have a chance. Let's be safe, smart, and respectful of the power behind the medicine.

15. Do you have an agreement about how to handle your finances?

Financial issues can be a major cause of grief in a marriage. In a survey by the Forum for Family and Consumer Issues, 39% of couples listed finances as the leading cause of marital conflict and 54% rated it as second.[92] Discussing your expectations and making and keeping good agreements on how to handle your finances can alleviate future problems. You may want to set out a one-year, five-year, and ten-year financial plan that reflects your present circumstances and your future goals with the realization that when children enter the picture, the priorities of your family's finances will change. For financial information, Suze Orman's *The Nine Steps to Financial Freedom*[93] is a great book: concise and easy to read. She emphasizes that how you approach money makes a difference. It isn't attracted to worries, reckless spending, or miserliness, but it does like to be treated with prudence and respect.

Begin by creating a realistic budget. List all income in one column and all of your expenditures in another. See if there are items you can cut to close budget gaps. Can you consolidate and pay down your debts? Include student loans, credit card debt and mortgages. It's a wise choice to pay off the debt with the highest interest rate first. Also, can you make changes in your spending habits to save up for something that you want? Decide if there will be one checking account or if each of you will have your own. Who will be responsible for paying the bills? How will you divide the earnings when both of you are working? Will there be a savings account? Are there retirement funds for both of you and a college fund for your children? If one of you is wealthy, will there be a pre-nuptial agreement?

Working out our financial plan is something that Robert and I did on a yearly basis. One of our arts and crafts shows where we sold our tie-dyed clothing was near Las Vegas, a nine-hour drive from home. Since we had plenty of time to talk on the way, I would bring our financial books along and crunch the numbers. We also spent time envisioning the future and thinking out of the box, talking over our long-range plans, like our dream to sail down to Mexico aboard our sailboat, *Harmony*. When our children were finishing up college and becoming self-sufficient, we became serious about our dream to cruise to the tropics. We rarely ate out and simplified our lifestyle. We did not renew our cable TV, magazine subscriptions, and even the local newspaper until we fulfilled our financial vision. We discovered that **it is not how much you make, but how much you spend.**

There is the old joke that you can either work forty hours a week at a job, or work eighty hours a week for yourself. Owning our own businesses, we did have to work hard. Actual vacations were non-existent, but we made interesting stops when we traveled to the craft shows. On weekends when we didn't have fairs, we returned home refreshed after spending time in nature in nearby places like Yosemite National Park and exploring the California coast.

With our large family and businesses to run, finances were often tight. I would sometimes lie awake at night mulling over how I was going to pay the bills coming due. Robert assured me that it was okay to wake him up if I was "tripping my brains out," about the budget. Even when it was 2:00 AM, we would talk it over and come up with solutions. Then both of us could sleep peacefully. When I shared my worries, I did not feel so overwhelmed. Needless worry actually inhibited my thought process, stifling original and innovative ways of managing the finances. By having a confident attitude that things would work out fine, I created a positive flow. Following Suze Orman's advice, I stopped worrying that I didn't have enough and, instead valued the income I had and treated it with respect. Our finances continually improved and my sleepless nights were history.

It helped to have our kids working at the craft shows with us and we talked openly with them about how we made, spent, and invested our income. Lively discussions were held about taxes, insurance, buying property, and the ins and outs of the world of finance. Our children knew how we paid for the mortgage and groceries. While working, they practiced skills like dealing with the public, making change, and "closing the deal." We paid our children well and they spent their earnings on clothes, transportation, and entertainment, and opened accounts for college expenses. It can be truly satisfying to study the numbers, make up a budget, see your debts go down, and your assets go up, and in effect, watch your dreams manifest into reality.

16. Is there a conflict concerning your religious beliefs?

George Bernard Shaw said, "There is only one religion, although there are a hundred versions of it." When you share the same beliefs, you generally view spirituality from a similar perspective that can enhance and deepen a relationship. When partners of two different faiths come together, there can be a larger planetary vision when they find common ground. It helps to agree on a unified belief system that includes the truths in both religions. One of you might even convert to your partner's religion.

Robert and I came from two different religious backgrounds, Judaism and Christianity, and together we searched out a common belief system that eventually expanded to include all religions and all peoples. In our family, we combined many of the customs and holidays of our backgrounds, celebrating Hanukkah, Christmas, Passover, and Easter.

Religion can be a delicate subject. Wars have been fought over which God is "right," and unresolved religious conflicts have spanned thousands of years of intolerance and conquest. Basic tenets like the Golden Rule and the Law of Karma like "Do unto others as you would have them do unto you," and "As you sow, so shall you also reap" are universal. However, if you hold on to the idea that my way is better than your way or I'm one of the chosen and you are not, there is likely to be trouble.

Openness, tolerance, and acceptance of each other's beliefs leads to happiness. Forcing ideas, belief systems, or a religion onto another person just doesn't work. Try to understand what your partner believes in his or her innermost heart. Find the points of agreement and build on your commonality. If children enter the picture, are you going to raise them in a specific religious faith? Will you celebrate religious holidays? Any conflicts about your beliefs need resolution before the marriage plans continue.

17. Is your partner frequently moody or depressed?

Depression is a mental illness and, like any physical illness, needs treatment before healing can take place.[94] Up goes the Red Flag! When the blues are left untreated, it will infect and destroy the marriage, or at the very least cause heartache and chaos. Also, it is not beneficial to have a heavy heart and suffer alone. Urge your partner to seek professional guidance before you make big plans. Be careful that you do not take your partner on as your "project" or your "patient," thinking that your love will provide the curative touch. That would be naive. You can be supportive, but he must do the difficult work for himself of finding out what will make him a happy and functional human being.

Perhaps your partner's attitude or moodiness makes it difficult for him to keep a job? Unemployment can be a depressing situation, but getting a job and keeping it can be one of the things that can contribute to a cure. Even if he starts with a low-level position, he could be on the road to finding his dream job. Each experience could advance him to the next level, especially if he follows directions, is timely, and works well with people, and most importantly, discovers his talents. If your partner should find himself unemployed, non-profit organizations are always looking for volunteers. Often a paid job will be offered once his skills, positive attitude, and good work habits are noticed. Certainly, the worst that will happen is he will be busy, have money in his pocket, and, hopefully, be tired enough at the end of the day to sleep well. If one job doesn't keep him busy enough, perhaps a second job will help.

Moodiness and boredom can be an indication of repressed hostility.[95] Is it a temporary condition or a chronic mental health issue that requires medication or therapy? Moodiness is often associated with holding back one's true feelings and not opening up and discussing what is troubling him. Try talking about it when your partner is not moody. If he is stubborn and insists on staying in a funk, refusing help from either you or anyone else, then the relationship is in danger of failure.

Consider reading about depression. For example, Terrence Real wrote the wonderful book called *I Don't Want to Talk About It.*[96] Terrence suffered from depression and, after hitting a low, began to study psychology. By working hard on his deepest hidden emotions, he was able to heal himself, his family and eventually many other people. His message is about hope. With determination and a search to the very depths of the soul, depression can be alleviated. Also, Byron Katie's book *Loving What Is*[97] describes a simple and helpful method of getting to the bottom of any problem and finding healing and true freedom.

18. Does your partner refuse to talk about issues that affect your relationship?

Refusing to discuss a problem will leave an open sore that festers and grows. Hoist the red flag! Avoidance or denial will not chase the problem away. If your partner is not willing to work through disagreements when they arise, s/he is not ready to nurture a relationship. Communication is a cornerstone of a successful partnership. With dedication to acquiring and developing "working it out" skills and a willingness to deal with the issues, your relationship will thrive.

See Chapter on Communications, Pg. 113-115

19. Are you uncomfortable with your partner's public show of affection?

A sweet embrace when you wake up, a kiss when you leave for work, and a hug at the end of the day is the oil that keeps a relationship running smoothly. When hugging, snuggling, and kissing is welcomed, spontaneous, sincere, and fun, you both enjoy the closeness. A loving touch should feel good. Are you always kissing in public, ignoring everyone around you? If something is inappropriate or awkward, let him or her know.

Depending on one's culture, a public show of affection can be either okay or objectionable. In many Asian and Muslim cultures it is not acceptable to display your love outside of closed doors.[98] In contrast, you can see Parisian and Roman lovers amorously intertwined just about anywhere. Set up subtle cues to let your partner know if something is objectionable for you in any given situation. When s/he respects how you feel, you can relax and be comfortable wherever you go.

20. Do you enjoy discussions about religion, philosophy, and spiritual matters?

When you are having a discussion about religion, current events, philosophy, things spiritual, and any other "hot" subject, having an open-mind is critical, and shows a healthy, mature relationship. Talking together about big ideas can lead to action that makes a difference in the world. When one of you brings up a subject, you may not know all the facts or even exactly where this new thought will take you. When you remain open to a new viewpoint, allowing it to expand instead of shutting it down before it has wings, new discoveries and concepts can evolve. When you think outside of the box, you may discover a bigger truth. This greater clarity can lead to exciting adventures for the mind. Problems come up when one of you refuses to allow the exploration of new ideas or sets limits on the conversation. Then stagnation sets in, a bane to a flowering relationship.

21. Are you taking an active part in the wedding plans?

In the United States marriage is a cooperative partnership, and in the eyes of the law you are both equally responsible. At this point, neither one of you has any reservations, right? The energy and stress levels usually mount when you set out on this amateur endeavor of planning a wedding. It can all seem overwhelming: the guest list, the caterer, how much is all of this going to cost, and, OMG, I forgot all about my dress and what about the cake and the flowers? Can you take a deep breath, relax, and laugh together? It is a big deal, but when you go into it with the attitude that you are going to have a wonderful party celebrating your love, you'll have a great time. What part of it interests you? How about the music? What kind of budget do you have to work with? Are you putting on the wedding yourselves, or are you going by the longstanding tradition of the bride's family paying for everything? What kind of wedding do you want to have: a small family affair, or are you going to go all out and invite all of your friends and extended family? Do you want a destination wedding or is it going to be at a local venue? If you are feeling that you are on the sidelines, do you need to step up, take more interest, and help with the details? A marriage is a two-way street and planning a wedding is one of those authentic tests for your new relationship.

Is one of your parents being difficult to deal with or is insisting on having it a certain way? Whose wedding is this?

You decide how involved the parents and in-laws are going to be. Let everyone know what they can do to help.

In our family, my daughter Rose and her fiancée, Ben decided to do all of the planning for their wedding. The bride and groom worked together to make their own invitations, lined up the caterer, and asked a friend to be their photographer. Ben wanted to do the flower arrangements including the bouquets. At first, Rose thought that he was taking on too much for the day of the wedding, but Ben did a beautiful job, kept costs down, and made it to the wedding on time! He also was in charge of the sound system and the dance floor lighting, while Rose arranged numerous things like the decorations and the music selections. They wrote their vows together and choreographed the ceremony. Delegating jobs to friends and family added to the party atmosphere. Using the Internet, they booked a honeymoon trip to Fiji, a romantic and surprisingly inexpensive spot. They both worked hard to make a beautiful wedding, their cooperative effort boded well for their relationship, and it turned out to be the party of the year!

This day is all about the two of you. It is your wedding, and everything is going to work out fine, with memories that will last a lifetime.

22. Is one or both of you a workaholic?

If you or your partner is studying for a degree or on a special job assignment working long hours, your marriage should be able to withstand this temporary inconvenience. But is this a situation that's going to become a permanent part of your lifestyle? A workaholic suffers from a form of addiction that is as harmful to a relationship as any other compulsion. However, it is unique because it is socially acceptable. Is he married to his work? Has it become his mistress? Is he never home? Will the children hardly know him? Is there not enough time to maintain the love connection? I've often heard that when you near the end of life, people wish they had spent more time with their family instead of doing all that work.

Certainly, a happy home is not sustainable without spending quantity and quality time with the children and special date nights with your lover. Is it okay with you to be responsible for maintaining the house, the children, the relationship, and everything else while your partner works a 60-plus hour week? Traditionally, this division of labor was the norm.[99] The husband went to work and was the breadwinner while the wife stayed home and cared for the home. Things have changed in the last few generations. In 1960, 70% of married women were stay-at-home moms, and in the modern world of 2014, 31% stay home with the children.[100] Rising costs often require two incomes to pay the bills, adding extra stress to a young family with children.[101] When both partners play an active role in nurturing the marriage, even though life is sometimes exhausting, there will be enough time and energy for everything.

23. Do you agree about whether or not to have children?

When one partner wants children and the other doesn't it could be a deal breaker. Hoist up the red flag! Some couples agree not to have kids and sometimes even believe that they have a noble purpose in helping reduce the population explosion.[102] If you choose this path, there are innumerable pursuits that you can put your energy into like finding a cure for cancer or do something wild like sailing around the world. But, if your partner wants a family, there will be an emptiness in his/her life if you don't have kids.

If you want to have a family, how many children do you want? How about your partner? Is it your idea to have a large boisterous family, or one or two kids that will allow you more time to pursue a career? When are you planning to start having children? Will you wait until after earning a degree, or getting a comfortable work situation so your partner can stay home with the baby?

What if you or your partner has fertility issues?[103] Do you want to adopt? Certainly, there are more than enough kids who need a stable family and a warm, loving home. Children are wonderful, expensive, mind-expanding, and a long-term responsibility, and you will be greatly rewarded with a child who you can help raise into an amazing person.

What if the agreement was to not have children but you became pregnant? Will you change your mind? Does there need to be a discussion about abortion or putting your child up for adoption?

Are you reluctant and afraid to become a parent because of your own unhappy childhood? Unless you make a conscious effort to do otherwise, parents tend to raise their children as they were raised. Fortunately, there are parenting classes to help prepare you for a positive experience. It will take concentrated effort and self-discipline to overcome the dysfunctional legacy of your family. When the old negative behaviors are not passed on, there is endless satisfaction to see your children grow up without that particular burden.

If there are serious differences in the way you think about children or if one of you wants a family, and one does not, then **now** is the time to call things off. One of you could end up very unhappy. This is supposed to be the partner of your dreams.

24. Do you work out your problems by having sex?

Having sex is a wonderful way to relieve tension that builds up from the stresses of everyday living. When the two of you make love, issues may seem to evaporate, but they probably remain. When you don't resolve problems that cause resentment or anxiety, eventually sex can lose its appeal. The "dirty laundry" piles up and inevitably interferes when you try to reach deeper levels of intimacy. Lovemaking is more satisfying after business has been taken care of. You free up vital energy when you resolve an issue or when an apology dissolves an old frustration. Straighten things out, and then the fireworks can really begin.

25. Does your partner make condescending remarks to or about you?

Up goes the red flag! Dating is the time when each partner is on his or her best behavior, and if your partner is belittling you now, chances are good that the condescending behavior will continue. **Warning**...there is trouble afoot! Is this a case of low self-esteem where your partner makes you smaller to make him/herself feel bigger and better? What attracted you to someone who does not respect or treat you well? If you ask to talk about the problem, and s/he responds with "I was just kidding," know that it is not a laughing matter. The abusive treatment won't stop. This level of stress will destroy the relationship sooner than later. If you are both determined to make changes to create a happy life, there is hard work ahead. Finding a counselor, who you both respect and appreciate, can help you get to the bottom of the problem.

26. Are there family members who will cause friction between you?

It is wonderful to have close family ties. When in-laws cause problems, there will be resentments. You might consider moving away from a toxic family situation. Although that might sound drastic, the idea is to create some distance from a situation that will add friction to the already challenging job of keeping a marriage together. A husband and wife who value their relationship and agreements above everything else especially the in-laws will have a better chance of a successful marriage.

Are you a "mommy's boy" or a "daddy's favorite little princess?" You may find yourself expecting and demanding the same doting and spoiling from your new partner that you enjoyed with your parents, but s/he may not want to play this role. As Harville Hendrix in *Getting the Love You Want* [104]speaks of so clearly, unconsciously we look for a partner who is the composite of our caretakers, both the positive and negative aspects.

Are you enmeshed in a family that is not inclusive or welcoming to your mate? The ideal situation would be to ask the family to meet with you to talk about a few troublesome issues. Let them know your concerns and hopefully they will listen to you, receive the message, and make the appropriate changes. Maybe there are concerns of theirs that are valid for you to hear. Meeting and talking would be to their advantage and hopefully would result in happier relations with you and their grandchildren. However, many people do not want to hear anything that might require them to change and you may not be able to come up with a happy agreement. This is a sad situation and it is up to you to decide what will be best for you as a couple. If things cannot be worked out, agree to disagree and keep things civil within the family. (Good luck.)

In our case, Robert and I had families who unfortunately, did not look favorably on our marriage. This situation made it difficult, and it was uncomfortable to hear the criticism. There was, of course, some truth in what our parents had to say, but it didn't make it easier to work through our problems. In the long run, this struggle helped us when we dedicated ourselves to work harder to create a resilient partnership.

It is wonderful to have grandparents and extended family to help out when children enter the picture. Hopefully your parents, grandparents, aunts, uncles, and cousins can be supportive, and everyone benefits from the intergenerational cooperation. Eventually when we started to have children, our parents visited us and we were happy to visit their homes and celebrate holidays together. Time does heal and grandchildren can work wonders.

27. Will your partner make a good parent?

Have you watched your partner interact with children? Do children love to be in his or her presence? Does s/he like holding a baby or enjoy playing ball with the kids? If this is the case, s/he will probably make a good parent. If, on the other hand, your partner shies away from interacting with children or has a condescending or aloof attitude, can you ask why? Perhaps it is a good idea to look at your partner's family and see how she was raised. Whatever she has learned from her childhood will show up in her treatment of your children. It's never too soon to start clearing hurts from an abusive childhood and creating a healthy environment for your family. If there is resistance to taking the steps to become a good parent, and you want to have children, this could be a deal breaker. Passing on an abusive legacy to your progeny will cause everyone unhappiness and regrets.

See the answer to #2 of the 101 Question Compatibility Test, Pg. 152.

28. Does your partner encourage you in your interests? (Your career, hobbies, sports, art, music, yoga, etc.)

You both bring an assortment of interests into this union, and things will go well when you encourage each other to do the activities that you are passionate about. Opposites attract. People are drawn to each other because of their similar interests and also for their differences. Spending time together doing what you both love is a wonderful way to enjoy each other's company.

If the differences cause tensions, what's the problem? Is your partner controlling you, deciding what activities you will do together that satisfies his or her desires, but stifles you and disregards your interests? Is he trying to make you into something that you are not? Are you not receiving the necessary support and encouragement for who you are and what you like to do?

Watching sports on TV, for instance, is often mentioned as a cause for tension. Robert and some of our children really enjoy the games. Although it did not interest me as much, I have watched enough football, baseball, and basketball to understand the rules. Robert really gets into it and is an enthusiastic commentator who explains the plays in understandable terms. I have fun going to watch our local "single A" baseball games from time to time. (Single A is the first professional step to the major leagues). We sit near the field in un-crowded bleachers and are able to have an up-close view of the action. Also, when there's a good game on TV, I love it when he calls me in for an exciting play and for the last few minutes of a tight game to see the final showdown. However, while he's watching, I generally like to do other things like read, write, cook, walk, or take a nap.

When we travel to different cities, we like to visit museums and galleries. Although it is not Robert's passion, he puts his heart into the experience and likes seeing me turned on by the creativity and talent. When I started my tie-dye business, he built me a studio and shop where I could do my art, not to mention keeping the washing machines and van in running order. Also, since my writing includes plenty of editing and re-editing, he has been most patient helping me with my not-so-great sentences. We also enjoy many activities together like sailing, gardening, swimming, cooking, reading, and walking. And, for six months of each year, we live on our boat in Mexico and look forward to this special time when we share our collective dream.

29. Have you talked about how you want to maintain your home and do your household chores? (The dishes, laundry, the lawn, vacuuming, cleaning the bathrooms, etc.)

Although the statistics suggest that women still handle most of the housework in a two-career household,[105] a more equitable agreement relieves tension and resentment. If you are privileged enough to be able to afford to have one parent stay home when your children are young, then naturally the person staying home takes care of the chores. While it is okay to divide up the work according to your preferences, an unpleasant chore shouldn't always land on one person's shoulders. If your partner has the attitude of "I refuse to do dishes," then you are going to have to shoulder the burden and that's not fair to you.

When you are busy doing the household chores, think of them as your yoga, your meditation. Seeing clothes and dishes go from dirty to clean and put neatly away brings satisfaction. In our household we share vacuuming, dish washing, and mopping the floors. Robert likes to mow the lawn, take out the trash, and clean the bathrooms. Also, he is my mechanical wizard on call when something around the house doesn't work. I balance the checkbook, do laundry, and pack the suitcases when we travel. We both like to cook. He is a wonderful short-order chef and his talents came in handy when there were hungry kids to feed. I was more likely to prepare a large pot of rice or potatoes, or bake pans of enchiladas or lasagna, to be on hand for the short order cook to jazz up and serve in a jiffy. No one is sitting around while the other person does 90% of the work.

When our kids were growing up, there was always a short window in each day when the house was in perfect order. We would post a chart so the kids could come home and do their chores whenever they could fit them into their busy lives. At other times, we would call a "blitz time," usually in the evenings before supper or on the weekends, and everyone would call out a chore they wanted to do until the house was clean again. Children who learn how to cook and keep house feel a sense of satisfaction when they contribute to the family's wellbeing. We considered chores to be everyone's responsibility and we didn't pay for keeping the house clean. Sharing the jobs builds good habits and their future partner will be most grateful.

Stereotypes have changed over the years. In the 50's and 60's television shows, Leave it to Beaver, and Ozzie and Harriet, Mrs. Cleaver and Harriet did all the housework and watched the children while the husbands worked from dawn until dusk, coming home to a clean home and dinner on the table. Today there is more sharing of the housework and the breadwinner is more involved. On the weekends, if your partner, for instance, works away from home, he can take on the chores and watch the children, enabling you to have a break or do the grocery shopping and other errands.

How clean do you want the house to be? Is one of you a neat freak and one a slob? If there are children, there are likely to be tents in the living room or an on-going Monopoly game on the table. If one of you wants things spotless and the other brings in mud on their shoes after working in the garden, can you find a solution that will satisfy both of you? Making easy-going compromises results in the chores being done and the household running smoothly.

Here's an interesting exercise for you and your partner. Each of you can write down what you expect to do and what you would like your partner to do when it comes to taking care of the house. Do you like the idea of blue and pink jobs (that is, traditionally male or female) or do you want the cooking, dishes, vacuuming, trash removal, laundry, lawn mowing, or toilet cleaning to be shared? Define how you want each of these chores taken care of and compare notes. Can you make agreements so that all the housework is done to your satisfaction? If your partner loves to cook, are you willing to do the cleanup? Resentment will not fester and you will enjoy a clean, happy home if the housekeeping chores are equitable.

30. Does your partner have certain habits that annoy you? (List them.)

Are these mannerisms or habits major or minor? Can you talk about the changes you would like to see? Is one of you always late? Is one of you a compulsive shopper, spending money that s/he doesn't have? Are jokes in poor taste? Does one of you become easily impatient, annoyed or angry? Does s/he drink too much or abuse harmful substances? Does s/he have strong dislikes about food? If there are habits that annoy you, talk about them before your wedding. Are you going to be able to live with these habits, or are you going to want some changes before you settle down together?

See the chapters on Subconscious, Pg. 102-109 and Communication, Pg. 113-115

31. Are you uncomfortable when you are with your future in-laws?

Several generations ago, marriages were sometimes arranged and love was not necessarily the primary concern. Wealth, a good job, or family ties were more important than the individual's feelings. The potential husband was required to provide for his wife financially, and it was a bonus if they fell in love.

In the U.S.A., men and women are on a relatively equal footing and the responsibility of looking out for one's own interest lands on the individual. Romance drives the dating ritual and the couple goes out together without having to check in with the family or take along a chaperone. However, sooner or later all of your close relatives will want to meet your new beau and give you their blessings. Inviting your partner to your parent's home usually causes nervousness, tension and discomfort. A new person who is entering the family might be quite different in appearance, culture, religion, economic status, or manners. Hopefully, everyone will be accepting, supportive, and tolerant. They will be curious, and it may feel a little awkward at first while they become acquainted, but this will change when they meet your partner on their own terms.

There are occasions when a new partner does not measure up to the image that the parents had in mind for their child. Maybe your parents will bring up a concern about negative qualities that they think could cause you trouble in the future. It doesn't hurt to take a look at what they are warning you about and thank them for their insight. In the long run, it is your decision and when they can accept the situation gracefully, hopefully things turn out all right. Parents have good intentions and time heals negative feelings. When grandchildren come, there is a new opportunity for tensions to ease.

Have you taken a closer look at your potential in-laws? How does Dad treat his wife and how does Mom act towards her husband? Is your partner respectful towards his or her mother and father? Parents are role models, and the way that they communicate and respect each other is an indication of how you likely will be treated by your partner.

What if the parents are not impressed and a warm welcome is not forthcoming? Ultimately, during the traditional marriage ceremony, the minister, priest, or rabbi might call for anyone who opposes this union to please speak up now or forever hold their piece. When objections are resolved before the ceremony, you avoid the drama of someone actually voicing a protest. What might the objections be? Do you need to have a discussion to iron out any problems? It can be illuminating to have a dialogue with the family about issues that they have. It is possible that they are off the mark, but it couldn't hurt to give their concerns adequate attention.

Most couples meet at school, work, or over the Internet far away from the family and home. The heat of romance may prevent you from seeing the potential problems obvious to those around you. If your parents' concerns are reasonable what kind of adjustments can you make? If the situation is strained, can you compromise enough to keep peace within the family? When there is respect, love, and an inclusionary attitude for the new member of the family, life is good. There is a joke about how every marital bed has at least six people in it, you and your partner, and each of your parents. Hopefully everyone can be civil and get along.

32. Do you feel pressure to choose a certain spiritual or religious path?

It's easy when you have common spiritual beliefs, but if that's not the case can you accept each other views? There are endless examples of couples from different religious backgrounds who have made a happy union. For millennia, the world has been at war over religion. You can fight this same war on the home front, and it can be terrible if neither one of you are willing to compromise. Why do that? Is animosity growing or can you both feel all right about your differences?

In my case, our Jewish/Christian union felt like a religious conflict with all of its tensions and cultural differences. Eventually, we discovered the secret of compromise that would lead to a lasting peace. We found a spirituality that included all religions and didn't dwell on the many differences that divide people. In choosing a multi-religious union, a couple may be choosing a battle that can be won, while helping (on a micro level) to create a world that is a more peaceful place. A cross-religious or cross-cultural marriage is usually never boring. It is a challenge to learn to see life from a different viewpoint, and it takes flexibility, tolerance, and patience. When there is mutual respect and a willingness to work it out and change, peace is attainable. See #3 in the 101 Questions Compatibility Test. Pg. 155

33. Is your partner jealous/possessive of you?

A possessive person is often inordinately insecure: someone who needs to have power and control over another human being. Is it because he feels a lack of power or control over his own life? Perhaps he is jealous of your individuality and freedom? Is he clinging and stifling, cutting you off from friends, family, and activities? A needy person may require more time to discover his individuality and self-confidence before he is ready for a lasting relationship.

What is the source of this envy and mistrust? Is he a control freak? Is he afraid that you will leave and is holding on tightly? Have you violated your partner's trust? Does he have a cultural belief that a wife is to be subservient to the husband? Can you live under different cultural norms? Can you talk about creating an equal relationship where there is life, liberty, and the pursuit of happiness for both of you? When there is honest communication between you, respect can grow and your partner can hopefully relax and let go of excessive control, mistrust and paranoia.

34. Are you or your partner not speaking to a member(s) of either of your families?

Unfortunately, there has been a major falling out between you and this relative(s) that seemingly cannot be rectified. What is the problem? What did they do that was so egregious and toxic that you have had to distance yourself from them? Have you dealt with this unpleasantness by closing the door and eliminating them from your life or have you tried to reach out with the olive branch of peace? Since the only thing that you can change is yourself, what could you do that might make the situation better?

Are you feeling like a victim of awful circumstances? When you glorify in your victimhood it keeps you from taking responsibility for your life. What did s/he do to you? How was s/he irresponsible or hurtful? You will stay enmeshed in this drama until you decide to forgive and let it go. When you take that big step, whatever happened in the past will not follow you around and haunt you, twisting your stomach up in knots every time you think of it. Forgiving this person and deciding to move forward with good will in your heart may be the hardest thing you've ever done, especially with someone who has caused you pain. However, then you can move to a higher level where you are in charge of your destiny. There are people who hold onto their hatreds throughout their lives, not realizing that they have the choice of whether or not to stay stuck in a bad movie.

Even though this person may have done dastardly deeds, it's your perception of this person as a monster that has become your "friend." You have created a destroying demon in your own mind who is not worthy of your attention and love. Are you blaming him/her for whatever isn't going well in your life? Can you step out of the victimhood role, and see this person as perhaps sad, pathetic, close-minded, abused, or angry? There may be a time when you can have a civil relationship with this person, and then maybe not. However, when you let go of your investment in being angry, you allow the situation to inevitably become more manageable.

The Noble Peace Prize recipient, Desmond Tutu from South Africa described the struggle that brought together instigators of brutality and their victims after the end of apartheid. He said, "Forgiveness gives a chance to make a new beginning."[106] It is possible to bring people together, maybe not to everyone's 100% satisfaction, but things can change dramatically and continue to evolve on a positive path.

Is there a possibility that you can work it out and have peace? If not, can you forgive and love him/her anyway?

Could what you dislike the most, in someone else, be a trait you have within yourself? Can mediation or reconciliation make everyone happy?

The classic situation involves a parent and a child who are estranged. Most parents want to be the best parents that they can and try to do good for their children. However, they might have been exemplary in some ways and terrible in others. The trick is to not make their negative issues your own. Whether parents are poor or rich, single or a couple, famous or Joe Average, they are human and make mistakes. Inevitably, they pass on their own issues to their children; working on these problems allows you to leave a sweeter legacy for your children.

35. Does your partner refuse to compromise on a particular issue? (List it.)

Innumerable situations arise during a marriage and if your partner will not openly look at all sides of an issue and be willing to compromise, there is going to be trouble. What is the problem? Why is s/he being stubborn? Are you going the wrong way down a one-way street? Maybe your partner has looked at all sides and still defends his/her viewpoint. Perhaps s/he has a valid argument that you are not considering? Can you both take a step back for a broader view and see what is happening? Is there a power struggle going on, where the more you push, the more s/he resists? Is this the time to bring in a third party to help sort things out?

See The Subconscious and Communication chapters, Pg. 102-109 and 113-115

36. Do you believe in the power of love to heal the body, mind, and spirit?

A relationship is enchanted when the sparkle in your partner's eyes says, "I Love you." This connection is filled with energy, synchronicity, telepathy, magic, clear vision, laughter, and miracles. Love is the passion and pleasure of sex and the miracle of childbirth. When you are full of love, it allows you to soar and touch the places that make life worth living. When coincidences occur, and synchronicity happens, joy is created and you know you are on the right track.

Love keeps a marriage together while you share your visions, dreams, and passions. With warmth and affection you can summon the strength and confidence required to make the big changes for yourself and each other. The walls come down and you are lifted out of the mundane into joyousness, prosperity, and longevity. When you create the happiness that you want, the spark of love stays with you for a lifetime.

37. Do you have 'my' and 'your' friends, but only a few who you share in common?

New relationships bring their old friends with them, and hopefully, you will find it easy to embrace each other's acquaintances. When you go from being a single person to becoming a couple, you will make new friends who share common interests like having children, and buying a home.

Some of your former buddies will also go with you to this next stage of life and marriage. Nurturing friendships and enjoying their company at gatherings will help keep your marriage vibrant and diversified.

Using your confidantes as the "complaint department," grumbling about how your relationship is doing, can create more problems than it solves. If the conversation turns into a whine session, it is usually undermining your partner instead of providing strength and support to repair the situation. However, when there are constructive conversations, everyone benefits. When your friends give positive advice and stories from their own experience that is supportive, they are just the type of allies you need.

Is the old gang of friends putting on pressure to do things you'd rather not? When there is peer pressure, do you keep your head and make the right choice despite what anyone else considers cool? Do you have a moral compass that gives you confidence to stand your ground? When you want acceptance from the in-group it is hard not to agree with their opinions and participate in their activities. Standing up to destructive peer pressure makes a difference. Watching how you manage a situation may give other individuals in the group courage. With your steadying force, you can be the one who sets the standard for what is cool. Can you let your partner know if someone is unpleasant or difficult to be around? An acquaintance of mine, for instance, mentioned that her boyfriend ran with a group of friends who would hit the booze hard every so often. She didn't think she could live with someone who smoked and drank to that extent. Her beau was in love with her and realized he wanted to distance himself from that crowd who were often caught up in unpleasant dramas. As a result, he decided to quit smoking and cut down to a beer a night or maybe two if it was party time. When he changed his habits, they attracted new companions who shared their family lifestyle. His old pals remained, but on a different level of intimacy. They continue to make new friends who often have children to play with theirs, allowing quality time for the parents to hang out together.

How are the Internet and social media affecting your friendships? In our age of instant technological communication, many people connect over the airways instead of face to face. It's common in public places to see people texting and talking on their phones, ignoring the live humanity around them. When it comes to social media like Facebook and Twitter, do you keep good boundaries? Do you keep your online presence and postings kind and courteous? Do you make time to do fun activities with your friends out in the fresh air, technology tucked away for another time? When you build long-lasting relationships you'll find a supportive group around you when you need help.

38. Do you believe that sex is an important part of marriage, and are you open to exploring the art of lovemaking with your partner?

When two people are in love, sex is the pot of gold at the end of the rainbow, the icing on the cake, and blissful heaven on earth. Physical joy in a relationship makes things run smoothly. Sex is your chance to totally give yourself to your partner. Certainly, lovemaking can take many forms and exploring all aspects of sex can be fun and exciting. On the other hand, when one of you is inhibited or too pushy, a struggle ensues that drains the fun out of it. You can achieve a balance so that love can flow. Often the issue is not about sex, but about some other problems, physical or emotional, that prevent you or your partner from relaxing. Also, reading or watching videos about lovemaking that describe foreplay, various positions, and the mental state when having sex can be helpful. Let your partner know what you like and what doesn't feel good. Lovemaking is an art learned through practice with a loving partner. "Practice, practice, practice," as my old piano teacher used to say.

39. Does your partner want to get married sooner than you do?

What is holding you back? Do you want to "live it up" a little more before settling down? Maybe you still want to be free and single, or is there something about your partner that bothers you and keeps you from saying yes? Maybe being with him or her has become too convenient, even though s/he is not "the One." Or do you have trouble with commitment and intimacy? Is your partner pressuring you, wanting the marriage to happen on his or her timeline? Is pregnancy pushing up your wedding date? Is this a classic case of "cold feet" where you need to be courageous and rise above your fear? Or are your fears and insecurities about this person valid? Can you discuss your feelings with someone you trust and receive some perspective about your doubts?

When you make a commitment to marry, it's like diving into the pool rather than sitting on the edge and just dipping your toes in the water. Perhaps you simply are not ready or mature enough, and that's okay too. Agreeing to marry should make you ecstatic, and if you aren't, take your time to make your decision. **When in doubt, chicken out**!

40. Do you agree about how you are going to discipline your children?

Couples who are planning a family need to talk about each other's ideas when it comes to disciplining children. What do you think about time-outs, spankings, or other punishments to teach a child? New enlightened ways of working it out with your kids are brilliantly discussed in *How to Talk to Kids So They Will Listen, and How to Listen to Kids So They Will Talk* by Faber and Mazlish (Revised 1999), and *The Five Love Languages for Children* by Chapman and Campbell (2012)

How were you disciplined as a child? What we know about child raising, both good ways and not so good, is mostly taught to us by our parents or guardians. Do you have traumas from your childhood? Were there betrayals, abandonment, insecurity and neglect, to mention just a few things that make you unsure of becoming a parent? If you or your partner came from a happy family, then you have only a few emotional scars. However, if there was abuse, whether verbal, emotional, physical, or sexual, then it's time for some dedicated therapy. Understanding these things and reconciling these deep hurts from an abusive childhood can create a healthy parent. Counseling and parenting classes can help you learn how to discipline your children in appropriate ways while consciously avoiding the destructive patterns of your upbringing.

See Answer to question #2 Pg. 152

41. Are you confident that your income will cover your expenses; can you live within your budget?

Rarely do two young people come into a marriage with their finances in perfect order. However, if you both have decent jobs, your economic situation will probably be comfortable. Then the ups and downs of life will come along: children, home purchasing, job loss, illness, recessions, bad investments, etc. Ask your partner what s/he would do in these situations. Can you curtail your spending and live simply? Are you both taking an interest in your financial affairs, even when one of you is the designated bill payer?

When you share the fiscal responsibility, it helps diminish the stress and pressures that often mount over matters economical. Do you or your partner spend compulsively? It can feel like a breach of trust when one of you buy, buy, buys, without the other's agreement. Is one partner stingy and won't allow spending for a needed vacation or a special purchase? Are there debts that need to be paid down, especially high interest credit cards? It is also good financial advice for you both to have a viable credit history so that when a big expense comes up like buying a car or a home both of your credit scores can be used to get a loan. When you need to decide how to invest your savings, it is helpful when you have been in the habit of talking things over and planning wisely.

If you are young, you may not be looking ahead to old age and retirement, but now's the time to start putting something away into your savings account so you will be covered when you want to stop working, maybe go on some adventures, and live comfortably into that good night.

See questions on finances. # 10, 15, 41, 50, 56, 63, 93.

42. Does financial help from your family have strings attached?

Loans from family members can be a mixed blessing. When they generously lend you money for a specific purpose, such as a down payment on a home or a low-interest loan to help you when you are just starting out, their financial help is a sign of their support and love. Certainly, have everything put in writing. The written agreement will state the terms of the loan, the interest rate, and when and how much the monthly payments will be. Simple loan forms or promissory notes are available on the Internet.

Is your family's financial help a way to manipulate you? Will your happiness be compromised for example, by obligations like visiting or helping out more often than is comfortable? When you talk about the details and write out any stipulations on the agreement form, perhaps you can come to an understanding that is fair for everyone.

43. Do you both have promising careers?

Are you still asking yourself what you want to be when you grow up? There may be a problem if one of you is ambitious and motivated, and one of you is not. Will one partner ride on the coattails of the other? Discovering your passions, and the directions you want to follow in life will create a spark that will empower you both to work in the fields that inspire you.

In the U.S.A., unlike many places in the world, both men and women are able to succeed in promising careers in their chosen fields. If one of you needs additional schooling, can your partner support you or do you need to take out loans? If you have to travel for your work, can s/he keep the home fires burning while you are gone? When you are supportive of each other's choices it enhances your careers as the relationship matures.

Then there is the decision to have children that can be a turn in the road that affects your, or your partner's climb up the proverbial career ladder. If the biological clock is ticking and children are scheduled for the near future, you have to adjust your lives and budgets. If you are pregnant, putting your career on hold will allow you to share in a unique process of discovery and learning that will benefit everyone in the long run. Several years ago, when our adult children became parents, they decided to tighten the economic belt so that one parent could stay home with the children until they went off to school. The days were spent going to the park, library, museums, and play dates with friends. These years go by surprisingly fast and then it will be possible to pick up where your career path left off, or new interests may take you in a different direction. Many of the things learned when raising a child translate into useful skills in the workplace. Self-confidence, maturity, a take-charge attitude, and the ability to multi-task can transfer into valuable assets on any job site.

In this day and age, when both partners may be on a promising career track, it's not unusual for a father to take time off from his career like Mom did in the past, enjoying the privilege of raising the children. It can slow down a career, but it is worthwhile. Whatever works for both of you. Does your company offer a flextime schedule, day care on site, or the possibility of telecommuting from home? Perhaps there is a grandparent or other relative who can watch the children when you both return to the workplace? There is always daycare or can you afford an au pair?

There are other options. Parents can work together with other families in the neighborhood to develop their own day care. With a little organization and agreements, you can create a unique and convenient system for you and your nearby friends. Do the adults work on different shifts where one parent can take the children to school and another can pick them up? Children thrive in a safe environment with their friends and trusted adults.

When our children were young, we lived in a household with other families and neighbors had kids close by. The mothers organized a baby-sitting group where we all could have at least two days a week to return to work. A career woman with one child might watch the children for only one day a week, but since I had an infant and two young sons, I'd watch the "kid-herd" three days a week and work for two days. A healthy balance was created when I had time with my children and still was able to partake of the adult world. Of course, this required that the work environment allow for flextime and part-time work. In our community, there was always somewhere that needed help whenever we were available.

When all of my children entered school, I started a tie-dyed art-wear business, called Harmony Enterprises, (What's a hippie to do?) While it was demanding of my time, it gave me an outlet for my artistic creativity and turned out to be profitable enough to keep our hungry teens fed. While I worked, our youngest daughter, Olivia, was part of a babysitting group and later a pre-school that was a good fit. As the kids grew up, they helped out at our craft shows, and the training that they received served them well when they went out looking for jobs. We were entrepreneurs and one of the by-products of forming my company was that we bought properties for our home and ever expanding businesses. Once we paid off the buildings, had made our last payment after sixteen years to the University of California regents, and sold our tie-dye company to our son, the real estate rentals became our principal source of income. Priorities shift as you age, and with creative planning you can realize your dreams.

44. Do you and your partner handle your personal problems in a reasonable way?

Difficulties inevitably arise. When love is pro-active, you can use your communication tools to sort out any craziness, and with practice your relationship skills will improve. Would it help to practice the hassle eliminators, apologizing and forgiving? How about working to change old patterns that sabotage a good relationship? Are you both sincere about resolving your differences? There will always be "something," a problem to solve, and when you handle it gracefully, the cooperation of two people working together builds a solid foundation. In the middle of the fray, relating to each other with courtesy, respect, and patience leads to intelligent problem solving. If one of you is stubborn or cannot communicate, compromise, or change, then the relationship needs a mediator. What is it that you want to hold on to so badly that you will jeopardize being together with your beautiful, intelligent, sweet, honorable, lovely, sexy mate?

See: The Chapter on Communication. Pg. 113-115

45. Does your partner's behavior at social events sometimes embarrass you?

Hopefully, your partner will act with civility everywhere you go, making you feel safe and secure. It's one thing to be the life of the party and enjoy the social whirl, but is that your guy with the lampshade on his head? Is he drunk, loud, and out of control? Is that her flirting? Isn't she supposed to be in love with you? Or is he the quiet and reserved one that doesn't interact at all? Do you belittle each other in public? Uh, oh, is there an alcohol or drug problem? When you are away from the party, find a quiet place where you can let him know that his behavior is not acceptable and that it embarrasses you. When you talk to her about her behavior, it will soon become obvious if s/he is willing to make changes. Disrespectful behavior builds resentment and is embarrassing and harmful. Can you make agreements about manners and interpersonal relations? Certainly, a couple should bring out the best in each other. Letting each other know what feels right and what doesn't is a first step.

46. Do one or both of you always have to be right?

No one is always right. When you are wrong, it's gracious to admit that, "Oops, Never mind, I was wrong." Often the best solution to an impasse is a compromise between your points of view. A receptive, humble attitude from both of you creates a workable arrangement and peace in the household. In contrast, stubbornness and inflexibility doesn't contribute to a happy relationship. Is there immediate resistance when your partner is trying to tell you something? Do you say "no," and defend or fight for your way? When you feel this happening, try holding back from your usual drama, take a breath, and let go of "I'm always right."

We all want it to go our way. At the next fork in the road, let your partner have his or her way and see where that takes you. You might find that you both want the same thing, but have different approaches to getting there. Trusting that you want the best for each other allows for innovative ways of doing things. The solution might turn out to be better than either of your original ideas.

47. Do you or your partner have a tendency to be lazy or unmotivated?

When your relationship is a dynamically evolving companionship, you are energized by the collective dreams becoming reality. If your modus operandi spirals down into being lazy, apathetic, or unmotivated, that will become the tenor of your household. You create your situation with your attitude. Are you bored? Is your boredom the "unenthusiastic hostility" kind?[107] Would you rather be playing video games or watching TV? How many hours were you on your phone and computer today? Are you feeling dispirited to the point that you are antagonistic to your own health and emotional wellbeing? If you are struggling with depression, can you take positive action to deal with this treatable illness? If you find yourself "nature-deprived" and action deprived, going for a walk, and clearing your head can do wonders for inspiring you with new imaginative ideas. Do you need to take a break and play Ultimate with your friends? When you can explore your hostility and turn it around to being a positive driving force in your life, you'll be on the right track. When you step out of yourself and look around, there are people who need you and things you can do that will begin to lift your spirits. Bored people are boring. What do you want that will make you passionate about life? Is there something that you are harboring that needs liberating so you can implement your desires and destiny? Redirecting your attention and changing habits will keep you busy, as well as reward you in ways that you could never imagine. Passion for life is contagious and putting out that extra effort to rise above your lethargy will infuse joy into your world. You might like taking the "Passion Test" (2008) by Chris and Janet Attwood[108] or read inspiring books that encourage you to take a step to follow your dreams such as *The Secret (2006)* by Rhonda Byrne,[109] and *The Divine Matrix* by Gregg Braden (2007).[110] The inspirational author, Louise Hay[111] writes, "Life is very simple. We create our experiences by our thinking and feeling patterns. What we believe about ourselves and about life becomes true for us." Mike Dooley, in his daily inspirations says that "Thoughts Become Things."[112]

See answer to question #17 on Depression and moodiness on Pg. 177.

48. Do you agree on how to furnish and decorate your home?

Perhaps one or the other of you has an interior design creative streak with an eye for color, decorations, and furnishings. Checking in with each other's opinions makes compromising easier and creates a relaxed, comfortable home. Do you have your areas, like he works in his garage or den? Or, do you both love to cook, and find the kitchen a great place to work together creatively? When Robert is ready to paint a wall or tile a floor, for instance, he consults with me about his vision and we both go to the store to pick out the colors and designs we want.

Is one of you a slob and the other a neat freak? Are you insistent about everything having its place and act as if you'll have a heart attack if milk is spilled on the floor? Or does your partner constantly leave a trail of dishes, dirty clothes, and other personal items all over the house? Did his Mom always pick up after him so he didn't learn to take care of himself? At some point when you've been out on your own, you realize you can no longer blame your parents for how they raised you. They did the best they were capable of and now it's your chance to improve on it. Changing your undesirable habits will bring happiness to your home no matter how it is decorated.

49. Do you know what is sexually satisfying for your partner?

Understanding the subtleties that can be shared with your partner brings you life-long pleasure. When each of you is giving 100% to the relationship, and feel satisfied, life is good! It's when problems crop up that the enjoyment diminishes. Does he want to have sex three times a day while you complain of a headache? Do you feel totally gratified during sex and leave her unfulfilled? You both know that women take about four times as long as men to become fully aroused?[113] That's not to say that a "quickie" isn't pleasurable and fun when you have a moment, but without later taking more time ("the five course banquet") to meet your partner's needs, she will be left unsatisfied. Does your sweetheart hint at what feels good and what doesn't? Can you turn the hints into an open and specific discussion on new positions and foreplay that s/he would like to try? Sometimes, we are not very adept at mindreading, and learning what your partner wants sexually will take away the guesswork. Then you can get right down to enjoyable and satisfying lovemaking.

50. Do you agree on how much of your budget will be spent on housing?

Let's pull out the paper and pencil and draw up a budget, including the rent or mortgage, and all the bills for food, clothing, gas, travel, taxes, insurance, car maintenance, and entertainment expenses. For example, when we were buying our home in California in the 1980s, the bank would not give us a mortgage if our payments would be over 30% of our income. Today that rule has relaxed a bit. Over 35% of homeowners now spend more than 30% of their budget on housing. In areas of the country that have high-priced real estate like New York or San Francisco, 20% of homeowners pay as high as 50%[114] and more. If this sounds like you, compromises will have to be made to live within your means. It can be difficult balancing the expenses with your income. Can you simplify your life in order to have time and money to pursue your dreams? When finances are tight, be imaginative and explore ways of stretching your paycheck, coming up with a second job, or let out the entrepreneurial genie. Let the ideas flow unimpeded, being flexible, and open-minded. Brainstorming won't cost you a dime. Can you move to a less expensive house or a less expensive area, find a higher paying job, go back to school to upgrade your skills, or start your own business? One of our daughters and her husband share the rent with another couple. Some friends of ours live on a boat in a marina not far from their work. Those may sound like wild ideas. What are yours? **It is not how much you make, but how much you spend.**

51. Are there homosexual, bisexual, or trans-sexual tendencies and preferences in your heterosexual relationship?

Talking openly and candidly about homosexual or bisexual tendencies that either of you might have is only fair to the relationship. It wasn't that many years ago that homosexual men and women in our society entered into heterosexual marriages in order to be socially accepted.[115] If in this day and age it still feels necessary to hide your sexual orientation, then it's time for you and your partner to at least have an honest conversation. There's no need to feel ashamed of being who you are. Most likely, sooner than later, you will be inspired to "come out" and follow your destiny.

There is a continuum of sexual tendencies easily compatible with a heterosexual and/or a homosexual relationship? [116] It's okay to try out your fantasies. Bisexuality might mean that you or your partner look forward to having an "open marriage" that includes other men and/or women sexually in your relationship. Will both of you be able to live with this arrangement that is more complicated than a two person relationship? There are pitfalls in an arrangement like this, like making sure that the sex is safe, and jealousy can be a thorny issue. The chances are rare of an agreement of this kind standing the test of time.[117] Do you know what you truly want? Two books on the subject of sexual preferences are John Money's *Gay, Straight, and In-Between: The Sexology of Sexual Orientation* and Simon LeVay's *The Sexual Brain.* [118]

52. Is it difficult to talk about your true feelings with your partner?

Communication keeps things vibrant and evolving. Why are you reluctant to talk? Have you closed off a secret corner of your heart? Your partner can feel the distance created by this piece of your life that you are holding back. Eventually the gap grows wider and the secrets that you harbor may breed resentment.

Expressing your true feelings and what you want in the relationship keeps you current, letting your partner know how much you appreciate him/her as well as what's bothering you. When your thoughts and feelings are out in the open, you can take care of any problems and then go about your business without an anchor weighing you down. Being open in a relationship is not easy; it can be one of the most challenging things you do. Neither Robert nor I came from a family where feelings were openly discussed, and we had to learn how to work through and arrive at a satisfactory conclusion. We stumbled, made mistakes, overreacted, came on too strong, didn't listen and had to apologize over and over before we got the hang of it. Maybe one of us said something unkind, or was in such a hurry that we overlooked what was important to our partner. Perhaps we were bossy, stubborn, fearful, or grumpy, to name just a few of those unhelpful ways of being. When we talk these things through, a burden is lifted from our shoulders, and life is filled with light and love again.

Are you afraid to express what you think and feel? Did you come from a family who kept their feelings hidden away out of fear or politeness? When you try to speak your true feelings, does your partner refuse to take you seriously? Are you intimidated because your partner is disrespectful to you? Does s/he refuse to listen to what you are feeling? Are you afraid if you give your point of view that your partner will run the other way and you will lose him/her forever? Your outlook is important and s/he needs to hear it. Be brave, speak the truth, and fear no man or woman.

53. Are you feeling pressured into marriage by the family?

For some reason, there are families that end up pushing their son's or daughter's into a marriage. Are they worried that their grown child will never find the right person? Is it a cultural tradition to have their children marry at a relatively young age? Are these parents anxious about wanting to have grandchildren? Is a positive pregnancy test speeding up the wedding date? Can you keep from being influenced by these pressures? Each of you is entering into this marriage of your own free will, right? Marriage is for two mature individuals who know what they want and are secure in knowing that they have made the right choice. You can stand up to anyone who is trying to manipulate you; this is a free country. If you have not agreed of your own volition, then the marriage will be starting out on a shaky foundation.

54. Do you worry that problems you experienced in childhood will affect the way you raise your children?

To prevent burdening your children with the same problems and hardships that you experienced, there is work to be done to change the patterns of the past. Did your family lean towards dysfunctional behavior? Were they violent, abusive or negligent? Was everything okay on the surface, but underneath there were unpleasant subjects and feelings kept hidden away? Did you grow up amidst a fog of lies? Is it easier to run away from your partner than to do the difficult work that is required to sort out your differences? Have your parents been divorced and remain unforgiving? The tendency is to find a partner who is a "composite of your caretakers." Does your partner have any of these destructive or negative traits?

Since you want a happy home, recognizing and understanding what caused your family to be dysfunctional are steps in the process of recovering from your unpleasant childhood. When you decide to grow beyond your family legacy, you make an agreement with yourself to actually work on changing long running patterns, so as not to pass the negative behavior down to your children. Fortunately, all your efforts to compromise, change your patterns, and create loving bonds will be worth it.

If your parents divorced, understanding the reasons for their separation is valuable to your recovery. See if you can find time to have a heart to heart conversation with each of them. When you tell them that you want a healthy marriage, hopefully, they will let you in on some of what they have experienced that taught them life lessons. Was the relationship so abusive that there was no other option but divorce? If they tried marriage counseling, what happened? Did one partner walk out? What were the irreconcilable differences?

If your partner is lucky enough to have come from a loving family, he or she can show you how to be a capable parent. Also, having a support group that backs you up when the going gets rough will be invaluable. There are always parenting classes, Mommy and Me groups, and marriage counseling available if you need these services.[119]

55. Are you nervous and uncomfortable about revealing your body to your future partner?

It has been over a hundred years since the Victorian Era, when women were taught that nothing existed below the neck, and there was uptightness around anything sexual. We have evolved over those years, but there are still inhibitions lurking around our beautiful bodies. Do both of you approach sex with eagerness and anticipation, glorifying in the enjoyment? Marriage is a union of body, mind, and spirit. Making love consummates a relationship and brings with it health and happiness. When you are comfortable in your own skin, you have accepted that you are the perfect whoever you are. When you are in love, you do not notice the physical flaws. When you can accept and love yourself exactly the way you are, you open the door to the possibility of making changes.

When you go slow with tenderness, hopefully you can alleviate any nervousness, fear, or low self-esteem that arises. Is your partner unresponsive to you during sex or in some way not treating you well? Did something happen to you that made you afraid or worried? Talk about your past experiences, feelings, fears, and concerns. Relationships are built on love, respect, security, trust and openness. By telling your partner what you want, you can let him know how to turn you on. Making love is one of the gifts of life and having fulfilling sex is a part of a successful union.

Is there something intimidating about your partner that makes it difficult for you to relax? What is it? Can you let him or her know? Was your childhood full of confusing messages about sex? Did your parents teach you that sexuality is bad, ugly, or sinful? Even though your parents had sex, they may not have necessarily approved of it or maybe they didn't want to let you know that it was cool. Breaking down these inhibitions can seem like a monumental task. If there has been childhood sexual abuse, professional guidance can help free you from the demons that stole away your childhood. There are many books on this subject and there are sex therapists who can help you with either a physical or emotional problem.[120] You want to enter into marriage ready to share your special gift. There is no place closer to heaven on earth than experiencing satisfying sex with your lover.

56. Can you count on your partner to be a good listener?

Conscientiously listening to each other is a sign of respect, trust, and caring. Does your partner have a short attention span? Does she find something else to do when you are trying to communicate? Is she so full of herself that she talks over you or interrupts? She needs to acknowledge that this is a problem and practice focusing her attention on what you are saying. Are you insisting on discussing something when your partner is tired, has just returned home from work, or is busy with a project? She might listen better if you make time to talk in unhurried and relaxed surroundings. Count yourself lucky if you have a partner with attentive listening skills.

57. Are you worried that you do not have adequate insurance coverage?

Insurance is one of the items in your budget, right? Most states require a minimum of liability insurance for your car and collision insurance is mandatory when you are purchasing a car on credit. Likewise, a mortgage company will require insurance on a home. Also, purchasing renter's insurance is relatively inexpensive and can protect your possessions against theft, fire, vandalism, and water damage. Life insurance is considered to be a wise investment after children are born, since the family depends on you for their support and security. Health insurance is now mandatory either through your workplace or through the Affordable Care Act. Shopping for insurance is made easier when you ask for referrals from your family and friends who usually have a long history with a reputable agent.

58. Do you and your partner trust each other with members of the opposite sex?

When you're in love and the communication between you flows, there is seldom a reason to mistrust your partner. If, however, your relationship is on shaky ground, even your partner's normal conversations with someone of the opposite sex might cause you to feel hurt and insecure. Sometimes suspicions appear out of fear and uncertainty rather than a real threat. Jealousy can be a noxious friend who is constantly creating anxiety and doubt. Can you banish that gnawing, stomach tightening, accusing voice? Unfortunately, what you fear most can actually come true; people tend to live up to expectations.

Sometimes there is good reason to feel jealous and insecure. Is your partner constantly flirting with every pretty girl around, thinking that the grass must be greener on the other side? Instead of confronting and resolving issues, does he run away, and find relief in someone else's arms? How do you catch his attention without chasing him away? It might be that your guy with the wandering eyes is too immature and not ready to maintain a lasting relationship. Talking openly and honestly can let you know where you stand. Make it good for you.

59. Are you unhappy with one or more of your partner's interests (career, hobbies, sports, etc.)?

When your partner takes part in dangerous or illegal activities, it can cause anxiety and distrust. If his/her interests come with a high cost or takes time away from you and your family, the relationship can suffer from money worries and estrangement. Why is your partner's project or hobby bothering you? Can you compromise about the time or money spent on this pursuit? Are you jealous that s/he is doing something enjoyable without you? Are you stifling your partner's creativity? It's a good idea to have your own interests when your partner is enjoying his/hers. If you are on opposing sides of this issue, is there a mid-ground where you can reach an agreement? Maybe you can learn how to take part in your partner's favorite pastimes and enjoy them together. Hopefully s/he will reciprocate.

60. Are you sometimes embarrassed by your partner's appearance?

Cleanliness and taking care of your appearance shows respect for yourself and your partner. Is s/he scruffy, wearing clothes that are dirty or have holes in them, (though torn and frayed edges can be stylish depending on the fashion of the day)? Do you dislike his or her style? Is this an issue about being a slob or is it a control issue? Do you want your partner to conform to your tastes? Everyone has a right to his or her style and part of your attraction was to his/her particular flair, hairstyle, clothes and shoes. However, clean health habits are an indication that a person cares about him/herself, and will by implication also have the same capacity to care for you. It might be enjoyable to go shopping together and help each other pick out clothes that you both like. When you can have fun giving each other a makeover, there are no unkind judgments going on to stifle creativity and personal expression.

61. Do you disagree about the type of wedding you want?

Despite the fact that a wedding is an important, life-changing event, it remains an amateur endeavor. The ideas that you might envision for your special day may not be the same as your partner's. Do you have disagreements about whether to have a small or large wedding, sit-down meal or buffet, who to invite or where to have it? Can this be a chance to compromise and practice the communication skills that create a happy marriage? When you do the planning, count on there being a hitch or two, but you will likely be able to look back even on the bloopers with fond memories and a few laughs. How much money do you have to spend on your party? Parents usually contribute to the cost of the wedding and when you add it all up, what kind of a budget do you have? Hopefully your families are graciously available to help and their contributions of bringing the drinks, the cake, or the flowers may be more valuable to you than money. What role do you want your parents, siblings and friends to play in the ceremony? A wedding is an opportunity for a family to show their support for your union. When everyone feels included, love flows and your special day will never be forgotten!

62. Do you try to avoid arguments or disagreements with your partner?

If you do not rock the boat, the boat is going to rock you. Do intimidation, fear, and insecurity keep you from talking to your partner? Did you come from a family that suppressed their feelings? If you bring up an issue, does your partner blow up, become abusive, or walk out the door? Is the security of your relationship contingent on avoiding conflict? If this is what is happening, **you are in an abusive situation.**

When a disagreement happens, you need to deal with it in a timely manner. Maybe your partner will surprise you with how willing he or she is to listen to what you have to say. Perhaps your timid approach has created the problem in the first place? On the other hand, if your partner cannot take feedback, or becomes angry and abusive during disagreements, then a third party is needed to help you sort it out. Standing up for what you believe and saying what you think and feel is a noble pursuit that brings equality and empowerment to the relationship.

63. Does your partner handle his/her finances responsibly?

Financial matters are often a contentious part of a marriage. You are going to share the expenses and pool your resources. If one of you is careless with money, it inevitably leads to financial difficulties. Do you feel like you have to hold tightly onto the purse strings or your partner will buy, buy, buy? Compulsive shopping can be an indication of deeper problems.[121] This parent/child-like struggle may prevent both of you from growing into equally responsible adults. So who is going to pay the bills? Can you agree on a budget?

A few tips can change the way you manage your budget and set you up for prosperity. "Smart money people" use their credit cards as a 30-day interest free loan by paying it off in full every month. You then use the card for the convenience it offers, rather than it using you. When it comes to buying an expensive item, try to negotiate the most reasonable terms. If you save up beforehand and pay in full when you make the purchase, you can often bargain for a better deal with cash in hand. Time and Attention are money. When you work smarter, not harder, you'll like the results.

Did you grow up in a family where money was tight, and are you worried that you will end up living in poverty again? Did your partner grow up in a wealthy family having whatever s/he wanted? How much are you both earning? What are the expenses and how much expendable income do you have? When you do these calculations, you can then see clearly what is available for discretionary purchases. When you take worry, hassle, careless spending, and stinginess out of the equation you'll find your bottom line improving. Generosity works magic and cultivates abundance.

64. What are your expectations for your children?

Parents introduce their kids to the myriad possibilities that come with life, and give them foundations of positive experiences, which will help them find their way in the world. Do you have certain expectations of what you want your child to become? Certainly, parents who live vicariously through their children bring unnecessary pressures onto the young person. There is the well-known example of the stage mother who will do anything to see her child become a famous actor, and then there is the dad who tries to live out his athletic dreams vicariously through his kids. Children can grow up feeling obligated to please their parents, and not follow their own interests. Everyone is born with his or her own innate talents, passions, and purposes. Parents who support their children's interests have the satisfaction of allowing them to reach for their (not your) highest potential and what brings them life-long happiness.

65. Do you have doubts about your love for your partner?

Everyone is looking for true love. Are you turned on when your partner is close by or when you hear his/her voice on the phone? Does s/he smell so good? There is a happily ever after, but you have to earn it. Nobody is perfect and we all have our issues. Dating and the engagement should last for a long enough time that you experience a few ups and downs. Is it a two-way street? Does your partner feel the same way about you? Do you feel like you are not ready or have doubts about traveling through life with him or her, through all the adventures and obstacles that lie ahead? When an enduring, unconditional love exists, even when the inevitable difficulties arise, then a solid, long standing relationship can prevail.

66. Are you uncomfortable with your partner's family or friends since you have come from a different cultural, social, or economic background?

If you are from a different race, culture, religion, or socio-economic background than your partner, consider how the two of you attracted each other out of the enormous pool of available choices. Are you drawn to each other because you find these major differences intriguing, attractive, and sexy? Is this the attraction of opposites? When you are traveling, there is often mystery and excitement discovering places where you have never been before. Falling in love with someone so different than yourself has a fascinating allure. Is he intellectually stimulating? Do you share the same interests? When you are in love, you overlook the differences. However, can your families overcome their prejudices? Spending time with her family will introduce you to new traditions, manners, customs, cultures, and expectations. She can help prepare you for what is acceptable and make you feel comfortable. Also, speaking a few phrases of her language will impress the parents. You may need to practice certain etiquettes, such as eating with chopsticks, your fingers, or know what to do with three different forks. If the families are on different continents, where are you going to live, especially if children enter the picture? She may decide that she wants to live closer to her Mama and family. Is that acceptable to you?

When your sweetheart is from the same social, cultural, or economic background, there will still be differences, but maybe not so exotic and unfamiliar. How does your partner feel about your family? Can s/he learn how to relate comfortably with them? These differences can be a chance for each of you to expand your horizons and learn how to fit into each other's way of life.

A friend of mine loaned me the book, *What To Do When You're Dating a Jew,* by Vikki Weiss and Jennifer A. Block,[122] that gave me a humorous and helpful look into my husband's roots. When I read to him about something that I thought was unusual, he considered it perfectly normal. His family could be vocal when expressing their feelings, while mine was reserved to a fault. Both families put out a righteous amount of guilt, stubbornness, and "we're never wrong," but in different flavors. When some attitudes have deep roots like "We're the Chosen People"(meaning everyone else is not) and "We are Saved," (and You are Not,)," there can be some head butting. These days we laugh when we talk about our cultural differences.

67. Can you count on your partner to give you support when you are feeling down?

When a couple is supportive of each other even when the storms of life knock them for a loop, you know that this relationship is going to work. It requires maturity and integrity for someone to help you through disappointing and tough times. Is there a tendency for her to run away when the going gets tough? On the other hand, are you tender and warm towards her when she is having a difficult time, making sure to create a safe and secure environment to help her cope with the obstacles along the path? Can you take on extra responsibilities in order to help her through a rough stretch? How we deal with the inevitable struggles in life can build our character, ripen our compassion, and deepen our love.

68. Is your partner too dependent on his/ her parents?

A healthy family benefits from reciprocal closeness even though everyone lives in their independent and self-sufficient world. A partner who is still dependent on her family, emotionally or financially, may not be mature enough to hold up her end in a marriage. Also, if your guy is on the phone to his mother every day, and is emotionally dependent on her, he will likely not be able to give his all to you. If your sweetie has been dependent on Daddy for her emotional or financial support, you will have a difficult time living up to her expectations. Everything can be going along just fine until you have a fight and then, instead of working it out, s/he may run home to his or her parents rather than diving "into the nitty-gritty."

On the other hand, it is a fortunate situation when you are close to your parents and have a gratifying adult-to-adult relationship. Your parents can give you insights from their own experiences based on how they handled their problems, their mistakes, and successes. In return, they may appreciate it when you spend time with them and help them with the many new advances in technology.

When the family can be supportive at times like the birth of children, sickness, or financial turmoil, it can be a win-win situation. When our grandchildren were born, we helped out by cooking, shopping, doing the dishes, and anything else that the household needed so the parents could enjoy their new baby. Letting the new mom know that she was doing great and that the baby was normal relieved gnawing, insecure feelings she had about her abilities or her worries when the baby was crying. As the children grew older, a "Nana check-up" gave the parents an unemotionally charged overview about a behavioral problem that had baffled them and opened discussions on ways to make things better. Grandparents make excellent babysitters for the grandchildren, giving you the occasional date night out with your sweetheart.

During the winter season, we make our sailboat, Harmony, available to our family to take a break from their busy lives and enjoy the warm waters of the tropics. There is nothing like swimming, fishing, snorkeling, building sand castles on the beach, and watching the dolphins to feel rejuvenated. Sitting around on deck with a cool drink, we talk about what's going on in our lives, and explore ideas or plans for a new endeavor. Everyone goes home to meet the everyday challenges with a rejuvenated and relaxed state of mind, body, and spirit.

69. Are you ready to accept the responsibilities of being a parent (3 AM feedings, a sick and crying child, "terrible twos," rebellious teens)?

The arrival of children brings another level of responsibility to a marriage, not to mention happiness that is beyond description. There are a myriad of challenges and yet the rewards are more than satisfying. A little person has entered your home, and she is totally dependent on you for her survival and sustenance, emotionally, physically, and spiritually. If you love and respect each other, your child will feel it and prosper in the stability of her world. However, when there is tension and disruption, she will be caught in the middle, and will feel the anguish and uncertainty of your world. When a couple is ready and looking forward to parenthood, there is a mutual understanding to give the children a positive start in life. 73% of people who are divorced attributed their separation to a lack of commitment.[123] When you are dedicated to your marriage, you will be able to weather the ups and downs of parenthood and appreciate the positive rewards that children bring. This is not to say you won't suffer from lack of sleep, or feel overwhelmed, anxious about your children's safety, health, and more, much more. When you consistently work towards having a warm, happy family that enthusiastically tackles problems, your children grow into self-confident, capable adults.

70. Is there a difference between love and sex?

The idea that sex and love are separate and unequal - with sex in some way dirty, nasty, or immoral - has been strongly entrenched in our Western, Judaic-Christian culture for thousands of years. The appearance of deadly diseases associated with sex like syphilis and AIDS reinforced the fear of unprincipled or "sinful" sex. Part of the dogma was that sex was designed for procreation alone and finding enjoyment in it was not a part of the equation. If you throw off the negative connotations attributed to sex, it becomes a beautiful medium by which two people can share an intimate connection.

In contrast, the word *love* embodies more than the physical act, including all the emotional and spiritual aspects of a relationship. The union of sex and love is the beautiful consummation that sustains a happy relationship on a high level. The healthy combination of sex and love is described in several well-known books about the art of Tantric Yoga,[124] where the beauty and wonderful emotional feelings are highlighted.[125] Couples are engaged in this dance of love, this merging into one, with emotional fireworks. Making love doesn't stop at the sexual act, but is about treating your partner with kindness and respect during the entire day and night. Sex is the physical culmination of the love you have generated in each interaction.

71. Are you comfortable with your partner's politics?

Politics can be a divisive issue. There are couples whose votes cancel each other out and then there are probably many more who think alike. Fortunately, two varying political viewpoints can co-exist in a marriage. Being informed about both sides of the issues keeps you up to date on local and national affairs. In your relationship, are there disagreements about highly charged issues such as gun control, climate change, abortion, immigration, marijuana legalization, gay marriage, racial profiling, health care, or the teaching of evolution in the classroom, for instance? If you can explore the details of the numerous issues while respecting each other's points of view, you will be able to find either compromise or at least an understanding of where your partner is coming from. Two individuals do not need to think alike, but if they are able to talk over their differences with civility then they can agree to disagree.

You may belong to different political parties, but hopefully you are respectful of each other's views about complex problems. Moreover, once you have children, you will want them to have a well-rounded viewpoint that includes all sides of an issue. When politics and world affairs are a part of a cordial family conversation, children can imagine achieving world peace and resolving environmental concerns.

72. Are TV and video games a satisfying and inexpensive pastime for you?

TV and all the other modern, electronic gadgets are wonderful inventions, but they can be addictive. Do you watch TV selectively, or is it left on for hours at a time and for background noise during meals? You and your partner don't want to become couch potatoes, do you? [126] There are inexpensive ways to keep your body fit while feeding your mind, such as participating in sports, taking walks or biking in nature, going to museums, attending concerts, exercising, reading, swimming, dancing, and gardening. A partnership is more than a pastime and requires connection and stimulation in ways a TV screen, video game or computer monitor cannot deliver. It's not that TV isn't wonderful, but it's a big world out there, with interesting places to go, activities to do, and creative ideas to share with new acquaintances and long-time friends.

73. When you are angry, do you say or do hurtful things to your partner?

Unresolved anger can erupt into emotional or physical violence.[127] Only by digging deep and understanding the source of your frustrations can you begin to alter your disruptive, emotional outbreaks. What are you doing to your partner? Try walking in her shoes and being treated the way you are treating her. You'd never stand for it or let anyone talk to her the way you do. If you truly love your partner, you will want her to be treated kindly and respectfully.

Acknowledging that you have an anger problem is a first step. Your feelings for fairness and justice may be valid, but your delivery leaves a lot to be desired. There are excellent books on the subject such as *The Dance of Anger* by Harriet Lerner,[128] and Gary Chapman and Ross Campbell's *The Five Love Languages of Children*. Counseling and anger management classes are available to help you free yourself from the hurt and disruption that uncontrolled rage brings to you and your family. Until this issue is addressed, there is a red flag on this relationship. See answer to question #13 on Pg. 168

74. Will your different educational backgrounds cause problems?

Our society emphasizes academic achievement, however, car mechanics, artists, or plumbers, for instance, can be equally brilliant and creative in their fields. Is there a big difference between the two of you intellectually? When there is enough commonality in a relationship, it can remain vibrant, and sharing stimulating discoveries with your thoughtful partner keeps both of you energized.

When Robert and I merged our intellectual styles it made for a compelling, cooperative force. I had a good memory and fit into the traditional classroom mold, being challenged by intellectual discussions and debates. In contrast, Robert never had much of a memory, but he has natural ingenuity and his creativity is hands-on. His talent of being his own boss, doing all the varied business things to keep Harmony Enterprises going, supported our family, and paid the kids' college tuition. On the other hand, I enjoy balancing a checkbook, doing the accounting, creating art, and planning our schedules. My partner is an entrepreneur who delves into the house remodels, fixes engines, and has what I like to call his "landlord gene." We were amazed when we melded my creativity with his business acumen, and were successful in the art world, a rarity considering all of the starving artists. We are both avid readers and our diverse interests lead to many moments when we read to each other, sharing our passions. When we hang out with friends, while I am having a stirring discussion about sub-atomic particles, Robert will be deep into the bilge discussing boat repair. Our separate outlooks on the world lead to exciting exploration into the workings of our minds, not to mention adventures where the broken engine is fixed and the selected weather window is excellent for sailing.

75. Have you talked about using birth control to plan your family?

If you are concerned about when to have children, what size family you want, and approximately how many years between children, then birth control comes into play. When you open up the discussion about family planning do you confront a storm of protest? If one or both of you have reservations, will you practice abstinence? Otherwise, there needs to be an understanding that children will arrive anytime and very likely, in large numbers creating a big family that can be a wonderful, happy, noisy, exciting, expensive, action-packed ride. Raising a large family of young people who are responsible world citizens to enhance our planet is an honorable calling.

One hundred years ago when many of us lived on farms, a large family was a necessity to do the numerous chores that ensured the survival of the homestead. There was also a higher infant mortality rate.[129] But in the 21st century, most couples in the U.S., if they are having kids at all, are having one or two children.[130] Discuss what you want and feel good about your compromises.

There is the old joke, "What do you call a couple who practices natural birth control?"

Answer: "Mama and Daddy."

76. Are you satisfied and happy with how your life is going?

When you are optimistic, you will be able to forge through life's challenges, despite obstacles and problems, finding a positive outlook even in the middle of upheaval. Every moment of every day you have the choice to affirm your life and create your own happiness. Why wouldn't you enjoy walking down that path towards your wildest dreams? What else can be as satisfying and exciting?

Unfortunately, some people are condescending or complaining, and they create unhappy dramas. Do you wake up in a grouchy mood? Does your partner? Do you snap at each other over little things? Do you whine or complain that life is not fair or that someone or something else is responsible for your problems? According to The Law of Attraction, bad vibrations generate more bad vibrations that often turn into unpleasant situations. Fortunately, you can opt to turn your life around by changing your attitude. When you use the power of choice and dial in your perspective to see the glass half-full, not half-empty, then you can sail along through the inevitable ups and downs, living life to the fullest.

77. Do you fear that you might be sexually impotent or frigid?

Sharing your sexuality with your partner can be a highlight in your relationship, not to mention the healing and relaxation that comes from having orgasms. If there is a physical or psychological problem, have you seen a doctor to diagnose your symptoms? Love, trust, and a tender partner might be able to help. Do you feel inhibited when it comes to your body? Are you able to talk about sex with him/her or is something keeping you from having this discussion? Can you relax in each other's presence? Can your lover ease your anxiety? Is there a time when you can unwind, turn off the TV and phone, and bask in the love that you have created? Letting him or her know how you would like to be touched will not diminish lovemaking or make your partner feel inadequate. Giving the love that you would like to receive generates enthusiasm and heightens the experience. If there are physical or psychological problems that you cannot resolve, there is the option of pursuing them with a respected doctor or sex therapist.

78. Are your ideas on raising children compatible?

It might seem too hypothetical to consider raising children before you are married or pregnant, but it is helpful to know each other's expectations. A common understanding about ethical values and discipline can alleviate some of the strain of bringing up children. For example, even with a solid agreement, kids will try to play one parent against the other. Taking a consistently unified position on values and boundaries creates a secure world for your child. If you and your partner have trouble compromising then the kids will feel insecure in the uncertainty.

Here are a few questions that might come up when you discuss how you would like to raise your children. How and where do you want to have the birthing? Does mom plan to breast-feed the baby? What religious teachings will you give your child? Will there be a baptism or circumcision? Is there an agreement about discipline? What kinds of schools are you interested in? Children blossom when parents are committed to nurturing their family in a loving environment.

79. Can you foresee problems resulting from an interracial marriage?

When you are in love and committed to each other, that should be all that matters. In the United States in 2010, 8.4% of married couples come from different ethnic backgrounds compared to 3.2% in 1980.[131] If you are an interracial couple, are you aware that there are some people, possibly relatives, friends, or even total strangers who may give you a difficult time? If you are confronted with negative attitudes, a sense of humor and a non-combative plan of action is a safe response, if you choose to respond at all.[132] Surrounding yourself with unprejudiced, open-minded people can hopefully help you avoid negative experiences. If you are lucky enough to know other interracial couples, you can be supportive of each other about issues that might arise. Most people want to be friendly despite superficial differences and their own unconscious biases. Fear and suspicion fade when you make personal connections.

As much as we would want racism to be out of the hearts of everyone, it still confronts us daily in a country that prides itself on equality for all. If children are in the plan, be willing to have open discussions about how they can stand up for themselves if they are met with any biased unpleasantness or bigotry. Teach them about the proud roots of your families and instill a sense of humor that will take them far.

Does your partner feel uncomfortable or anxious when he wants you to meet his family? Is it like that great movie, *Guess Who's Coming to Dinner?* It's not just racial, but there are cultural, ethnic, and religious differences that can also be a source of contention. Hopefully this is not the case, but if it is, dealing with the situation civilly and living your life to the fullest is the best way to handle it. Joel Crohn, Ph.D wrote a helpful book entitled *Mixed Match, How to Create Successful Interracial, Interethnic, and Interfaith Relationships.*[133] In the end, love does conquer all, and if you are both set on making your relationship work, than this can become a minor obstacle that you can talk about, laugh about, and continue on with your happy life despite what anyone else might think.

80. Is there a conflict about your views on adoption?

For one reason or another, you may have decided not to have your own biological children or perhaps you are not able to. If you are considering adoption, what are the disagreements? Can you find an equitable solution? Resolving any conflicts about parenting your new child before you adopt will make the transition easier for all. Consider consulting with the many adoption agencies that come with good references.[134] It might help to speak with couples who have adopted children to help you understand the process and what to expect. There is a lot of information available about your options including websites, books, and adoption clinics. [135] It's never an easy process, and building a supportive group around you may ensure a positive experience. Fortunately, there are babies and children waiting for a loving family.

81. Is your partner involved in community activities at the expense of you and the family?

Your relationship is shortchanged when an outside activity takes priority over your family. Many community projects and political activities, even those that are altruistic or bring power and prestige, inevitably end up keeping one partner away from the family for extended periods of time. The responsibility of raising children then shifts to the partner remaining at home. Is s/he on board to back you up on this endeavor? When you keep a balance between your family time and your other pursuits you will have more energy for both. Can you delegate certain responsibilities that take up too much of your time? Do you feel that you are indispensable and there will be a huge gap created if you don't do this extra work? Since our life expectancy is longer these days, there is usually a chance to pursue all of your goals at the right time with everyone's support. When the children are young, they benefit when both parents have time to spend with them. When they become teenagers, they are more preoccupied with their own activities, leaving you time to follow your calling in the public sector. There can be a sense of satisfaction when your older children participate in your outside pursuits. High schools often give extra credit for community service. Perhaps it's a good idea to discuss with your family your ideas about what will take up so much of your time to see if it's feasible. Compromising will be the key when making it good for everyone concerned.

82. Does your partner support your future goals and ambitions?

Sharing your wildest dreams and ideas is usually a high point when you are dating. Your optimistic visions of the future, your ambitions and goals may give your partner an intimate view into what the future with you could look like. During what ideally will be a long and happy lifetime, you can help each other fulfill your goals. What sounds so crazy that it makes your partner hold back his/her enthusiasm? A wholehearted, supportive partner is what you are looking for.

On our first date, my future husband and I talked about living on a boat and sailing off to the tropics. Thirty years later after raising our children and running our businesses, we were able to sail Harmony to the cruising grounds of Mexico and as far south as Ecuador. I support him in his wild sailing adventures and he is also an enthusiastic editor of my writing and has spent countless hours helping me rework my manuscripts. After my book, *Harmony on the High Seas, When Your Mate Becomes Your Matey* was published, he helped me give seminars at boat shows and yacht clubs. It's wonderful to have someone who takes an active role in your dreams and helps turn them into a reality.

83. Are your partner's eating habits a source of contention?

During childhood we are raised on a certain diet that usually becomes our comfort food. Were you brought up on meat and potatoes while the person you are dating is a vegetarian? Is one of you a devotee of junk food while your new love won't touch the stuff? An unhealthy diet inevitably leads to health issues later in life. Is there a weight problem associated with poor eating habits? Is one of you picky about trying new foods? If one or both of you has a family history of diabetes, high cholesterol, cancer, heart disease, obesity, hypertension, etc., can you agree to cut down on certain foods that exacerbate these conditions even if they taste "sooo good?" Have you struggled with anorexia, bulimia, yo-yo dieting, or overeating? Can you agree on a program for a healthy life style?

A finicky eater might find the courage to taste a bite of unfamiliar foods instead of rejecting them, (Like in Dr. Seuss' *Green Eggs and Ham*). It's not conducive to good digestion when there's tension and drama around the dining table.

84. Can you talk with each other about any subject?

A marriage is an open book. If there are topics that are taboo or unspoken, then you may be missing pages that can generate insecurity and contention. During the dating and engagement stage of a relationship, feel free to discuss everything that comes to your mind. Postponing touchy subjects creates gaps in communications that can easily result in distance and estrangement. What can't you talk about and why? Talking through sensitive issues will expose problems that you can then put to rest.

85. Do your partner's prejudices bother you?

If your partner has an underlying dislike of certain people, cultures, races, religions, or those who may have a different way of thinking, raise the red flag! Children absorb their parents' views of the world. Biases, intolerance, and bigotry usually stem from someone who feels like they have to lift themselves up by tearing other people down. Bigotry is usually a sign of low self-esteem. Sometimes these feelings can come from an unpleasant experience with someone from another race or culture, and you stereotype the whole group because of the actions of one person. Martin Luther King, Jr. said it so well: "I look to the day when people will not be judged by the color of their skin, but by the content of their character."[136] These same prejudices may eventually be directed towards you and your children. Do you want to continue passing down this legacy of intolerance? It is always easier to find fault with someone else than to notice and work on your own frailties.

86. Will getting married solve some of your problems?

There are problems that getting married actually can solve. It will be easier to pay the rent or mortgage with dual incomes; you can share the housework, and hopefully you won't be lonely. However, it doesn't take a marriage agreement to straighten out financial issues or make a smooth-running household. Roommates can live together and receive these same benefits. Ideally, marriage is an agreement to build intimacy through a loving, working relationship that will last a lifetime. Such an alliance will then be resilient enough to bring children into a secure and happy home. To think that by being married, problems will vanish into happily-ever-after is indeed a fairy tale. New issues inevitably surface, and bringing them to a satisfactory resolution will be a lifelong endeavor. You both gain maturity by doing what it takes to negotiate through the rough spots along the way. A realistic approach to marriage keeps you from being disillusioned when you have to navigate through those difficult times.

87. When you have time off, does your partner choose all of the activities?

If he is always insisting that you do his choice of activity, dominance, self-centeredness, and control are now thrown into the equation. When this happens, resentment inevitably builds and the happiness quotient sinks.[137] Even though you may have different interests, spending quality time together doing things that you both like makes for a balanced connection.

A relationship has a good chance of success when the partners are close friends with common interests. If you are congenial and cooperative, you can be entrepreneurs and do outrageous endeavors together.[138] In the sailing world, for instance, we found that usually the men had the sailing dream and the women came along for the ride. However, we have met many women who had fallen in love with the lifestyle, who became sailors and navigators, and are part of this fun-loving community. When the adventure is over, the couple returns home to become involved in other pursuits. They have accomplished a dream and there's satisfaction from that experience. Even when your interests are different from your mate's, encouraging each other to follow your passions will bring energy and enthusiasm into your lives.

Taking an interest in your partner's endeavors may involve you in something outside of your comfort zone. He needs your support and you may be surprised to find that you have hidden talents. Hopefully, it will be reciprocal and he will go along with your interests as well. Sharing in each other's pursuits increases the possibility of a balanced relationship.

88. Do you agree that both of you will be working outside of the home?

The financial benefits of two paychecks are obvious when you can save up for a house, pay off your debts, and if you choose, go on that adventure you have been dreaming about, or take time off to start a family. When you both have careers, you return home to share stories of your day. Having someone outside of your workplace to talk about the triumphs and disasters, the personalities and changes gives you perspective that can help when there are difficulties.

What will happen if children join your family? Who is going to spend time with the baby? Is childcare an option at your workplace? Babies and young children thrive when their parents are close by. Even though there are competent childcare centers, it is advantageous in the long run when parents are able to raise their own children during those young impressionable years, a relatively short time in the scheme of things.[139] Making financial sacrifices to allow one or the other parent to stay home during these formative years is beneficial if you can afford it. Couples who can find compromises at work like arranging flextime schedules, or telecommuting from home are at an advantage. Imaginative brainstorming with your partner can introduce possible scenarios that could work out well. Let's suppose that Mom's employer provides certain benefits that make it logical for her to keep working, then Dad might become Mr. Mom. The ideal is for both parents to spend quality and quantity time with their children.

Wouldn't it be nice if your workplace provided daycare so you could visit your child during lunch and breaks? Perhaps this can be the model for workplaces of the future. Here and now, couples have changed their shifts to allow one parent to always be at home, or a grandparent can fill in when needed. If you can telecommute, working out of your home permits you to make your own schedule and take a turn with the children. If it is financially possible, the satisfaction that you will have from being with your kids while they grow from infant to school age will bring you joy and be beneficial for them as well. The health of our families will make it all worthwhile in the long run. Good luck with this planning.

89. Do you embrace the basic principles of the traditional marriage vows?

There's a reason why the traditional marriage vows say, "For better or for worse, for richer and for poorer, in sickness and in health, until death do us part." It is saying that you are making a lifetime commitment to stay together, no matter what. If there are any doubts, perhaps you can find a quiet place and think about what is keeping you from taking on this responsibility. At this stage of the relationship, are you sure of what you want?

Did you come from a divorced family? Here are a few interesting statistics compiled by Nicolas Wolfinger of the University of Utah. The divorce rate is 50% higher than average when one spouse comes from a broken home, and there is a 200% higher risk if both come from a split family. Children whose parents are separated are 50% more likely to marry another child from a fractured family. These adults have seen the vows and commitments go up in smoke and will want to find that place deep within that breaks the intergenerational cycle of divorce and creates an enduring marriage.[140]

Why are you afraid to commit? Is this the right relationship for you? Are the red lights flashing, warning you of danger? What is your gut telling you? Your partner wants to hear you say, "I do" from your heart. With your family and friends watching, you want to be sure of what steps you are taking. These are the people who you invited to your wedding, who are there to celebrate your happiness. Everyone witnesses your love, hears you say those vows, and when problems arise they are the ones who will ask, "Can we help?"

You can change the words of the traditional vows, perhaps say them more poetically using phrases that have a special meaning to you and your partner. The spirit of the vows is a reflection of your commitment. In reality, the marriage vows are simply words, and it's not about the words, but about how you and your partner keep your promise each day.

90. Are you and your partner on the same sleep cycles?

A compatible relationship is built on having things in common. When one of you is a morning person and the other a night owl is that going to be a problem? Work and school have usually required you to wake up early whether you are a morning person or not. If you like to party until late into the night and your partner likes to go to bed early, how are you going to manage? Does absence make the heart grow fonder? When children arrive, these varying sleep patterns might even come in handy especially if you work on a different shift. Can you talk about your expectations and make compromises?

91. Will the physical and mental health of one or both of you cause any problems?

A marriage commitment includes caring for each other when there are health issues as well as when everything is going along perfectly. Illness can severely challenge that agreement and stretch your limits of endurance, courage, and compassion. Major life changes can emerge after experiencing a debilitating health problem and you may find yourself on a journey to find your next true purpose.

After nearly twenty-five years of raising my children and running a business, my back pain was impacting my enjoyment of life. I decided that doing my tie-dye business exacted too heavy a toll on my body, (long hours on my feet taking care of customers, and setting up the booth). Listening to the message of my aching back was the impetus for us to choose another path, and we discovered an escape route. We recalculated our finances until we found a way to throw off the dock lines and sail *Harmony* south to Mexico. I was able to swim in warm water almost every day and managed to live with less stress for six months out of each year for the next four years. When we returned to the U.S. we worked fewer craft shows which allowed me to heal. It turned out that it was inexpensive to live the cruising lifestyle and eventually, we sold our business to our son and were able to live comfortably managing our rental properties.

If you enter a relationship knowing that you or your partner has a physical or mental health issue are you aware of the extent of the health care required? Meeting with a doctor or therapist will clarify what is involved to make your relationship work. It is possible to have many years of happiness when one partner agrees to take care of the other in exchange for the gifts of companionship, love, and shared interests.

If you are the primary caregiver, do you set aside time for yourself to renew your own health and energy? Finding a support group for caregivers usually makes life easier. When you enter this relationship, if you fully understand the expectations and the challenges, each of you can have a life full of love and contentment.

92. Does your partner place too much emphasis on neatness?

There are certain people who like everything to be neat with things in their proper place. It can verge on compulsiveness. Is this okay with you? When I was first married, I kept a neat home, but when children entered our family, I realized that it was more important to spend my time playing or reading with them than to be overly concerned about housekeeping. As our children grew older, they helped with the chores, but with all of us busy with work and school, our house remained comfortably lived in. At one point we even hired a maid to do a once over every week. Compulsive cleanliness can be okay if it's fine with everyone, but when a two year old enters the scene, she has her own ideas. When the priority of the home is a happy family where each person feels like they have the freedom to relax and enjoy life, an immaculate house may not be that important.

On the other hand, if your partner is constantly leaving his dirty clothes on the floor, never volunteers to do the dishes or clean the bathroom, an imbalance exists in your relationship that requires a compromise. A certain level of cleanliness is required for health and happiness. If one of you refuses to do his or her share of the chores, it begs the question, "When are you going to take on some of the responsibility?"

One of you may want a white couch in a living room with a spotless white carpet while your partner may prefer a more easy-going lifestyle. Can you negotiate an agreement to satisfy both of you? We have a friend who fortunately has enough space to have a white living room used for special occasions and a den or recreation room to hang out in.

However you manage to work it out, make it satisfying for each of you.

93. Do you have trouble agreeing on major expenditures, (House, car, vacation)?

Making agreements about the big financial expenditures usually tests you and your partner's ability to talk things through and come to a satisfying compromise. When you discuss possibilities, share your dreams and evaluate the pros and cons, it will become clear what choices are best for you both. Let us take purchasing a home for an example. According to Moneying.com, the general rule for buying a house is that it is financially viable to buy a house if you plan on living in it for at least five years and the PITI (mortgage principal, interest, taxes and insurance) is reasonable and affordable.[141] Is this a favorable time in the housing market to buy? Is there enough saved up for a down payment with wages coming in monthly to afford the mortgage payment and your other bills? Is this where you want to settle down? Will your job require your family to move? When you rent in the area where you want to purchase a house, you see if you like the schools, the shopping, the neighbors, etc. It helps to listen to trustworthy family and/or friends who are knowledgeable about real estate.

When you come up to the big decisions, make sure both of you are on the same page. It may feel stressful, but by working together you will be satisfied with your choice. Is one of you tight with money? Are you scared to commit to the payments and the upkeep of a home? When you talk about major expenditures, it helps if you are both organized with your finances and flexible when you do your brainstorming. An excessively cautious partner can stifle an adventurous move, while risk takers can make mistakes and cause havoc to the family's security. Success usually follows if a visionary entrepreneur is allowed to pursue his dreams while his partner keeps a close eye on the finances.

94. In the middle of a heated argument, can you agree to a cooling-off period before you try to resolve the issue?

When you are in the middle of a raging squabble it isn't easy to stop the show and ask for a time-out. It's even more difficult to come to a satisfactory compromise. A cooling-off period is a welcomed break as long as you deal with the issue eventually and do not ignore it, allowing it to fester and come back to haunt you later. Avoiding problems can trap a couple in an unhappy situation while issues accumulate. In the meantime, it often seems as if love has disappeared. Each of you has the choice to apologize; it is a good way to start things off on the path to reconciliation. Don't forget to keep humor on the front burner.

Can we try it again, only nicer? Perhaps you can agree to disagree until you seek an outside opinion. When disputes persist, there is nothing wrong with consulting a trusted third party who you both respect.

See: Communication and The Subconscious. Pg. 113-115 and Pg. 102-109

95. Are you living too close to the parents?

A warm and close family is what we all work towards, but that is not always the reality. There's the old joke, "Why do grandparents and grandchildren get along so well?" Answer: "They have a common enemy." When in-laws "behave" themselves, paying attention to the appropriate boundaries, they do not intrude on a couple trying to set up their own household. They are not overbearing about how they think things should be done, and they allow the family its space and time to be together. Grandparents can be helpful and a source of information that comes from experience. They also make excellent baby sitters. In many cultures such as in Mexico, having family members watch the kids while the parents work is the primary way that children are cared for. Youngsters usually prosper when nurtured by members of an extended family.[142]

Has your family been welcoming to your significant other? Is it pleasant for your new amour to visit? If there's been tension have you tried to work things out? When they are not receptive and nobody wants to hear what you have to say, creating distance between you and your parents is unfortunately the usual solution. You do need a little time to let the dust settle. Hopefully this will only be temporary and visits will remain civil and courteous.

96. Were you physically, emotionally, or sexually abused as a child?

When you pursue the path towards truth and healing, you can find peace. The abuse was not your fault; you were a child, not an adult. There is work to do to understand how the abuse affects you now, including anger to work through, forgiveness to nurture, and relieving yourself of blame and shame. A counselor or a supportive group can give you valuable advice and courage.[143] People who were denied love as children have an enormous potential to give and receive.

When you are dating someone who has been abused, you are in a unique position to help. You can encourage him/her to track down ways that can help alleviate the trauma that s/he has been through. This is a tall order and, of course, s/he has to be in total agreement that this is the path to take. If you decide to get married and have children, you definitely want to do the difficult work that it takes to prevent this legacy of violence from entering your lives and being passed on to the next generation.

See Answer #55 on Pg. 220 and Footnote #120

97. Has pregnancy affected your marriage plans?

Pre-marital pregnancy has a way of changing the course and velocity of the marriage plans. In the past, if a woman became pregnant before she was married, there might be what was referred to as a "shotgun wedding."[144] That's when Dad, with his shotgun poised to back up his demands, would insist that the man marry his daughter since she is pregnant and he is now responsible for providing for mom and baby. Another old scenario was that the pregnant woman might be shuffled off to a convent or a relative's home in a distant town. Eventually she would have the baby and, not wanting to tarnish the family's reputation, would put the newborn up for adoption.[145] Regardless of whether you are getting married or not, once you decide to have the child, you are committed to provide for the baby, physically, emotionally, and financially. If you decide to remain unmarried, is the baby's father going to help you care for your child? Should marriage wait until you have completed school, or secured a steady job? The stakes are high and your family and friends are hoping that the two of you are mature enough to take on the responsibility of raising your child. Maybe there are major issues that indicate that this marriage would be a disaster. Whichever decision you make, your baby is a tie that will always bind you together, and hopefully you can carry out your parental roles responsibly and respectfully with the child's wellbeing a priority.

If a marriage is not advisable, joint custody is preferable if both parents want to have a presence in their child's life. The courts today tend to award joint custody, which means both of you will participate in the raising of your child. It was not too long ago when it was a rare occasion for custody to be awarded to the father, but times have changed. Your child can thrive when both parents stay involved in his/her life, particularly if the parents abstain from using the child as a bargaining chip in a contentious custody agreement. To have a child caught up in the battle between warring parents is a form of emotional incest, where the young person has to hear insults about the two people in his life that mean the most to him. Most children are not mature enough to be able to understand what is going on and don't want to choose one parent above another. When you speak kindly about your former partner, you encourage your child to learn about his mom or dad's good qualities. If one parent refuses to accept responsibility, or would be a danger to the child, (is abusive or violent) hopefully you and the courts can agree on an acceptable solution that is in the best interest of the child.

When a couple is not ready for marriage or the responsibility of raising a child, there are some difficult choices to be made. Would you consider adoption? There are many parents who are unable to conceive and you could fulfill a couple's dream with your beautiful child. In today's progressive world there are even adoptive parents who allow the biological mother to be a part of the child's life.

And then there is the morning after pill (used in the first 72 hours after intercourse) and abortion in the early stages of pregnancy that are legal options for terminating an unwanted child. These choices are not without emotional, physical, and psychological stresses, so think carefully before proceeding towards this major life decision. Whenever I conceived a child (Seven times), it was a beautiful experience, and abortion did not enter my mind. I might have thought differently if there had been negative circumstances, but in any case, I wanted the choice to be my own.

See: Birth Control, Pregnancy, and Abortion, Pg. 73.

98. Have you had sex before this relationship?

If you have had sexual intercourse with someone other than your current partner, have you taken a recent HIV and STD (Sexually Transmitted Diseases) test, and have a clean bill of health? Even though you practiced safe sex, you still should take the tests.[146] **The nastiest thing you can do to your partner is pass on a fatal disease.**

If the pre-marital sex was good, hopefully a wonderful and compassionate partner initiated you into the joys of intimacy. Did s/he teach you the subtleties of your body with a delicate touch and gentle manner? If you have had a positive experience and your partner is accepting and not jealous, it can bode well for the relationship. If perhaps it was not a good experience, hopefully, you can explore lovemaking together and find the sweetness that you both deserve.

See: References for where to get testing, Pg. 76

99. Are you in agreement about how you like to spend your vacation and holidays?

Do you have different ideas about what your dream vacation would be? A child's warmest memories are often of the fun things that happened when his/her family was out camping or traveling together. Maybe you want to relax on a beach and read a book while your partner would rather raft down the Colorado River through the Grand Canyon. If there is a radical difference in your ideas of rest and relaxation that a compromise will not cure, is it okay to take separate vacations? Each of you could return home rejuvenated, and happy to be back. If you vacation together, any destination that you pick has a plethora of activities for both relaxation and adventure.

Holidays are a special time to spend with your family, especially after the children arrive, and it's likely that both sets of grandparents will want to be with you and the kids. Can you spend Thanksgiving with one family, and winter holidays with the other? It's a chance to be free from work, a time to nurture the family bonds and create lasting memories.

Celebrations, visiting with friends and family, and giving and receiving gifts are traditional events during these shortest days of the year. Does one partner choose not to participate? Is somebody being stingy like Dr. Seuss' *The Grinch* whose "heart is two sizes too small" or Ebenezer

Scrooge's "Bah Humbug" in Charles Dickens' *The Christmas Carol*? Possibly he dislikes the consumerism of our culture around the holidays and does not want to indulge in the entire Buy, Buy Buying Circus. However, the holidays can be magical times and having Ebenezer in your house brings everyone down. Let's hope that old Scrooge transforms into a generous and caring man, laughing and dancing with the kids.

Holidays are hopefully happy times that create lifelong memories. On Christmas morning at our house, excited children gathered around a tree surrounded by brightly and carefully wrapped gifts. We had a tradition to give every gift its due and opened only one at a time. There was happiness and laughter down to the smallest gift. When the children were grown and out on their own, Robert and I realized a dream and sailed to Mexico for the winter months. We decided to buy airline tickets instead of gifts, so the family could vacation with us on our boat.

100. Have you talked about how your life will be after the wedding?

Do you still view your future husband as Prince Charming or your future wife as the Beautiful Princess? After marriage, do you expect to "live happily ever after?" Unrealistic expectations can go Poof in an instant. Eventually you will see each other as a human being, with flaws, problems, highs and lows. Becoming well acquainted before you are married allows you time to discover the strengths and weaknesses of the relationship. Perhaps you need to experience more of life before you take on the challenge? Who is going to do the dishes? Can you agree about the finances? What will you do when a child is sick and needs attention at two in the morning? Will your life-long dreams and passions fit into both of your ideas of a wonderful life together? If you look at a marriage as a long-term commitment, do the hard work when it's needed, you will evolve into that Prince Charming and Beautiful Princess, a fabulous and unforgettable adventure.

101. Do you feel relaxed and comfortable with your partner?

Having a close friendship with your partner sustains the relationship when times are tough. When you encourage him to be who he is, you are able to celebrate his uniqueness and individuality. When you are unhappy with your mate, you might need an occasional reminder of what the attraction was in the first place. If there is constant tension between you to the point that you are walking on pins and needles and unable to say what is on your mind then it's time to work it out. If you are afraid to bring up something that is causing you discomfort, bringing in a third party to help mediate might bring satisfaction.[147] Don't you want the person who you chose to live with for your lifetime to be your best friend?

I Love You, You're Perfect, Now Change

How did The Test go for you? Did you address your conflicting answers and talk about the issues? Do you share similar views on the big questions like finances, children, and your visions for the future? Can you sort through disagreements and come out the other side still loving each other? Are you learning how to operate your relationship respectfully? Are your communication skills improving?

Some of you may at this point decide to live together and pool your resources. Keep in mind, that when you share a household, you become entwined emotionally and physically, whether there is a ring to symbolize it or not. Eventually at least one of you will want more of a commitment. Would you get a learner's permit and then never apply for your driver's license? If you have come from a divorced family, are you worried that you may follow a similar path? Is one of you looking for security and a life-long agreement, while the other is indifferent or nervous about this whole marriage thing?

You might like to review the chapters on The Subconscious and Communication for more guidelines to help discussions remain kind, helpful, and compassionate instead of escalating into discouraging, angry bickering and frustrated shouting matches.

Can you talk about anything? Have you both had to make some changes? Has it been done for the good of you individually and for the health of your relationship? There's no doubt that when your partner shares her concerns, it sometimes feels as if she is smashing your whole world, but if you decide to forego this process of working it out, inevitably, you will continue to come up against the same issues.[148] To a new couple, this can be alarming and you may want to give up or run away. Fortunately, with practice, you can learn how to let go of deeply rooted habits, and evolve towards having a greater capacity for love and happiness.

"The Sword of the Peaceful Warrior is Love."
Gary Amirault

Fortunately, with practice, you can learn how to let go of deeply rooted habits, and evolve towards having a greater capacity for love and happiness.

Breaking Up is Hard to Do

The romance was intense and incredibly gratifying for a while, but then things started to deteriorate, implode, and finally fall apart. What happened to that turned-on love that was so nice? Where is that person who you wanted to be with every minute of the day? Did the passionate sparkling hearts and flowers turn into passionate daggers? (There's still passion but it's gone to the dark side). Usually, the first impulse is to say that it is your partner's fault. He changed for the worse or did not evolve as you did, but let's face it, it takes "two to tango." Was one of you not ready for a serious relationship; in that case, did the other push too hard for it to happen? Or were you just out for a good time with no intention of committing? Did you end up disempowered and dumped, with your energy depleted? Somehow you also created this scenario that spiraled down into emptiness and animosity. What can you do? Once the crying and anguish subsides, and you have pulled yourself together and forgiven yourself and your partner, you can then consider it a class in Life Experience 101.

Fortunately, there are things you can do. Do you want to try again to work things out and see if you can revive your drowning relationship? Or do you want to break up, leave it behind and learn from your mistakes. If you decide to separate, can you leave on good terms and not allow your anger and resentment to grow and fester? You didn't build up insurmountable walls that will prevent you from having a cordial friendship in the future, did you? These choices require a lot of contemplation and forgiveness for both yourself and your partner, but you can let go and move on, gaining understanding and resiliency from life's curve ball.

Couples inevitably come to this crossroad. Is your relationship worth it or is it time to break up? If there is a major flaw like domestic violence, or infidelity, and one of you refuses to do the difficult work to repair the problem, then it is time to admit that it's over.

A trial separation isn't a bad idea since you are both unable to live together without it quickly deteriorating into an argument. Is it time to return to the peace table and work out the details? Asking a third party to mediate the strife that caused the separation allows for an objective viewpoint. Can your heart open back up to accept and give love again? What originally attracted you to him/her? Why did you enter into this relationship in the first place? Is it possible for both of you to eliminate the negative habits that ruined this once beautiful love affair? Will you forgive and allow him or her to forgive you? Can you forgive yourself? During this time of separation, are you able to make new agreements and commitments while you go through your changes? Can you rebuild your love for each other, and create a union that is stronger than it was before? This sturdier foundation will take you into a deeper friendship and perhaps transform it into the blissful, happily-ever-after that you always dreamed of. In a stable and loving relationship, working it out and changing for each other becomes part of the routine. Issues are brought up and accepted with respect. It doesn't mean that things don't sometimes get heated, but when the agreement is to work it through until you reach satisfaction, the ugly feelings disappear.

If two people decide to permanently separate, healing can happen after all is said and done. You might be able to meet on neutral ground and celebrate the time that you spent together. Let him/her know how grateful you are for the good times, the positive lessons, the adventures, and the love you experienced. If you can drop the resentments and anger and let the relationship go in peace, you will both be happier people for it. When there are children involved, your future meetings for scheduled weekends, graduations, weddings or birthdays will be civil and the children will suffer less. It is already hard enough on the kids; let's not make it worse.

In a stable and loving relationship, working it out and changing for each other becomes part of the routine. Issues are brought up and processed with respect. It doesn't mean that things don't sometimes get heated, but when the agreement is to work it through until you reach satisfaction, the ugly feelings disappear.

Moving In

When you move in with your lover, you are making a large emotional investment. Are you investing wisely? Cohabitation is more or less like being engaged. Are you moving in together out of convenience? The problem for women is that without a commitment, living together can become a disempowering situation. You are giving the guy all the goodies, with only a questionable assurance that he will stick around when things get heavy. In the long run you will be grateful when you stand up for yourself and make it good for you.

With living expenses sky high, it's no wonder that you want to share the costs of rent, utilities, groceries, and more. Have you been through some ups and downs with your partner and been able to work through your disagreements until both of you are satisfied? Did that give you confidence that you could live together and keep your love vibrant? It's a good idea to set down practical ground rules for your new home, like who's going to pay the bills and who will do the dishes before you carry in your clothes, computer, and furniture.

A promise ring or an engagement proposal represents a commitment to make the relationship work for the long term. Moving in together is a trial run to see how well you will share a household. Inevitably, you will run up against problems you never imagined; working through them will be your challenge. If you both are able to solve problems as you go, you will enter a life-long relationship confident that you have made the right choice.

We know a couple that lived together for thirty-four years before they made a permanent commitment! The wife said with a smile, "I knew after that long it would be a happy marriage."

When you move in with your lover, you are making a large emotional investment. Are you investing wisely?

Love keeps a relationship together while you share your visions, dreams, and passions. With warmth and affection you can summon the strength and confidence required to make the big changes for yourself and each other. The walls come down and you are lifted out of the mundane into joyousness, prosperity, and longevity. When you create the happiness that you want, the spark of love stays with you for a lifetime.

The Proposal

Congratulations! You and your partner have taken *The 101 Question Compatibility Test* and talked about the answers that showed up as potential problems. Hopefully, the questions brought up topics that inspired you both and led to insightful discussions. Are you feeling good about looking deeply into what is involved in this life-changing commitment? Are you ready for the next step of your journey? You don't have to; there's still time to be single and enjoy yourself without a sincere promise. Or do you want more than anything in the world to be with your love, and are ready to make the big move?

There is a tradition in the Vietnamese culture, where the suitor comes to his girlfriend's home to speak with her father about marrying his daughter. Her brothers and cousins have been alerted, and they are excited to be a part of the up and coming hazing, giving the potential new member of their clan a hard time before they allow him inside. There are hoops to jump through to win their sister's hand.

However, in our Western culture, family is usually far from the romantic setting, where the polished beau presents his sweetheart with a ring and asks her to marry him. He showers her with love and promises to take care of her for the rest of their lives.

When our adult children announced their engagements and showed off their rings, there was an excitement that was unprecedented. After our daughter Rose had exchanged promise rings with her sweetheart Ben, they joined our family for our annual Thanksgiving feast. After dinner, Ben surprised us by telling us that he planned to propose to Rose, and wanted to ask the family if it was all right with everyone. It was an exciting moment and we congratulated them, and asked about their plans. Rose's siblings quizzed them with a few tough questions. The happy couple was gracious in the hot seat and handled it with humor. Several weeks later, at sunset below the iconic lighthouse at Half Moon Bay, California, Ben proposed to Rose. When the time comes for you to make your heartfelt proposal to your sweetheart, you will be standing at the threshold of a most exciting, life-long adventure.

"Love is Friendship that has caught fire. It is quiet understanding, mutual confidence, sharing and forgiving. It is loyalty through good and bad times. It settles for less than perfection and makes allowances for human weaknesses. " Ann Landers

The Engagement

Your engagement is the next step leading up to marriage, a special time to enjoy the interlude of romance and elation that comes with the agreement to be wed. A young couple will often allow themselves a year or so before the date when they want to walk down the aisle. You can take weekend trips to beautiful spots to pick out your venue, a place in nature perhaps, on a beach or in a forest, a house of worship, a wedding hall, or a retreat center. If you have a larger budget, you might consider a destination wedding where your family and friends come together for a week of exploring an exotic location before your ceremony. Within that year, there are deadlines and arrangements to make like, who will cater the food, and when to send out the save the date cards and then the invitations. There are so many choices to make and a budget to keep. But think of all the fun you'll have!

Congratulations on your engagement!!! Book 2 is my take on Marriage and the Art of Raising Children. It will be published as soon as I get it together between babysitting my grandchildren, cruising with Robert in Mexico, and enjoying life. May love be with you always.

Acknowledgements

I want to thank Ina May Gaskin and the late Stephen Gaskin, and everyone on the intentional spiritual community known as The Farm, who played a large part in my life and the lives of my family. I particularly want to thank you for all of those late nights when you truly lived the practice of helping us sort out the intricate workings of our psyches. There were times when your words made the difference, when you taught me the meaning of unconditional love, and you empowered me when you once told me to "tie myself to the mast during the storm and hold on."

My gratitude is also boundless for The Farm midwives who delivered our children into a world filled with love and support while being surrounded by the beauty of nature.

My deepest appreciation goes out to our son and daughter, Saul and Olivia Gleser, who gave of their busy schedules to edit my manuscript and give valued insights from their youthful perspectives. Thank you, Rose Platt for the cover picture taken at sunset on Ocean Beach in San Francisco. My sincere gratitude goes to our daughter-in-law, Irene Song who helped me with the layout and cover design. Special thanks goes to Deanna Roozendaal who edited my manuscript in the middle of her cruising season, giving me positive and supportive feedback from her English professor background. Margaret Murray also edited my manuscript and helped bring this book into reality. John Klink and Richard Maldonado of Rush-It Graphics were our helpful and creative graphic designers. Thank you all for your interest in re-birthing this book.

I want to thank our children, Sunyah, Brian, Eugene, Saul, Audrey, Roseanna, Caitlin, and Olivia for all of their love and support while I worked on this project. Appreciation also goes to our grandchildren, Madison, Tobias, Coral, Onyx, Leif, and Lillien who bring us joy, sweeten our lives with their kindness, beauty, humor, and intelligence, and ensure bright prospects for the future.

Appreciation, Gratitude, Celebration!

Thank you all!

Bibliography

Ackroyd, Eric. *A Dictionary of Dream Symbols.* London, UK: Blandford, 1993.

Andreas, Connirae and Tamara. *Core Transformation.* Moab, Utah: Real People Press, 1994.

Arntz, William; Chasse, Betsy; Vicente, Mark. *What the Bleep Do We Know.* Deerfield Beach, FL: Health Communications, Inc., 2007.

Attwood, Janet and Chris. *The Passion Test, The Effortless Path to Discovering Your Life Purpose.* New York, NY: Penguin Group, 2006.

Barbach, Lonnie and Levine, Linda. *Shared Intimacies, Women's Sexual Experiences.* New York, NY: Bantam Books, 1989.

Bradshaw, John. *Homecoming.* New York, NY: Bantam Books, 1990.

Bradshaw, John. John Bradshaw on: *Healing the Shame that Binds You.* Deerfield Beach, FL: Health Connections, Inc., 1988.

Braden, Gregg. *The Divine Matrix.* Carlsbad, CA.: Hay House. Inc., 2007.

Byrne, Rhonda. *The Secret.* New York, NY: Simon and Schuster, Inc., 2006.

Byrne, Rhonda. *The Power (The Secret).* New York, NY: Simon and Schuster, Inc., 2010

Chapman, Gary. *The Five Love Languages: The Secret to Love that Lasts.* Chicago, IL: Northfield Publishing, 2015.

Chapman, Gary and Campbell, Ross. *The Five Love Languages of Children.* Chicago, IL: Northfield Publishing, 2012.

Chapman, Gary. *The Other Side of Love.* Chicago, IL: Moody Press, 1999.

Coelho, Paulo and Clarke, Alan R. *The Alchemist.* New York, NY: Harper Collins Publisher, 1998.

Coelho, Paulo. *By the River Peidra I Sat Down and Wept.* New York, NY: Harper Collins Publishers, Inc., 1997.

Darling, Lynn. *For Better and Worse*. Esquire. May 1996, pg., 58-66

DeAngelis, Barbara. M.D. *Secrets About Men Every Woman Should Know*. New York, NY: Dell Publishing, 1990.

Dooley, Mike. *Choose them Wisely: Thought Become Things.* New York, NY: Simon and Schuster. www.tut.com 2009.

Dooley, Mike. *The Top Ten Things Dead People Want to Tell You.* www.hayhouse.com, Hay House. 2014.

Edelman, Hope. *Motherless Daughters, the Legacy of Loss.* New York, NY: Dell Publishing, 1994.

Faber, Adele and Mazlish, Elaine. *How to Talk to Kids So Kids Will Listen and Listen So Kids Will Talk.* New York, NY: Avon Books, Inc., 1980, Revised. 1999.

Franquemont, Sharon. *You Already Know What To Do,* New York, NY: Penguin Putnam, Inc., 1999.

Gaskin, Ina May. *Ina May's Guide to Childbirth*. New York, NY: Bantam Dell, 2002.

Gaskin, Ina May. *Spiritual Midwifery*. Summertown, TN: The Book Publishing Company, 1977.

Gaskin, Stephen. *This Season's People.* Summertown, TN: The Book Publishing Company, 1975.

Gleser, Virginia. *Harmony on the High Seas, When Your Mate Become Your Matey,* Modesto, CA: Harmony Publishing, 2011.

Grey, John. *Men are From Mars, Women are from Venus: The Classic Guide to Understanding the Opposite Sex*. New York, NY: Harper Collins Publishers, Inc., 2012.

Gurian, Michael. *The Wonder of Boys.* New York, NY: Penguin Putman, Inc., 1996.
Gurian, Michael. *The Wonder of Girls.* Atria Books, New York, NY: Simon and Schuster, 2002.
Hafen, Bruce. *Marriage and the State's Legal Posture Toward the Family.* Vital speeches of the Day. Oct. 15, 1995, pg., 17-19
Hay, Louise L. *Heal Your Body.* Carlsbad, Ca.: Hay House, Inc., 1982.
Hay, Louise L. *The Power is Within You.* Carson, Ca.: Hay House, Inc., 1991.
Hendrix, Harville. Ph.D. *Getting the Love You Want.* New York, NY: Henry Holt Company LLC., 1988.
Jeffers, Susan, Ph.D. *Feel the Fear and Do It Anyway.* New York, NY: Fawcett Columbine, 1987.
Katie, Byron and Mitchell, Stephen. *Loving What Is: Four Questions That Can Change Your Life.* New York, NY: Three Rivers Press, 2002.
Katie, Byron, with Michael Katz. *I Need Your Love - Is That True?* New York, NY: Three Rivers Press, 2005.
Kornfield, Jack. *After the Ecstasy, the Laundry, How the Heart Grows Wise on the Spiritual Path.* New York, NY: Bantam Books, 2000.
Lawler, Michael. *Doing Marriage Preparation Right.* America. Dec. 30, 1995-Jan 6, 1996, pg., 12-14
Lerner, Harriet Goldhor. Ph.D. *The Dance of Anger.* New York, NY: Harper and Row Publishers, 1985.
The Miami Herald. May 19, 1980. Archives.
Miller, Matthew. *The Sacred "M."* The New Yorker. Oct. 1995, pg., 9-10
Moore, Robert and Gillette, Douglas. *King, Warrior, Magician, Lover.* New York, NY: Harper Collins Publishers, 1990.

Myss, Caroline, PH.D. *Why People Don't Heal and How They Can*. New York, NY: Three River Press, 1997.
The New York Times Magazine. Oct. 8, 1995, pg., 51-63, 74-106
Northrup, Christine, M.D. *The Wisdom of Menopause*. New York, NY: Bantam Books, 2001.
Northrup, Christine, M.D. *Women's Bodies, Women's Wisdom*. New York, NY: Bantam Books, 1994.
Orman, Suze. *The Nine Steps to Financial Freedom*. New York, NY: Crown Publishers, 1997
Peters, Edward. *Too Young to Marry*. American. June 22, 1996, pg., 15-16
Ramsey, Angus. *Sally's Gift*. Create Space, 2014.
Ramsey, Angus. *The Secret to Political Happiness*. Create Space, 2016.
Ramsey, Dave. *The Total Money Makeover*. Nashville, TN: Nelson Books, 2013
Real, Terrence. *I Don't Want to Talk About It*. New York, NY: Fireside, 1997.
Rosin, Hanna. *Separation Anxiety*. The New Republic. May 6, 1996, pg. 14-18.
Scmitz, Anthony. *The Secret to a Good Marriage*. Health. March/April 1995, pg., 50-56.
Simsion, Graeme. *The Rosie Project* and *The Rosie Effect*. New York, NY: Simon and Schuster, 2013.
Spector, Barry. *Madness at the Gates of the City: The Myth of American Innocence*. Berkeley, CA.: Regent Press, 2010.
Stiriss, Melvyn. *Voluntary Peasants*, Parts 1-5, A Goodreads Author, available on Amazon Kindle, 2014-2016
Tutu, Desmond. *No Future Without Forgiveness*. New York, NY: Doubleday Books, 1999.

Warren, Neil Clark. Ph.D. *Finding the Love of Your Life.* Wheaton, IL.: Tyndale House Publishers, 1992.
Wolf, Sharyn. C.S.W. *How to Stay Lovers for Life.* New York, NY: Penguin Books, USA, Inc., 1997.

Appendix A: Cross Reference to the 101 Compatibility Questions and Answers by Subject

Children – 23, 40, 64,75, 78, 80, 96, 97.

Family -- 3, 26, 31, 34, 42, 53, 66, 68, 95, 96.

Finances -- 10, 15, 41, 42, 50, 57, 63, 93.

Friends -- 5, 37, 58, 66.

Homemaking – 11, 29, 48, 83, 92, 95.

Parenting -- 2, 9, 23, 27, 40, 54, 64, 69, 75, 78, 80, 96.

Relationship -- 4, 6, 7, 12, 13, 14, 17, 18, 19, 20, 21, 22, 24, 25, 28, 30, 33, 35, 36, 38, 39, 41, 44, 45, 46, 47, 51, 52, 54, 56, 58, 59, 60, 62, 65, 67, 70, 71, 72, 73, 74, 75, 76, 79, 81, 82, 83, 84, 85, 86, 87, 89, 90, 91, 92, 94, 96, 97, 99, 100, 101.

Religion -- 3, 16, 20, 32.

Sex -- 8, 12, 24, 38, 49, 51, 55, 70, 75, 77, 98.

Wedding -- 21, 39, 53, 61, 79, 86, 89, 97, 100.

Work -- 1, 22, 43, 47, 81, 82, 88.
Working It Out -- 4, 6, 7, 12, 13, 17, 18, 19, 22, 24, 25, 30, 33, 35, 44, 45, 46, 52, 54, 58, 59, 60, 62, 65, 67, 73, 84, 85, 86, 87, 90, 92, 93, 94, 96, 99.

Appendix B: Reading References by Subject

Loving Yourself

Carolyn Myss's book, *Why People Don't Heal and How They Can*: "Regardless of what needs surface as you learn to know and love yourself, the important points is to give yourself the **right of choice, self-expression, and self-respect**."[149]

The complex subject of change has attracted many great authors over the years like Jon Kabat-Zinn who wrote the great book, *Wherever You Go, There You Are.* [150]

In the book, *Core Transformation* by Connirae and Tamara Andreas,[151] there are exercises that teach you how to parent the child of your youth.

What the Bleep Do We Know written by William Arntz, Betsy Chasse, and Mark Vicente,[152] is a fascinating book that was also turned into a great movie.

Byron Katie's book *Loving What Is* [153] describes a simple and helpful method of getting to the bottom of any problem and finding healing and true freedom.

You might like taking the *"Passion Test"* (2008) by Chris and Janet Attwood [154] or read inspiring books that encourage you to take a step to follow your dream such as *The Secret (2006)* and *The Power, (The Secret)* (2010) by Rhonda

Byrne,[155] and *The Divine Matrix* by Gregg Braden (2007).[156] The inspirational author of many books, Louise Hay[157] writes, "Life is very simple. We create our experiences by our thinking and feeling patterns. What we believe about ourselves and about life becomes true for us." Mike Dooley, in his daily inspirations says that "Thoughts Become Things."

A great group of fun exercises to tap into how to make changes for yourself are found in Sharon Franquemont's *You Already Know What To Do.*

Terrence Real wrote the wonderful book about dealing with depression called *I Don't Want to Talk About It.*[158]

Relationships

Harville Hendrix in his book *Getting the Love You Want* has you delving deep into from where your relationship problems derive.

Byron Katie's book *Loving What Is*[159] and *I Need Your Love, Is that True?* Describes a simple and helpful method of getting to the bottom of any problem and finding healing and true freedom.

Two books on the subject of the continuum of sexual preferences are John Money's *Gay, Straight, and In-Between: The Sexology of Sexual Orientation* and Simon LeVay's *The Sexual Brain.* [160]

Joel Crohn, Ph.D wrote a helpful book entitled *Mixed Match, How to Create Successful Interracial, Interethnic, and Interfaith Relationships.*[161]

Your Body, Health, and Sexuality

An excellent source of information for women is Dr. Christine Northrup's book, *Women's Body, Women's Wisdom.*[162]

Jed Diamond has also written a number of books with information about men's cycles including *The Irritable Male Syndrome: Managing the Four Key Causes of Depression and Aggression.*[163]

A book that can give you a look at a wide range of women's sexual experiences is *Shared Intimacies, Women's Sexual Experiences* by Lonnie Barbach, PH.D and Linda Levine, A.C.S.W.

National HIV & STD Testing at https://gettested.cdc.gov, and Anonymous testing at www.planned parenthood.org/learn/stds/std-testing-hiv-safer-sex/hiv-aids/hiv-testing and free STD testing at www.freestdcheck.org.

Handling Your Anger

The Dance of Anger by Harriet Goldhor Lerner Ph.D.[164]

Raising Children

New enlightened ways of working it out with your kids are discussed in *How to Talk to Kids So They Will Listen, and How to Listen to Kids So They Will Talk* by Faber and Mazlish (Revised 1999), and *The Five Love Languages for Children* by Chapman and Campbell (2012)

Gary Chapman and Ross Campbell in their book, *The Five Love Languages of Children* and Gary Chapman in his book, *The Other Side of Love* are resources on understanding rage, and how to distinguish between valid and distorted anger. [165]

Financial Advice

Suze Ormond's, [166] *The Nine Steps to Financial Freedom,* and Dave Ramsey's[167] books are both easy to read with a no-nonsense, balanced attitude about financial matters.

Abusive Childhood

Adult Survivors of Child Abuse at www.naasca.org/010111-Recovery.htm, www.Isurvive.org, www.psychecentral.com, www.adultchildren.org, and Rape, Abuse and Incest national Network at http:/www/rainn.org/adult-survivors-of-childhood-sexual-abuse. [168] Byron Katie's, *Loving What Is* also is a valuable resource.

Appendix C - Copy of The 101 Question Compatibility Test

Mark each sentence with: Agree, Disagree, Unsure, Yes, No or Maybe

Below you will find the 101 Question Compatibility Test for you and your partner to complete. Answer the questions with Agree, Disagree, Unsure, Yes, No, or Maybe. Be prepared to talk about why you chose these answers. While you go through the test, place a star by any questions that make you uncomfortable or that you would like to discuss further.

1. Do you enjoy your work?
2. Will you make a good parent?
3. Are your future in-laws comfortable with your culture or religion?
4. Does your partner's sense of humor sometimes bother you?
5. Do you enjoy spending time with your partner's friends?
6. Do you have any doubts that you have made the right choice?
7. Are you concerned about the significant age difference between you?
8. Have you grown up with a healthy attitude about sex?
9. Do you agree on your roles of caretaker and/or breadwinner when rearing your children?

10. Do either of you have large debts?
11. Do you know where you are going to live?
12. Have issues concerning premarital sex, former lovers, and/or ex'es caused you problems?
13. Does your partner become angry, making you afraid that s/he will hurt you?

14a. Are you worried about you or your partner's use of tobacco, alcohol, or other addictive substances?

14b. Do one or both of you enjoy drinking or using recreational drugs in moderation?

15. Do you have an agreement about how to handle your finances?
16. Are there conflicts concerning your religious beliefs?
17. Is your partner frequently moody or depressed?
18. When there are problems to be discussed, does you partner refuse to talk about them?
19. Are you uncomfortable with you partner's public show of affection?
20. Do you enjoy discussions about religion, philosophy and spiritual matters?
21. Are you taking an active part in the wedding plans?
22. Is one or both of you a workaholic?
23. Do you agree about whether or not to have children?
24. Do you work out your problems by having sex?
25. Does your partner make condescending remarks to or about you?

26. Are there family members who will cause friction between you?
27. Will your partner make a good parent?
28. Does your partner encourage you in your interests? (Your career, hobbies, sports, art, music, yoga, etc.)
29. Have you talked about how you want to maintain your home and do your household chores? (Doing the dishes, laundry, the lawn, vacuuming, cleaning the bathrooms, etc.)
30. Does your partner have certain habits that annoy you? (List them.)
31. Are you uncomfortable when you are with your future in-laws?
32. Do you feel pressure to choose a certain spiritual or religious path?
33. Is you partner jealous and possessive of you?
34. Is your partner or you not on speaking terms with a member(s) of your family?
35. Does your partner refuse to compromise on a particular issue? (List it.)
36. Do you believe in the power of love to heal the body, mind, and spirit?
37. Do you have 'my' and 'your' friends, but only a few who you share in common?
38. Do you believe that sex is an important part of marriage, and are you open to exploring the art of lovemaking with your partner?
39. Does your partner want to get married sooner than you do?
40. Do you agree about how you are going to discipline your children?

41. Are you confident that your income will cover your expenses; can you live within your budget?
42. Does financial help from your family have strings attached?
43. Do you both have promising careers?
44. Do you and your partner handle your personal problems in a reasonable way?
45. Does your partner's behavior at social events sometimes embarrass you?
46. Do one or both of you always have to be right?
47. Do you or your partner have a tendency to be lazy or unmotivated?
48. Do you agree on how to furnish and decorate your home?
49. Do you know what is sexually satisfying for your partner?
50. Do you agree on how much of your budget will be spent on housing?
51. Are there homosexual, bisexual, or trans-sexual tendencies and preferences in your relationship?
52. Is it difficult to talk about your true feelings with your partner?
53. Are you feeling pressured into marriage by the family?
54. Do you worry that problems you experienced in childhood will affect the way you raise your children?
55. Are you nervous and uncomfortable about revealing your body to your future partner?

56. Can you count on your partner to be a good listener?
57. Are you worried that you do not have adequate insurance coverage?
58. Do you and your partner trust each other with members of the opposite sex?
59. Are you unhappy with one or more of your partner's interests (career, hobbies, sports, etc.)?
60. Are you sometimes embarrassed by your partner's appearance?
61. Do you disagree about the type of wedding you want?
62. Do you try to avoid arguments or disagreements with your partner?
63. Does your partner handle his/her finances responsibly?
64. What are your expectations for your children?
65. Do you have doubts about your love for your partner?
66. Are you uncomfortable with your partner's family and friends since you have come from a different social, cultural, or economic background?
67. Can you count on your partner to give you support when you are feeling down?
68. Is your partner too dependent on his or her parents?
69. Are you ready to accept the responsibilities of being a parent, (3 A.M. feedings, a sick and crying child, "terrible twos," rebellious teens)?
70. Is there a difference between love and sex?

71. Are you comfortable with your partner's politics?
72. Are TV and video games a satisfying and inexpensive pastime for you?
73. When you are angry, do you say or do hurtful things to your partner?
74. Will your different educational backgrounds cause problems?
75. Have you talked about using birth control to plan your family?
76. Are you satisfied and happy with how your life is going?
77. Are you afraid that you might be sexually impotent or frigid?
78. Are your ideas about raising children compatible?
79. Can you foresee problems resulting from an interracial marriage?
80. Is there a conflict about your views on adoption?
81. Is your partner involved in community activities at the expense of you and the family?
82. Does your partner support your future goals and ambitions?
83. Are your partner's eating habits a source of contention?
84. Can you talk with each other about any subject?
85. Do your partner's prejudices bother you?
86. Will getting married solve some of your problems?

87. When you have time off, does your partner choose all of the activities?
88. Do you agree that both of you will be working outside of the home?
89. Do you embrace the basic principles of the traditional marriage vows?
90. Are you and your partner on the same sleep cycles?
91. Will the physical and/or mental health of one or both of you cause any problems?
92. Does your partner place too much emphasis on neatness?
93. Do you have trouble agreeing on major expenditures (House, car, vacation)?
94. In the middle of a heated argument, can you agree to a cooling-off period before you try to resolve the issue?
95. Are you living too close to the parents?
96. Were you mentally, physically, emotionally or sexually abused as a child?
97. Has pregnancy affected your marriage plans?
98. Have you had sex before this relationship?
99. Are you in agreement about how you like to spend your vacation and holiday times?
100. Have you talked about how your life will be after the wedding?
101. Do you feel relaxed and comfortable with your partner?

Appendix C – Copy of The 101 Question Compatibility Test

Mark each sentence with: Agree, Disagree, Unsure, Yes, No or Maybe

Below you will find the 101 Question Compatibility Test for you and your partner to complete. Answer the questions with Agree, Disagree, Unsure, Yes, No, or Maybe. Be prepared to talk about why you chose these answers. While you go through the test, place a star by any questions that make you uncomfortable or that you would like to discuss further.

1. Do you enjoy your work?
2. Will you make a good parent?
3. Are your future in-laws comfortable with your culture or religion?
4. Does your partner's sense of humor sometimes bother you?
5. Do you enjoy spending time with your partner's friends?
6. Do you have any doubts that you have made the right choice?
7. Are you concerned about the significant age difference between you?
8. Have you grown up with a healthy attitude about sex?

9. Do you agree on your roles of caretaker and/or breadwinner when rearing your children?
10. Do either of you have large debts?
11. Do you know where you are going to live?
12. Have issues concerning premarital sex, former lovers, and/or ex'es caused you problems?
13. Does your partner become angry, making you afraid that s/he will hurt you?
14a. Are you worried about you or your partner's use of tobacco, alcohol, or other addictive substances?
14b. Do one or both of you enjoy drinking or using recreational drugs in moderation?
15. Do you have an agreement about how to handle your finances?
16. Are there conflicts concerning your religious beliefs?
17. Is your partner frequently moody or depressed?
18. When there are problems to be discussed, does you partner refuse to talk about them?
19. Are you uncomfortable with you partner's public show of affection?
20. Do you enjoy discussions about religion, philosophy and spiritual matters?
21. Are you taking an active part in the wedding plans?
22. Is one or both of you a workaholic?
23. Do you agree about whether or not to have children?
24. Do you work out your problems by having sex?

25. Does your partner make condescending remarks to or about you?
26. Are there family members who will cause friction between you?
27. Will your partner make a good parent?
28. Does your partner encourage you in your interests? (Your career, hobbies, sports, art, music, yoga, etc.)
29. Have you talked about how you want to maintain your home and do your household chores? (Doing the dishes, laundry, the lawn, vacuuming, cleaning the bathrooms, etc.)
30. Does your partner have certain habits that annoy you? (List them.)
31. Are you uncomfortable when you are with your future in-laws?
32. Do you feel pressure to choose a certain spiritual or religious path?
33. Is you partner jealous and possessive of you?
34. Is your partner or you not on speaking terms with a member(s) of your family?
35. Does your partner refuse to compromise on a particular issue? (List it.)
36. Do you believe in the power of love to heal the body, mind, and spirit?
37. Do you have 'my' and 'your' friends, but only a few who you share in common?
38. Do you believe that sex is an important part of marriage, and are you open to exploring the art of lovemaking with your partner?
39. Does your partner want to get married sooner than you do?

40. Do you agree about how you are going to discipline your children?
41. Are you confident that your income will cover your expenses; can you live within your budget?
42. Does financial help from your family have strings attached?
43. Do you both have promising careers?
44. Do you and your partner handle your personal problems in a reasonable way?
45. Does your partner's behavior at social events sometimes embarrass you?
46. Do one or both of you always have to be right?
47. Do you or your partner have a tendency to be lazy or unmotivated?
48. Do you agree on how to furnish and decorate your home?
49. Do you know what is sexually satisfying for your partner?
50. Do you agree on how much of your budget will be spent on housing?
51. Are there homosexual, bisexual, or trans-sexual tendencies and preferences in your relationship?
52. Is it difficult to talk about your true feelings with your partner?
53. Are you feeling pressured into marriage by the family?
54. Do you worry that problems you experienced in childhood will affect the way you raise your children?

55. Are you nervous and uncomfortable about revealing your body to your future partner?
56. Can you count on your partner to be a good listener?
57. Are you worried that you do not have adequate insurance coverage?
58. Do you and your partner trust each other with members of the opposite sex?
59. Are you unhappy with one or more of your partner's interests (career, hobbies, sports, etc.)?
60. Are you sometimes embarrassed by your partner's appearance?
61. Do you disagree about the type of wedding you want?
62. Do you try to avoid arguments or disagreements with your partner?
63. Does your partner handle his/her finances responsibly?
64. What are your expectations for your children?
65. Do you have doubts about your love for your partner?
66. Are you uncomfortable with your partner's family and friends since you have come from a different social, cultural, or economic background?
67. Can you count on your partner to give you support when you are feeling down?
68. Is your partner too dependent on his or her parents?
69. Are you ready to accept the responsibilities of being a parent, (3 A.M. feedings, a sick and

crying child, "terrible twos," rebellious teens)?

70. Is there a difference between love and sex?
71. Are you comfortable with your partner's politics?
72. Are TV and video games a satisfying and inexpensive pastime for you?
73. When you are angry, do you say or do hurtful things to your partner?
74. Will your different educational backgrounds cause problems?
75. Have you talked about using birth control to plan your family?
76. Are you satisfied and happy with how your life is going?
77. Are you afraid that you might be sexually impotent or frigid?
78. Are your ideas about raising children compatible?
79. Can you foresee problems resulting from an interracial marriage?
80. Is there a conflict about your views on adoption?
81. Is your partner involved in community activities at the expense of you and the family?
82. Does your partner support your future goals and ambitions?
83. Are your partner's eating habits a source of contention?
84. Can you talk with each other about any subject?
85. Do your partner's prejudices bother you?

86. Will getting married solve some of your problems?
87. When you have time off, does your partner choose all of the activities?
88. Do you agree that both of you will be working outside of the home?
89. Do you embrace the basic principles of the traditional marriage vows?
90. Are you and your partner on the same sleep cycles?
91. Will the physical and/or mental health of one or both of you cause any problems?
92. Does your partner place too much emphasis on neatness?
93. Do you have trouble agreeing on major expenditures (House, car, vacation)?
94. In the middle of a heated argument, can you agree to a cooling-off period before you try to resolve the issue?
95. Are you living too close to the parents?
96. Were you mentally, physically, emotionally or sexually abused as a child?
97. Has pregnancy affected your marriage plans?
98. Have you had sex before this relationship?
99. Are you in agreement about how you like to spend your vacation and holiday times?
100. Have you talked about how your life will be after the wedding?
101. Do you feel relaxed and comfortable with your partner?

Endnotes

[1] www.cdc.gov, Center for Disease Control and Prevention and Huffingtonpost.com. According to the CDC marriage rates are 6.8 per 1000 and divorce rate was 3.6 per 1000 in 2013. In 2009 in a Huffington Post article 46% of more recently married couples failed to reach their 25th anniversary. A young couple marrying for the first time today has a lifetime divorce rate of 40%. 8.8 years is the average length of a marriage in the U.S. States vary on divorce rates.

[2] www.aauw.org/research/the-simple-truth-about-the-gender-pay-gap 78% average pay gap between men and women in nearly every occupation both female-dominated, gender-balance and male-dominated workplaces. 91% pay gap in Washington, DC to 66% gap in Louisiana.
www.catalyst.org/knowledge/women's-earnings-and-income
www.pewresearch.org/fact-tank/2015/04/14/on-equal-pay-day-everthing-you-need-to-know-about-the-gender-gap/.

[3] See Note 2.

[4] Adapted from a quote by the Roman philosopher, Seneca the Younger (4 BC-AD 65) who was quoting his friend Demetrius the Cynic. En-wikiquote.org/wiki/Seneca_the_Younger. Gregory K. Ericksen attributed the quote to Seneca in his book, *Women Entrepreneurs Only: 12 Women Entrepreneurs Tell the Stories of Their Success*.pg. ix. (1999)

[5] Wilcox, Bradford. The Evolution of Divorce. National Affairs, Issue # 1, Fall 2009. From 1960-1980 divorce doubled from 9.2 per 1000 to 22.6 per 1000 marriages. In 2007 there were 17.5 per 1000 divorces so it is improving. 20% of couples married in 1950 divorced while 50% married in 1970 divorced. 11% of children saw their parents divorced in 1950 and 50% of

children saw their parents divorced in 1970. Demographer, Nicholas Wolfinger found that there is an intergenerational cycle of divorce and children of divorce are 89% more likely to divorce compared to adults who were raised in intact, married families.

[6] See Note 2. Vanessa Martins Lamb, The 1950's and the 1960's and the American Woman: the Transition from the Housewife to the Feminist, History. 2011 <dumas-00680821>

[7] www.Safehorizon.org, National Domestic Violence Hotline, 1-800-799-SAFE, Violence, Statistics and Facts. "1 in 4 women will experience domestic violence during their lifetime." History of Battered Women's Movement, Table 1. Herstory of Domestic Violence. www.icadvinc.org.

[8] See Note 2.
www.Blackloveandmarriage.com, James Walsh, Live-In Relationships vs Marriage: The Advantages and Disadvantages of Both, "Couples who live together have a divorce rate 50% higher than those who don't." Live-in arrangements are devoid of commitment vs commitment and stability in marriage. "A family void of commitment is not good for children." www.Firstthings.org. What You Should Know About Living Together. "Couples who participate in a premarital program experience a 30% increase in marital success over those who do not."

[9] Hubpages.com Paul Swendson, author, The Ultimate Generation Gap of the 1960s
En.wikipedia.org/wiki/Generation_gap "Baby Boomers seemed to go against everything their parents had previously believed in music, values, governmental and political views."

[10] See Note 2.

[11] See Note 2. Discusses how no-fault divorce and the emphasis on the "self-oriented ethic of romance, intimacy, and

fulfillment" of the 1960s and 70s changed the landscape of our family relationships from "the prisms of duty" where "intimacy was an important good, but also child rearing, shared religious faith, mutual spousal aid, a decent job, and a well-maintained home."

[12] www.uky.edu Brief History of the Gay and Lesbian Rights Movement in the U.S. – 1969 Stonewall Riot in New York City. sixties-social movements @.wikispaces.com/Gay Liberation, "In the 1960's homosexuality was against the law.

[13] En.wikipedia.org/wiki/Lavender marriage. Mixed orientation marriage where one or both partners were homosexual or bisexual. In 1920's in Hollywood they were marriages of convenience known as a Lavender marriage.

[14] See Note 12.

[15] Sophie Montgomery Crane. *Family Stories,* Published through Lulu.com, 2012. pg. 39.

[16] Charles Joseph Gross. *American Military Aviation: The Indispensable Arm.* Self-published. 2002. Jack Edward McCallum. *Military Medicine: from Ancient Times to the 21st Century.* Santa Barbara, CA: ABC-CLIO, Inc. 2008.

[17] Former Defense Secretary, Robert S. McNamara, Brian Van de Mark. *In Retrospect: The Tragedy and Lessons of Vietnam.* New York, NY: Random House, Inc. 1995.

[18] Melvyn Stiriss wrote a five part history of The Farm in *Voluntary Peasants*, on Amazon's Kindle. 2014-2016, En.wikipedia.org/wiki/History-of-the-hippie-movement ABCNew.go.com Oliver, Libaw. *Hippie Culture Just Keeps Truckin' On.* 2015

[19] Contributed by my yoga teacher, Debbie Wolski, teacher and owner of Village Yoga Center in Modesto, Ca.

[20] Myss, Caroline, PH.D. *Why People Don't Heal and How They Can.* New York, NY: Three River Press, 1997.

[21] Arntz, William; Chasse, Betsy; Vicente, Mark. *What the Bleep Do We Know*. 2007, Used by permission from Health Communications. Inc., Deerfield Beach, Fl.
[22] Paulo Coelho. *By the River Piedra I Sat Down and Wept.* New York, NY: Harper Collins Publisher, Inc., 1997.
[23] Robert Frost, *The Road Not Taken.* Frost's Early Poems. www.sparknotes.com/poetry/frost/section7.rhtml. "….Two roads diverged in the woods and I-
I took the one less traveled by, And that has made all the difference."
[24] Martha Stout. *The Sociopath Next Door.* New York, NY: Broadway Books, 2005
[25] Connierae and Tamara Andreas. *Core Transformation.* Moab, Utah: Real People Press, 1994.
[26] www.safehorizon.org/page/child-abuse-facts-56.html Child Abuse Facts: 1/3 of those who were abused as children grow up to be abusers of children.
[27] The Serenity Prayer written by Reinhold Niebuhr 1892-1971 and adopted by Alcoholics Anonymous and other twelve-step programs. En.wikipedia.org/wiki/Serenity-Prayer
[28] Gregg Braden, *The Divine Matrix.* Carlsbad, CA: Hay House, Inc. 2007.
[29] En.wikipedia.org/wiki/Cato-the-Elder/quotes, en.wikipedia.org/wiki/Plutarch, Plutarch was a biographer of Cato the Elder, giving many of his famous quotes. He lived from AD 46-127.
[30] www.goodreads.com. Quote by Eleanor Roosevelt. Thedailywayhome.com/achievement-byproduct-happiness-way-around
[31] https://www.score.org/
[32] www.sba.gov/content/follow-these-steps-starting-business, www.entrpreneur.com/article/235224, John Rampton. *50 signs*

You Need to Start Your Own Business. www.forbes.com/fac/welcome_mjx.shtml, Marin Zwilling. 10 Reality Checks Before Starting Your Own Business.

[33] Paulo Coelho and Alan R. Clarke. *The Alchemist.* New York, NY: Harper Collins Publishers. 1998.

[34] En.wikipedia.org/wiki/L._M._Boyd, www.newspapers.com/newspage, L. M. Boyd lived from 1927-2007. The Love and War Man.

[35] www.personalfutures.net.id65.h6ml, www.orchidrecoverycenter.com/hormone-therapy/hormonal-therapy-and-the-4-hormonal-stages-in-women,

[36] www.newportacademy.com/teenage-hormones-and-sexuality Gonadotropin (GnRH) -releasing hormone triggers pituitary gland to secrete follicle-stimulating hormone (FSH) and luteinizing hormone (LH) in both girls and boys. In girls FSH instructs the ovaries to begin producing estrogen, one of the primary female sex hormones and eggs.

[37] En.wikipedia.org/wiki/Comparison-of-birth-control-methods and www.plannedparenthood.org/learn/birth-control/withdrawal-pull-out-method charts to show statistical probability of getting pregnant with all types of birth control or withdrawal method.

[38] Margaret Nofzinger, *A Cooperative Method of Natural Birth Control.* Summertown, TN., The Book Publishing Co., 1992. The Natural Family Planning method that I used was called the Basal Body Temperature (BBT) Method taking a thermometer reading every morning and charting each day for each month to determine when ovulation had taken place. Having sex after ovulation (a spike and then a steep drop in temperature) and before menstruation is considered a safe time to have sex. Due to travel, stress, illness and other conditions, regular cycles can become irregular and difficult to gage.

[39] See note, 31. www.newportacademy.com/teenage-hormoes-and-sexuality In boys the FSH and LH hormones tell the testes to begin producing testosterone, the male hormone, and sperm.
[40] Jed Diamond. *The Irritable Male Syndrome: Managing the Four Key Causes of Depression and Aggression.* Holtzbrinck Publishers, Rodale, 2004, Jed Diamond. *Male Menopause*. Amazon.1997, www.medincine net.com/script/main/art.asp?articlekey=53725, www.theirritablemale.com, goodmenproject.com/featured-content/the-good-life-do-men-have-a-monthly-cycle, www.newparadigmjournal.com/May 2007/monthlyemotionalcycle.htm. The Monthly Emotional Cycle in Every Man or Woman: Rexford B. Hersey's Remarkable Paradigm by David Alan Goodman.
[41] www.lawcore.com There were 6 million wrecks in the US in 2013 with 3 million injuries and 40,000 fatalities. ½ of the fatalities were not wearing seat belts. 40% of the fatalities involved drunk drivers, 30% contributed to speed, and 33% to recklessness.
[42] Psychecentral.com/media-manipulation-of-the-masses-how-the-media-manipulates/ by Samuel Lopez De Victoria, PhD. www.forbes.com/whatis-media-manipulation, by Ryan Holiday, author of *Trust Me, I'm Lying: Confessions of a Media Manipulation.* New York, NY: Penguin Group, 2012.
[43] En.wikipedia.org/wiki/Media_manipulation, The techniques used even in the seemingly trusted news media, are staged action, inferred slander, "logical fallacies, and propaganda techniques, and often involve suppression of information or points of view by crowding them out, diverting attention elsewhere and inducing people to stop listening to certain arguments."

[44] Mike Dooley, a featured teacher in the international phenomenon, *The Secret,* by Rhonda Byrne, (see Bibliography) www.tut.com/about mikedooley, www.kripatu.org/presenter/V0006554/mike_dooley.
[45] Stephen Gaskin. *This Season's People.* Summertown, TN: The Book Publishing Co., 1975. Pg. 29.
[46] www.guttmacher.org/pubs/gpr/09/3/gp.090308.html, *Abortion and Mental Health: Myths and Realities*, by Susan A. Cohen. www.carenetpregnancycenter.com/abortionprocedures-and-risks.htm, www.plannedparenthood.org/files/8413/9611/5708/Abortion_Emotional_Effects.pdf, americanpreganancy.org/unplanned-pregnancy/abortion-emotional-effects.
[47] www.hhs.gov/ash/oah/adolescents-health-topics/reproductive-health/stds.html, www.cdc.gov/std/stats/
[48] www.hhhs.gov, Title X Family planning clinics.
[49] See Note: 48
[50]www.azlyrics.com/lyrics/who/mygeneration.html., en.wikipedia.org/wiki/my-Generation
[51] www.popsci.com/science/article/2013-01/did-penicillin-kickstart-sexual-revolution
[52] www.cnn.com/2011/HEALTH/05/25/edmund.white/hiv.aids/, *HIV in the '80s: People Didn't Want to Kiss You on the Cheek* by Elizabeth Landau, men'shealth.intoday.in/story/aids-sex-relationship-love-health/1/116797-html, www.askmen.com/entertainment/austin_300/328_we-missed-the-slut-generation-html, *Where's Our Free Love Generation,* by Ryan McKee
[53] En.wikipedia.org/wiki/Rosie_the_Riveter, www.yale.edu/ynhtl/curriculum/units/2002/3/02.03.09.x.html, brittanyhillman.hubpages.com/hub/Rosie-the-Riveters-impact-

on-society, www.sfgate.com/news/article/WWII-meant-opportunity-for-many-women-oppression-2501118.php.

[54] Moore, Robert and Gillette, Douglas. *King, Warrior, Magician, Lover.* New York, NY: Harper Collins Publishers, 1990.

[55] Hendrix, Harville. Ph.D. *Getting the Love You Want.* New York, NY: Henry Holt Company LLC. 1988

[56] www.thelawofattraction.com/love Quote from Ralph Waldo Emerson, "Love and you shall be loved." Positivity, gratitude, being thankful, loving yourself all clears the way for attraction and love to happen.

[57] www.clemson.edu/fyd/Asssets/Adobe_Acrobat_files/tcct-resolving-family-conflict.pdf, www.helpguide.org/article/relationships/conflict-resolution-skills.htm.

[58] See Note 21.

[59] www.staroversky.com/blog/three-minds-consious-subconscious-unconscious, Corsini, R.J. and Wedding, D. Current Psychotherapies (9th ed.). Belmont, Ca: Brooks/Cole, 2011. www.health.harvard.edu/blog/unconscious-or-subconscious

[60] www.geniusintelligence.com/nature of the subconsciousmind.htm, www.gurusoftware.com, www.ebtx.com/ntun/ntunsub.htm, www.sacred-texts.com/nth/yfhu/wfhuo6/htm

[61] www.johngottman.com and Wikipedia on John Gottman and his Institute. From the 2002 Report. How couples fight and make up.

[62] www.robertsrules.com The Official Robert's Rules of Order Web Site

[63] Philosophyonthemesa.com/2010/11/01never-apologize-its-a-sign-of-weakness/ by Nina Rosenstand. Quoting an article by

Elizabeth Bernstein in the Wall Street Journal about two studies from the University of Waterloo in Ontario, Canada written up in the Journal of Psychological Science.

[64] www.quora.com/Why-is-saying-I'm-sorry-a-sign-of-weakness-to-some, www.essense.com/2012/02/28/real-talk-are-apologies-a-sign-of-weakness/,

[65] Lyrics by Stephen Stills, www.azlyrics.com/lyricsstephenstills/lovetheoneyourewith.html.

[66] Dictionary.reference.com/browse/ego – means self-esteem, feelings.

[67] By Virginia Gleser, *Harmony on the High Seas, When Your Mate Becomes Your Matey,* Modesto, CA: Harmony Publishing, 2011. Excerpt by permission of the author.

[68] Miami Herald, 1980. www.newpaperarchive.com

[69] www.marriagesavers.com and www.wikipedia.org on Michael McManus. Also http://www.reduceddivorce.org, www.pbs.org./wgbh/pages/frontline/shows/marriage/etc/script.html

[70] See Note: 25.

[71] www.pewforum.org, academic.udayton.edu/race/04needs/s98alouis.htm, http://contemporaryfamilies.org…/2014_Symposium_Civil_Rights.doc

[72] www.confused.com/press/releases/why-four-years-four-month-is-the-ideal-age-gap.

[73] www.webmd.com/baby/guide/pregnancy-after-35

[74] Erik Erikson's 8 stages of Life. Web.cortland.edu/ERIK/sum, en.wikipedia.org/Erikson's-stages-of-development

[75]https://www.plannedparenthood.org/learn/sexally/masturbation www.theatlantic.com/health/archive/2013/06/, https://en.wikipedia.org/wiki/Masturbation

[76] www.alternet.org/sex-amp-relationship/orgasm-gap-real-reason-women-get-less-ofen-men-and-how-fix-it
[77] Intuitive mothers, Lynn Macpherson, *Intuitive Mothering: Trusting Your Own Child Rearing Instincts,* Australia: New Holland Publishers, Ltd., 2006 people.aapt.net.au/lynmacpherson/im/book.html, www.ceciljane.net/intuitive-mothering, www.coreawareness.com, Liz Koch. *Intuitive Mothering.*
[78] Ncsu.edu/ffci/publications/2008/v14-nl-2008-spring/Washburn-Christensen.php, finance.yahoo.com/news/10-money-mistakes-ruin-marriage-095503587.html Ten Money Mistakes that can Ruin Your Marriage.
[79] En Wikipedia.org/wiki/prenuptual_agreement, www.nolo.com
[80] Orman, Suze. *The Nine Steps to Financial Freedom.* New York, NY: Crown Publishers, 1997
[81] Dave Ramsey, www.daveramsey.com, enwikipedia.org/wiki/Dave_Ramsey
[82] www.census.gov and Geographical Mobility/Migration 2007 report.
[83] www.waitingtillmarriage.org/4-cool-statistics-about-abstinence-in-the-usa/
[84]www.azlyrics.com/lyrics/stephenstills/lovetheoneyourewith.html
[85] www.clarkprosecutor.org/html/domviol/effect.htm, www.safehorizon.org/page/domestic-violence-statistics--facts-52.html
[86] Lerner, Harriet Goldhor. Ph.D. *The Dance of Anger.* New York, NY: Harper and Row Publishers, 1985
[87] www.libraryindex.com/pages/2066/Treatment-Male-Batterers-RECIDIVISM-RATES.html, www.americanbar.org/groups/domestic.violence/resources/statistics.html

[88] Gary Chapman and Ross Campbell. *The Five Love Languages of Children.* Chicago, IL: Norfield Publishing. 2012 Gary Chapman. *The Other Side of Love.* Chicago IL: Moody Press. 1999.
[89] www.cdcgov/tobacco/data-statistics/fact_sheets/secondhand-smoke/health.effects/
[90] www.webmd.com/heart-disease/news/20100621/how-red-wine-helps-the-heart
[91] Alcoholrehab.com/drug-addiction/self-medication-substances-abuse/, www.psychologytoday.com/blog/addicted/201208/addiction-self-medication by MarcLewis Ph.D 2012
[92] See Note 78. Ten Money Mistakes that can Ruin Your Marriage.
[93] See Note 80.
[94] www.dbsallliance.org/ www.nami.org/Template,cfm?Section&Depression&template=contentmanagment/contentdisplay.cfm&ContentlD+67727
[95] See Note: 94
[96] Real, Terrence. *I Don't Want to Talk About It.* New York, NY: Fireside, 1997
[97] Katie, Byron, *Loving What Is: Four Questions that Can Change Your Life.* New York, NY: Three Rivers Press, 2002. Katie, Byron, with Michael Katz. *I Need Your Love – Is That True?* NewYork, NY: Three Rivers Press, 2005
[98] En.wikipedia.org/wiki/Public_display_of_affection
[99] www.wic.org/misc/history.htm, *Women's History in America* by Women's International Center. Dailycaller.com/2013/05/30/study-says-traditional-gender-roles-may-be-thing-of-the-past
[100] See Notes: 53 and 99

---

[101]https://www.americanprogress.org/issues/economy/report/2014/09/24/96903/the-middle-class-squeeze/, https://www.lsnj.org/PDFs/RCL2013.pdf

[102] www.npg.org/npg-comments/choice-Childfree-increasing-factor-u-s-population-growth-html, 1970 – 90% of American women had at least one kid, 1976 – average was 3 kids, 2012 – 16.8% women had not given birth. 68% increase since 1970. Up to 49% are delaying until their 30's. www.forbes.com/sites/ericagles/2011-10-31/why-im-not-having-kids-and-you-shouldn't-either by Erica Gies

[103] See Note: 38.

[104] See Note: 55

[105] www.huffingtonpost.co.uk/2014/10/06women-housework-compared-men_n_5937536.html, time.com/2895235/men-housework-women/, by Alexandra Sifferlin

[106]Desmond Mpilo Tutu. *No Future Without Forgiveness,* New York, NY: Doubleday. 1999. www.brianyquotes.com/quotes/quotes/d/desmondtut/112366.html, "Hope is being able to see that there is light despite all of the darkness."

[107]Amy E. Dean, *Peace of Mind, Daily Meditations for Easing Stress.* New York, NY: Bantam Books. 1995, books.google.com/books?id+L3N4UZPB_RIC&pg=PA13&1Pg=PA13&dq=unenthusiastic+hostility&source=bl&ots=G21bpFmM7v&sg=E

[108] www.thepassiontest.com, by Chris and Janet Attwood. *The Passion Test, The Effortless Path to Discovering Your Life Purpose.* New York, NY: The Penguin Group. 2006

[109] Rhonda Byrne. *The Secret*, New York: Simon & Schuster, Inc., 2006, and *The Power (The Secret)* 2010.

[110] Gregg Braden. *The Divine Matrix*. Carlsbad, CA.: Hay House, Inc. 2007.

---

[111] www.hayhouse.com, Louise Hay. *The Power is Within You.* Carlsbad, CA.: Hay House, Inc. 1991. Louise Hay. *You Can Heal Your Life, The Movie*
[112] Dooley, Mike. *Choose them Wisely: Thought Become Things.* New York, NY: Simon and Schuster. www.tut.com 2009.
[113] www.menshealth.com/mhlists/top-sex-secrets/pmtu.php, www.bustle.com/articles/34770-how-long-should-it-take-a-woman-to-come-how-to-stop-worrying-and-start-orgasming, by Vanessa Marin, friendsandlovers.com/for-women-only-htm
[114] www.bloomberg.com/bw/articles/2014-07-17/housings-30-percent-of-income-rule-is-near-useless
[115]Axel Madsen, *The Sewing Circle: Hollywood's Greatest Secret: Female Stars Who Loved Other Women.* 1995
[116] John Money. *Gay, Straight, and In-Between: The Sexology of Sexual Orientation.* New York, NY: Oxford University Press, 1988, Simon LeVay. *The Sexual Brain.* Cambridge, MA: MIT Press, 1993.
[117] www.ibtimes.com/gay-mormons-heterosexual-marriage-are-more-likely-divorce-study-1782124,
[118] See Note: 116.
[119] Charles L. Whitfield. *Heal the Child Within: Discovery and Recovery for Adult Children of Dysfunctional Families.* Deerfield Beach. FL: Health Communications, Inc., 2006. www.MDJunction.com/dysfunctional-families, www.actionfamily.org/content/supportgroups, www.psychcentral.com/lib/adult-children-of-dysfunctional-families/00017543, www.landmarkworldwide.com
[120] Adult Survivors of Child Abuse at www.naasca.org/010111-Recovery.htm, www.psychecentral.com, www.Isurvive.org, www.adultchildren.org, Rape, Abuse and Incest national Network at http:/www/rainn.org/adult-survivors-of-childhood-

---

sexual-abuse. http://mainweb-v-musc.edu/vawprevention/general/saunders.pdf, www.health right360.org/what-we-do-summery-of-programs, fsa-cc.org/survivors-healing-center/, naasca.org/Groups-Services, www.pandy's.org/articles/innerchild.html/ by Melinda, Healing Your Inner Child after Sexual Abuse, wwwlucidpages.com/healing.html. - Healing from Childhood Sexual Abuse. Ellen Bass and Laura Davis. *The Courage to Heal: A Guide for Women Survivors of Child Sexual Abuse*. New York, NY: Harper Collins Publishers, Inc., 1994. Wendy Meltz. *The Sexual Healing Journey*. New York, NY: Harper Collins, 1991.
Robin D. Stone. *No Secrets, No Lies: How Black Families Can Heal from Sexual Abuse*. Harmony Publisher. 2007. Support services: www.aftersilence.org, www.ascasupport.org, www.psychecentral.com, www.havoca.org.
[121] Compulsive shopping disorder: Jon E. Grant, Christopher B. Donahue, Brian L. Odlaug. *Treating Impulse Control Disorders: A Cognitive-Behavior Therapy Program*. New York, NY: Oxford University Press, 2011. www.healthline.com, www.addictionrecov.org/Addictions/?AID+34, en.wikipedia/wiki/compulsive-buying-disorder, www.indiana.ed/-engs/hints/shop.html, see also Note: 143.
[122] Vikki Weiss and Jennifer A. Block. *What to Do When You're Dating a Jew*. New York, NY: Three Rivers Press, 2000.
[123] www.patch.com/georgia/marietta/the-top-10-reasons-marriage-ends-in-divorce-14370092, by Mary Montgomery.
[124] www.yogainternational.com/article/view/tantra-and-the-teachings-of-Abhinavagupta
[125] www.dictionary.reference.com/browse/tantra+yoga
[126] www.urbandictionary.com/define.php?term=couch+potato

[127]www.healthyplace.com/blogs/verbabuseinrelationships/20112/anger-management-likely-to-increase-domestic-violence, www.danielsonkin.com/articles/anger.html

[128] See Notes: 86 and 88.

[129] www.Jn.nutrition.org/content/131/2/4015.short, www.kff.org/global-indicator/total-fertiltity-rate/

[130] www.census.gov/hhes/families/files/graphics/FM-3.pdf

[131]En.wikipedia.org/wiki/interracial_marriage_in_the_United_States.

[132] www.richona.net/2011/12/27/10-pitfalls-about-interracial-relationships, www.fullerton.edu/universityblues/interracial/challenges.htm, www.pbs.org/wgbh/pages/frontline/shows/secret/discuss/melt1.html, www.facebook.com/notes/interracial-loving/four-things-to-avoid-in-an-interracial-marriage-relationship/296801883501

[133] Joel Crohn, Ph.D. *Mixed Match, How to Create Successful Interracial, Interethnic and Interfaith Relationships.* New York, NY: Ballantine Books, 1995.

[134]http://www.childwelfare.gov/topics/adoption/adoptive/finding-agency, www.adoptionhelp.org, www.americanadoption.com, www.gladneycommunity.com, information@beaconhouseadopt.com, National Foster Care and Adoption Directory Search

[135] www.whattoexpect.com/family/becoming-an-adoptive-parent.aspx, www.webmd.com/parenting/features/kids-health-adoption-april13, www.legalzoom.com/articles/foreign-adoption-what-to-expect-when-you-adopt-abroad.

[136]www.brainyquotes.com/quotes/quotes/m/martinluth297516.html

[137] the-happy-side.com/hq.php, en.wikipedia.org/wiki/Gross_National_Happiness, liveawholelife.net/happiness-quotient/

---

[138] See Note: 31.
[139] www.psycologytoday.com/articles/200704/daycare-raising-baby, circle of moms.com/stay-at-home-moms/staying-at-home-vs-daycare-420456, www.babycenter.com/childcarae-options, www.slate.com/articles/doublex/thekids/2013/08/day_care_in_the_United_States_is_it_good_or_is_it_bad_for_the_kids.html
[140] Mom.me/parenting/6576-effect-divorced-parent-child's-future-relationships, - Daughters of divorce have 60% higher divorce rates, sons have 35% higher rate. www.psychecentral.com/blog/archives/2012/11/09/is-my-marriage-doomed-if-my-parents-get-divorced-when-i-was-a-kid/ by Leslie Doares. www.cnn.com/2010/LIVING/09/22/divorced.parents.children.marriage/ Children of Divorce Vow to Break Cycle, Crate Enduring Marriage. by Stephanie Chen. 50% higher divorce rate when one spouse comes from a divorced home, 200% higher risk when both do. Children of divorce are 50% more likely to marry another child of divorce. Statistics by Nicholas Wolfinger, University of Utah- author of *Understanding the Divorce Cycle: The Children of Divorce in Their Own Marriages.* New York, NY: Cambridge University Press. 2005
[141] Moneyning.com/housing/the-five-year-rule-for-buying-a-house. Depending on the location of the house matters. Includes not paying closing costs too often. Since you pay interests at first and little towards principal, it comes out about the same as renting until after five years when you'll be paying more on the principal.
[142] See Note: 119
[143] See Note: 120, National Domestic Violence Hotline, 1-800-799-SAFE, www.helpguide.org/articles/abuse/domestic-violence-and-abuse.htm, www.bandbacktogether.com/emotional-abuse-resouces,

www.healthyplace.com/abuse/emotional-psychological, stoprelationshipabuse.org/educated/types-of-abuse/emotional-abuse, psychecentral.com/21-warning-signs-of-an-emotionally-abusive-relationship, www.springtideresources.org/resources/emotional-abuse-assessment-guide

[144] En.wikipedia.org/wiki/shotgun_wedding

[145] See the movies, The Magdalene Sisters directed by Peter Mullen, 2003 and Philomena directed by Stephen Frears, 2013

[146] National HIV & STD Testing at https://gettested.cdc.gov, and Anonymous testing at www.planned parenthood.org/learn/stds/std-testing-hiv-safer-sex/hiv-aids/hiv-testing and free STD testing at www.freestdcheck.org.

[147] See Note: 120, 143.

[148] Blogs.psychecentral.com/relationships/2011/03/the-laws-of-change-and-the-subconscious-mind/ by Athena Staik

[149] Myss, Caroline, PH.D. *Why People Don't Heal and How They Can*. New York, NY: Three River Press, 1997.

[150] Kabat-Zinn, Jon. Wherever You Go, There You Are: Mindfulness Meditation for Everyday Life. New York, NY: Hyperion Books, 1994.

[151] See Note: 70.

[152] Arntz, William; Chasse, Betsy; Vicente, Mark. *What the Bleep Do We Know*. 2007, Used by permission from Health Communications. Inc., Deerfield Beach, Fl.

[153] Katie, Byron, *Loving What Is: Four Questions that Can Change Your Life.* New York, NY: Three Rivers Press, 2002. Katie, Byron, with Michael Katz. *I Need Your Love – Is That True?* NewYork, NY: Three Rivers Press, 2005

[154] www.thepassiontest.com, by Chris and Janet Attwood. *The Passion Test, The Effortless Path to Discovering Your Life Purpose.* New York, NY: The Penguin Group. 2006

[155] Rhonda Byrne. *The Secret*, New York: Simon & Schuster, Inc., 2006, and *The Power (The Secret)* 2010.
[156] Gregg Braden. *The Divine Matrix*. Carlsbad, CA.: Hay House, Inc. 2007.
[157] www.hayhouse.com, Louise Hay. *The Power is Within You.* Carlsbad, CA.: Hay House, Inc. 1991. Louise Hay. *You Can Heal Your Life, The Movie*
[158] Real, Terrence. *I Don't Want to Talk About It.* New York, NY: Fireside, 1997
[159] Katie, Byron, *Loving What Is: Four Questions that Can Change Your Life.* New York, NY: Three Rivers Press, 2002. Katie, Byron, with Michael Katz. *I Need Your Love – Is That True?* NewYork, NY: Three Rivers Press, 2005
[160] See Note: 116 and 118
[161] See Note: 131, Joel Crohn, Ph.D. *Mixed Match, How to Create Successful Interracial, Interethnic and Interfaith Relationships.* New York, NY: Ballantine Books, 1995.
[162] Northrup, Christine, M.D. *The Wisdom of Menopause.* New York, NY: Bantam Books, 2001
Northrup, Christine, M.D. *Women's Bodies, Women's Wisdom.* New York, NY: Bantam Books, 1994
[163] Jed Diamond, *The Irritable Male Syndrome: Managing the Four Key Causes of Depression and Aggression.* Rodale Inc., Roadale Wellness.com. 2005
[164] Lerner, Harriet Goldhor. Ph.D. *The Dance of Anger.* New York, NY: Harper and Row Publishers, 1985
[165] Gary Chapman and Ross Campbell. *The Five Love Languages of Children.* Chicago, IL: Norfield Publishing. 2012 Gary Chapman. *The Other Side of Love.* Chicago IL: Moody Press. 1999.
[166] Orman, Suze. *The Nine Steps to Financial Freedom.* New York, NY: Crown Publishers, 1997

[167] Dave Ramsey, www.daveramsey.com, enwikipedia.org/wiki/Dave_Ramsey

[168] See Notes: 120 and 143

www.ingramcontent.com/pod-product-compliance
Lightning Source LLC
Chambersburg PA
CBHW062159270326
41930CB00009B/1584

9780964724747